Deaf American Literature

Deaf American Literature

FROM CARNIVAL TO THE CANON

Cynthia Peters

Gallaudet University Press
Washington, D.C.

Gallaudet University Press
Washington, DC 20002

Library of Congress Cataloging-in-Publication Data

Peters, Cynthia.
   Deaf American literature : from carnival to the canon / by Cynthia Peters
     p. cm.
   Based on the author's thesis, George Washington University, 1996.
   Includes bibliographical references and index.
   ISBN 1-56368-094-7 (alk. paper)
     1. American Sign Language. 2. Interpreters for the deaf. I. Title.

HV2471 .P38 2000
419—dc21

                                     00-031523

Contents

Acknowledgments   vii

Chapter 1

Is There Really Such a Thing as Deaf American
Literature?   1

Chapter 2

Carnival: Orature and Deaf American Literature   17

Chapter 3

Deaf Carnivals as Centers of Culture   32

Chapter 4

The Oral Tradition: Deaf American Storytellers
as Tricksters   52

Chapter 5

Literary Night: The Restorative Power of Comedic
and Grotesque Literature   78

Chapter 6

Deaf American Theater   96

Chapter 7

Islay: The Deaf American Novel 121

Chapter 8

Poetry 147

Chapter 9

From Orature to Literature: The New Permanence
of ASL Literature 173

Chapter 10

Conclusion 201

Index 207

Acknowledgments

THIS VOLUME is an extensive reworking of my dissertation, "Deaf American Literature: A Carnivalesque Discourse" completed in 1996 at George Washington University. I am most grateful to Lois Bragg for planting the seeds and Dan Moshenberg of GWU for providing invaluable assistance and encouragement. The following people also plowed through preliminary drafts, supplied valuable information, and/or responded to numerous e-mail inquiries: Patrick Graybill, Shirley Shultz-Myers, Clayton Valli, Sam Hawk, Joseph Grigely, Ben Bahan, Donald Bangs, Willy Conley, Bob Daniels, Bernard Bragg, Barbara Kannapell, Mike Kemp, Dirksen Bauman, and Lynn Jacobowitz.

At Gallaudet University Press, I wish to thank Ivey Pittle Wallace, Christina Findlay, and Alice Falk for their boundless patience, unwavering support, and great facility with the written word.

Finally, I wish to dedicate this volume to Graham Peters—Australian, thespian, husband—and to Stephen Ryan, Jester par excellence.

Chapter

1

Is There Really Such a Thing as Deaf American Literature?

IN HIGH school and college, we learn how to analyze fiction: we chart a work's plot, ponder its theme or themes, dissect character motivation, and hold a magnifying glass to the author's use of language, symbolism, and imagery. Having seen to the basics, we then go on to genre considerations and note how our narrative is like or unlike the typical short story or novel. Next, we set our narrative alongside the author's entire oeuvre to see if it is another chip—or not—off the old block. From there we move to the author's historical and cultural milieu and compare the author's writing with that of his or her contemporaries. We bear in mind the general philosophical outlook at the time—rationalism, romanticism, classicism, modernism, or postmodernism—and how our short story or novel figures in the whole cultural matrix. In these days of heightened ethnic and gender awareness and empowerment, we may wish to speculate on the writer's possible allegiances and prejudices.

If our narrative is by an American writer, we come up against the broader question of what American literature *is* and how we

1

should discuss it as a whole. What in a novel by, for instance, Ernest Hemingway or Edith Wharton leads us to pronounce it an "American" novel? How is American literature differentiated from European literatures—particularly British literature, from which it derives and within which it is often subsumed? Witness the large number of American college and university students past and present majoring in *English* and studying the masters: Chaucer, Shakespeare, Milton, and so on. In what ways is American literature similar to the (former) mother literature and in what ways has it evolved away from its parent? What useful approaches might these admittedly debatable distinctions offer as we examine our "American" novel or short story?

As we look a little more closely, we may find that our short story or novel is by an African American writer or a Hispanic writer. American literature is a smorgasbord that includes Native American literature, African American literature, Chinese American literature, and Hispanic literature. Such smaller literatures are also "American" but have features that distinguish them from literature considered mainstream. Thus any analysis of such work should explore how the ethnic writer has borrowed from both the ethnic rhetorical tradition and the canonical literary tradition, and in the process merged the two. We must endeavor to look to the ethnic culture itself for our approach to a particular ethnic—and hybrid—body of works.

Our short story or novel may be even further removed from the mainstream: it may be by a Deaf American. This brings us to the question of what Deaf American literature—or "deaf lit," as it is colloquially termed—*is*, and what steps should be followed in analyzing it or discussing it. We need to keep in mind that Deaf Americans are, like the American colonists, a smaller group descended from a larger group; like Native Americans and other contemporary minority groups, they also are a smaller group *within* a larger group. And just as American writing is both British and American, and Native American literature is both "Indian" and American, so Deaf American discourse is both American and "Deaf." We can compare it to mainstream American literature as well as to other American minority literatures by examining, for example, how a

Deaf American short story is both like and unlike a "typical" American short story.

In fact, critics have paid relatively little attention to the unique language and discourse (including "literature") of Deaf Americans as a whole. One reason is the widely held misconception that limits deaf lit to what is on paper: that is, the poetry, stories, and plays that reflect the biculturality of Deaf Americans. Most have been instructed in English and English literature as a part of twelve or more years of schooling, and many young Deaf Americans dream of writing and publishing stories and poems in English—whether or not they are proficient in English and even though they are very fluent in their native language, American Sign Language (ASL). Thus, the local school library may boast rows of novels, plays, and poetry by Deaf American writers in English (or English translations). This large collection would probably include the poetry of Rex Lowman, Laura Searing, and Linwood Smith; the narratives of David Wright and Douglas Bullard; and the plays of Gil Eastman, Bernard Bragg, Eugene Bergman, and Willy Conley—writers on whom many instructors focus in their high school or college courses on "The Deaf in Literature." However, their focus on printed works excludes the vast majority of work that can be considered Deaf American literature.

Deaf American literature is not solely or primarily these written works, but also the ASL stories and ASL art that have been passed down through the years. These constitute the storytelling or vernacular tradition, kept alive by numerous ASL artists and storytellers all over the country. Like Native Americans, Deaf Americans have their own language and their own vernacular stories and art forms. Their culture includes artists who sign in ASL and artists who write in English, as well as those who consciously or unconsciously mix the vernacular tradition in ASL with the literary tradition in English. Therefore, the rhetoric or discourse of this minority group offers a wide range of rhetorical forms. We have ASL stories and art; English stories, novels, and poems; and hybrid forms, such as those created for or adapted to videotape.

The result may seem very like a Hispanic literature, in which two cultures (Spanish and American) and two literary traditions intermix. A Hispanic writer who grew up in the United States has most likely been exposed to both Spanish or Mexican literature and American literature. He or she is bicultural, with one foot in Spanish culture—as it has evolved in Mexico and the Southwest—and one foot in mainstream American culture. Such an author may write about life along the Tex-Mex border, in a narrative format that approximates the conventional short story form and in a prose spiced with *tejano* words and expressions. Deaf American writers or ASL artists, too, are exposed to both Deaf American and mainstream American culture while growing up. As a result, they are both Deaf and American and use both sign language and English. In coming up with their own stories or poetic forms, they may draw on two cultures and rhetorical traditions. These stories or poetic forms may be in English but treat the Deaf American experience; they may be in sign language but draw on the literary form of the short story.

Yet in this case, the intermixing is not simply a confluence of two cultures and their two literary traditions but a coming together of "opposites." While Deaf Americans are visually oriented, most people are, of course, aurally oriented. Moreover, and somewhat paradoxically, although mainstream society is aurally oriented, it favors written communications. In contrast, because their visual vernacular necessitates face-to-face communication, Deaf Americans are primarily a "talking" people; indeed, ASL has no written form in widespread use. Consequently, Deaf Americans are technically an "oral" people; their lives are dominated by face-to-face "talk." As a result, their *orality* is opposed to *literacy*, the communication by way of reading and writing characteristic of mainstream society. Deaf culture is largely an oral culture: that is, a culture that has not fully developed, or cannot easily or wholly adapt to, literacy.

Deaf American literature is not unique in this regard; Native American literature displays similar contradictions. Much early Native American literature was actually an *orature*, or oral literature, because Native American languages had no written forms. Therefore, Native Americans have a vernacular tradition that consists of stories and other cultural forms in their native language. But because Native Americans have also been exposed to the mainstream literary tradition, those writers conversant in both the tribal vernacular and the majority language mix opposites—the oral and the literary—in their writings. Therefore, in Native American literature, we can see features of the oral culture along with features of the mainstream literary tradition.

Likewise, these same opposites have come together—felicitously or not—in a bicultural, bimodal, bilingual Deaf American literature. As Harlan Lane documents in the *Gallaudet Encyclopedia of Deaf People and Deafness*, the two languages, "oral" ASL and aural English with its written form, have intermixed to varying degrees down through the years.[1] Beginning in the nineteenth century, elements of English and Old French Sign Language intermingled with the home signs of various small communities (particularly the deaf community on Martha's Vineyard).[2] All these various threads first came together at the American School for the Deaf in Hartford, Connecticut. In school, the children undoubtedly learned English, read poems and stories, and attempted to produce for their teachers their own poems and stories in written English. At the same time, among themselves they came up with vernacular narratives and other art forms in ASL. This scenario was surely repeated at many of the other schools for the deaf subsequently established across the country in the nineteenth and early twentieth centuries.

As part of their instruction in English, Deaf children were encouraged to read that culture's literature. Because their teachers praised and marveled at this literature, the children were entranced by stories, poetry, and drama in English. In these works, they were taught, were to be found excellence, linguistic artistry, profound themes, and human pathos. If Deaf children (and adults) wanted to make their own attempts at such artistry and profound human communication, the only language available to them was English; ASL, which then was not considered a language, could hardly be a suitable vehicle. Thus, in the past many Deaf Americans wrote poems and stories much like those found in standard literature anthologies. Their sonnets, lyrics, epics, and the like have the usual stanzaic divisions, rhyme, alliteration, symbolism, and imagery.

Many of these stories are conventional both in genre—adventures, bildungromans, science fiction, romances, and so on—and in form, containing the usual beginning, middle, and end, as well as dialogue in English.

These writings in English in the early nineteenth century were undoubtedly the earliest Deaf American literature. Around this time, however, vernacular forms very likely were beginning to flourish on the margins as children and adults told each other stories in sign language and began to manipulate the steadily evolving language. Moreover, once the language was in widespread use and sufficiently sophisticated—probably in the second generation after its standardization by Laurent Clerc and Thomas Gallaudet—much translation and adaptation of mainstream works into sign language occurred. Thus the vernacular tradition of storytelling has existed for nearly two hundred years alongside written works in English, signed adaptations, and, more recently, a modern ASL literature.

These numerous ASL narratives and other vernacular art forms have for a long time been considered a kind of folklore or "deaflore," studied and documented by various folklorists including Simon Carmel and Karen Baldwin.[3] Of particular note is Susan Rutherford's 1987 dissertation, which focuses on storytelling, ABC story-poems, and other vernacular forms of expression.[4] Rutherford also looks into the diglossic nature of ASL: one variety being high or literary (a signed form of English) and the other low or colloquial. She also delineates the different functions that this "folklore" serves in the community: acting as a metaphor for the group's experience; transmitting group customs, values, and behavioral norms; serving to educate in specific competencies; and maintaining group identity. Throughout her analysis, Rutherford assumes that ASL is a language used by a minority group. But the traditional forms that she examines remain a kind of folklore—an art form that many consider less important than written literary works.

When ASL became recognized as a legitimate language in the 1960s and Deaf Americans were shortly thereafter acknowledged as a minority group, an effort got under way to produce an ASL literature comparable to mainstream literature. Many Deaf Americans have felt this to be a crucial step. For ASL to gain full recognition as a language in its own right, there must be greater public awareness that an ASL literature exists.[5] To be a literature, it must have the properties or qualities of the paradigmatic literature presented to Deaf Americans in school: that is, English literature. Therefore, Deaf Americans have attempted to produce ASL works of art that, like written literature, are of a high standard.

To this end, many have begun to use ASL in artistic and literary ways. Rather than creating stories and poetry in written and spoken English (and signing them in English word order), Deaf Americans now strive to create poetry and narratives in ASL that are as excellent as any composed in written English.[6] For instance, at the same time that Rutherford was investigating vernacular art forms, artists such as Bernard Bragg, Dorothy Miles, Ella Mae Lentz, Clayton Valli, and Patrick Graybill were fashioning amazingly complex ASL poetic forms. Noting that written poetry has rhyme, rhythm, compactness, symbolism, and so forth, these ASL artists attempted something comparable albeit visual-kinetic. This was a gradual effort and required a bit of experimenting and a bit of retooling. Some of these artists wrote their poems in English and then translated them into sign language; some composed in ASL but used English glossing to help them remember their "lines." But, gradually, many of their works became less English and more ASL, while still retaining the "literary" properties seen in the majority language and literature.[7]

Therefore, modern ASL literature has been developing, evolving, and unfolding. Just as Western poetry was the first art form to gain sophistication, followed by Western drama and narrative, so the same pattern seems to have held for artistic ASL.[8] A number of community theaters, including the Fairmount Theater of the Deaf in Ohio, mounted original ASL productions in the 1970s and early 1980s; but it was the flowering of ASL poetry in the late 1980s and the 1988 Deaf President Now movement (both in the D.C. area) that gave real impetus to modern Deaf American drama outside postsecondary institutions. Deaf American drama really took off in the early 1990s; under the leadership of Don Bangs and Patrick Graybill quite a few original full-length productions were staged in

Washington, D.C., including *Institution Blues* and *A Deaf Family Diary*.[9] At about the same time, complex ASL narratives on video-tape began to emerge. Most noteworthy was the first installment in Ben Bahan and Sam Supalla's videotaped ASL Literature Series, which contained two lengthy and highly artistic ASL narratives.[10] Since then, ever greater numbers of sophisticated ASL productions, particularly poetry and prose, have been produced and distributed on videotape all over the country.[11]

In these sophisticated works, the "literary" and the indigenous Deaf American not only come together but jostle and parry, often at the expense of the English language and conventional literary properties. Such spirited interaction has been termed *polyglossic* by Mikhail Bakhtin, the influential Russian sociolinguist, whose notion of *polyglossia* can be defined as the interanimation and nego-tiation of two or more unequal languages in diverse works and pro-ductions.[12] This playful interanimation, with the vernacular bounc-ing off and vying with the majority language and vice versa, has often characterized multilingual, multicultural societies through the centuries, particularly when a dominant or majority culture encompasses a smaller culture.

We can find polyglossic discourse during the days of the ever-expanding Roman Empire; the feudalistic Middle Ages; European empires in the East, Middle East, and Africa; and the newly estab-lished American republic—and it continues to occur in modern-day America. To varying extents African American, Hispanic, and Native American literatures can all be considered polyglossic. Mainstream discourse and ethnic discourse square off on a daily basis, particularly when minority writers and artists try to maintain their culture and cultural forms. In their rhetoric, as in the work of Deaf Americans, we cannot fail to perceive the two languages and rhetorical traditions playing off each other. Similarly, despite and because of the influence of conventional Western literature, many ASL artists have been endeavoring to maintain their culture and rhetorical tradition.[13]

Here the Deaf American artist is a twentieth-century Trick-ster—a figure like the Native American Coyote and the African monkey god.[14] So too were the oracles, seers, bards, minstrels, jongleurs, and court jesters of yore tricksters of one kind or another. The mythical and ubiquitous Trickster down through the centuries has been a master of style and stylus. Trickster has been the one who translates, who interprets, who mediates, and who distributes knowledge. Just as Trickster mediates and thereby unites opposed forces, so too does Trickster mediate between mainstream and Deaf cultures and interpret one to the other. As Henry Louis Gates elaborates in detail in *The Signifying Monkey: A Theory of Afro-American Literary Criticism*, Trickster in ancient times and ancient lands—whether Monkey or Coyote—was the messenger who conveyed the needs and desires of humans to the gods and, conversely, interpreted the will of the gods to humans.[15] The Deaf American Trickster functions analogously in interpreting the will and foibles of the majority culture to Deaf Americans and in turn communicating to the hearing world the needs, desires, and aspirations of the smaller group. Trickster also appears whenever there is a quest for meaning and for freedom from the restrictions of law, custom, and circumstance.

Because written literature is a comparatively recent development, Trickster is traditionally known for his or her rhetorical skills in oral communication. With exceptional linguistic facility Trickster can effectively supply, even model, useful strategies, stratagems, and coping behaviors. Such guidance is helpful when one is faced with two worlds (i.e., those of the minority and majority), whether dealing with a single person, a group, or a culture as a whole. In *using* and *manipulating* the language and the rhetorical tradition, Trickster communicates in a manner that inspires communal pride and emulation. What Trickster has to say and how he or she says it embodies the culture and its rhetorical tradition.

Returning to literature per se, we see that our Deaf American Trickster—let us call him or her Jester—mediates, challenges, and interprets. Jester, our ASL storyteller, ASL poet, ASL artist, intermixes two rhetorical traditions and in the process gives rise to a Deaf method of literary criticism: in the writing or the telling, Jester is simultaneously functioning as a "literary critic." The way an ASL artist, for example, puts together a particular work says something about the work itself and about Deaf Americans and their literature as a whole. It tells us something, as Gates points out, about the way language is used (rhetorical strategies, discourse structures) within the minority culture in relation to the mainstream literary tradition and the vernacular ASL tradition *both.*

Again, when—as in our two-world milieu—multiple languages and rhetorical traditions are in use, often becoming interanimated, polyglossia ensues. To better understand what happens, we need only visualize a carnival or fair where different people of different income levels, ethnic groups, and dialects come together and interact. Even better, visualize a harvest festival during the Middle Ages. As Bakhtin pointed out in his seminal *Rabelais and His World*, harvest festivals, market days, regional fairs, religious feast days, and other festivities during the Middle Ages—what he generically terms *carnivals*—were a vital component of the culture.[16] People of all socioeconomic levels came together: the aristocrats, the church leaders, the merchants, and the peasants mingled as equals. As all these different strata intermixed, their diverse modes of communication (high Latin and the various vernaculars) became interanimated. In this context, jesters, minstrels, bards, fools, and jongleurs were the tricksters.

So too do Deaf Americans get together for gatherings large and small: the National Association of the Deaf (NAD) conventions, the Deaf Way festivals, bowling tournaments, and reunions. So too do they have their storytellers and ASL artists who function as the guides and interpreters—the tricksters—in the culture. Carnival in general and medieval carnival in particular is thus an apt analogy, or rather an appropriate paradigm, for Deaf American culture and discourse.[17]

Instead of viewing and then judging Deaf American literature from the standpoint of Western literary conventions, we should see Deaf American literature for what it is: a mixture of this and that, whose elements all compete and vie with one another in a polyglossic interaction. After all, a visual-kinetic vernacular with no written form is very different from a spoken language with a written form, even though here they somehow come together. Thus, Deaf American discourse needs to be recognized as being both oral and literate, both ASL and English, in proportions that will vary with the particular work or production. It also needs to be viewed as a minority literature, a literature created by people who live in two different worlds. While mainstream society is blithely unaware of this two-world condition, many Deaf Americans have grown very—perhaps too—accustomed to it.

My intent here is not to *invent* a Deaf American theory (and thus make overriding claims) but to explore how the Deaf American tradition has theorized about itself. A number of scholars have taken a similar approach to other minority literatures. For example, Gates's *Signifying Monkey* proposes a critical discourse drawn from the culture itself to analyze and comment on African American literature. As noted above, the pivotal figure in this critical discourse is the signifying monkey, a centuries-old trickster figure: and it is in tricksters and their doings and communications that we see an indigenous literary criticism at work. This belies the notion that "nonliterary" cultures have little or no ongoing analysis of vernacular art forms. Rather, the analysis takes place within the vernacular art forms themselves, as the storyteller both tells the story (or is the main figure or character) and at the same time offers a commentary.

The viewers in the audience also do not sit passively, but rather actively engage in the process. A number of Deaf Americans and mainstream critics have noticed that there has been little formal criticism of Deaf American literature. However, there is an "oral" criticism of this literature, although it is by nature evanescent.[18] Most of the "literary criticism" occurs *during* the "literary event." Reactions to storytelling, for example, are immediate, for members of the audience respond to the ASL presentation as it is taking place, and praise or condemn it immediately afterward. Thus, the storyteller is constantly adjusting his or her presentation according to the feedback of a particular audience.

As we have already seen, Deaf American literature is carnivalesque, with two languages, two rhetorical traditions, and two cultures at play. A focus on that carnivalesque quality—exhibited by the writer or signer him- or herself—and on the play in the literature is an approach drawn from within the culture. As writer or storyteller, Jester manipulates both languages, rhetorical traditions, and cultures—thus analyzing and interpreting while writing or telling. This manipulation is itself literary criticism, and Jester is the Deaf literary critic in action.

When "deaf lit" is mentioned, Deaf Americans are frequently bemused. "What on earth is deaf lit?" they ask. Many have been so busy reading written works of mainstream literature that Deaf American works in English are still unknown to them. Thus they have never heard of *Islay*, responded enthusiastically to Gil East-man's *Sign Me Alice*, or sighed over Rex Lowman's poems.[19] Many Deaf Americans do not realize that deaf lit also encompasses ASL narratives and other art forms, including the little number "stories" in ASL; many have not heard of or thrilled to *My Third Eye*, the ASL poetry of Peter Cook, or the videotaped narratives by Ben Bahan and Sam Supalla.[20] This book is an effort to provide a general overview that will familiarize Deaf Americans and others with Deaf American literature.

Deaf American literature, like all minority literatures, should be recognized as unique; it is a mixed, rebellious, and playful dis-course, containing other minorities within it. It therefore needs to be judged on its own terms. As a Deaf American, a graduate of a residential school for the deaf and Gallaudet University, I have taken in with great enjoyment and appreciation many ABC stories, gone faithfully to plays produced by the National Theatre of the Deaf, and been transfixed by Clayton Valli's ASL poetry. Like many of the older students at the Maryland School for the Deaf in the late 1960s, I was a member of the New Era Club, which put on plays and various short skits. I have seen sign language adaptations of English narratives, songs, and poems such as "The Star-Spangled Banner" and Robert Frost's "The Road Not Taken." At Gallaudet, I have been among many who delighted in Phi Kappa Zeta Literary Night productions, Kappa Gamma vaudeville productions, and numerous ABC story-poems composed for homecoming festivities. At anniversary parties, school reunions, and conventions, I have been inspired by the many ASL works performed and produced.

As a college instructor and doctoral student specializing in twentieth-century American literature, including African American literature, Native American literature, and women's literature, I have come to see Deaf American literature as a complex body of works in its own right. It has many similarities to other American minority literatures, especially those with oral roots. I have read of others' attempts to approach the two worlds in which they live and the manifestations—literary and not so literary—arising out of and reflecting that peculiar existence. Similarly, as a child of an oral deaf father and a hearing mother, mainstreamed in the public school system for seven years and then transferred to a school for the deaf for three years, I have been keenly aware of the two-world condition in which we Deaf Americans find ourselves and from which our carnivalesque literature grows. I have seen a need to come up with an approach that is all-embracing.

The following chapters take a look at this carnivalesque literature as a whole, including various writings in English, sign language adaptations, ASL literature, and vernacular art forms. We note how ASL artists utilize the language in vernacular art forms with great dexterity and artistry, often manipulating it at the expense of the English language and the Western literary tradition. In the videotaped ASL narratives of Ben Bahan and Sam Supalla we see an intermingling of narrative strategies from both the vernacular storytelling and the Western narrative tradition.

Coming at this confluence from the other direction, we examine Doug Bullard's *Islay*, a Deaf American novel in English. Deaf drama has had an especially interesting history, for it includes sign language adaptations of plays such as Shakespeare's *Othello*, original but conventional stagings such as *Sign Me Alice*, vaudevillian forms such as *My Third Eye*, and hybrid productions such as *Institution Blues*. Likewise, we note how Clayton Valli, Patrick Graybill, and Debbie Rennie draw on the vernacular tradition of ASL art and the tradition of Western poetry to come up with a very complex ASL poetry. The carnivalesque nature of Deaf American literature can be seen particularly clearly in the popular form known as "Literary Night," a mishmash of everything: ASL and English, ASL vernacular art forms and adaptations, orality and literacy, visuality and aurality, performance and literature, Deaf American and American. All of these interact and play off one another, all facilitated by our Deaf American Jester.

Notes

1. Harlan Lane, "Sign Languages: American," in *Gallaudet Encyclopedia of Deaf People and Deafness,* vol. 3, ed. John Van Cleve (New York: McGraw-Hill, 1987), 54.
2. See Nora E. Groce, *Everyone Here Spoke Sign Language* (Cambridge, Mass.: Harvard University Press, 1985). The Martha's Vineyard community of the early nineteenth century is known for having integrated its Deaf members into the social fabric; many hearing islanders were able to sign.
3. See Simon Carmel and Leila F. Monaghan, "Studying Deaf Culture: An Introduction to Ethnographic Work in Deaf Communities," *Sign Language Studies* 73 (1991): 410–20; Karen Baldwin, " 'The Lumberjack and the Deaf Tree': Images of the Deaf in Folk Narrative," *Kentucky Folklore Record* 28 (1980): 1–2, 6–11. See also *Deaf Folklore,* prod. Gallaudet College Television, Washington, D.C., videocassette, 80 min., 1980.
4. Susan Rutherford, "A Study of American Deaf Folkore" (Ph.D. diss., University of California, Berkeley, 1987).
5. A 1993 promotional flyer for the ASL Literature Series put out by DawnSignPress notes, "The lack of awareness of American Sign Language (ASL) literature has been a stumbling block to the acceptance of ASL as a foreign language. ASL, the language in the deaf community, is becoming increasingly popular and deserves to have its literature recognized and developed."
6. Since a large percentage of Deaf Americans in the nineteenth and early twentieth centuries were postlingually deaf, their sign language works, particularly when adapted from the mainstream, were fairly dignified and English-like. These adaptations were neither manually coded English nor ASL, but they displayed much visual enhancement. In the 1960s and 1970s (the Total Communication or Sim-Com era), aural properties were emphasized—for example, by accompanying the sign language with a great deal of mouthing. More recently, two trends have predominated: works and adaptations that pay no heed to English and its aural properties, and very artistic and literary ASL works that try to approximate mainstream literary qualities (albeit in a visual way).
7. See Jane Kelleher, "Literature of Deaf Iowans: Linguistic Form and Social Function" (Ph.D. diss., University of Iowa, 1986), abstract in *Dissertation Abstracts International* 47 (1988): 4391A.

8. For Western poetry, drama, and narrative, I have in mind primarily modernist productions, specifically those of the United States, Ireland, and Great Britain. Poetry, particularly Continental poetry, became increasingly symbolic around the turn of the century. The poem became more overtly an art object—something put together artistically and artfully. Henry James then set out to make the novel as artistic and sophisticated as poetry with works such as *The Golden Bowl* (1904). Drama, as Eugene O'Neill's *Hairy Ape* (1922) demonstrates, also became more abstract and obscure. On artistic ASL in Washington, D.C., the *Poetry in Motion* videocassette (discussed in chapter 8) of Clayton Valli, who was on the Gallaudet faculty in the 1980s, came out in 1990. Ben Bahan and Sam Supalla appeared in the first installment of the ASL Literature Series in 1992, and Don Bangs and Pat Graybill produced *Institution Blues* in 1993 and *A Deaf Family Diary* in 1994.

9. *Institution Blues*, scripted by Don Bangs and Jan DeLap, dir. Don Bangs, prod. SignRise Cultural Arts, Publick Playhouse, Cheverly, Md., October 1, 1993; *A Deaf Family Diary*, script by Don Bangs, dir. Patrick Graybill, SignRise Cultural Arts, Publick Playhouse, Cheverly, Md., February–March 1994.

10. Ben Bahan and Sam Supalla, *Bird of a Different Feather and For a Decent Living*, ASL Literature Series, prod. Joe Dannis, San Diego, Calif., Dawn Pictures/DawnSignPress, videocassette, 60 min., 1992.

11. At Gallaudet, Gil Eastman developed the two *Sign Me Alice* plays in 1973 and 1983 respectively, and Steve Baldwin wrote some original plays at Southwest Collegiate Institute for the Deaf in Texas in the early 1980s.

12. See the editor's glossary to M. M. Bakhtin, *The Dialogic Imagination: Four Essays*, ed. Michael Holquist, trans. Caryl Emerson and Michael Holquist (Austin, Tex.: University of Texas Press, 1981), 431.

13. To be sure, the printed form of English has also benefited Deaf Americans, providing an inexpensive means of communicating over a distance. When they phone or e-mail one another, they use English (along with a TTY or computer). They rely on newsletters such as the *Hessian Post* (the alumni publication of the Maryland School for the Deaf) and national publications such as *Deaf Life*, the *NAD Broadcaster*, and the *Deaf American*. Regional publications such as *Dee Cee Eyes* in the Washington, D.C., area keep the community abreast of local events and activities.

14. On the Coyote figure, see Paul Radin, *The Trickster: A Study in American Indian Mythology* (London: Routledge and Kegan Paul, 1956); Bo Scholer, ed., *Coyote Was Here: Essays on Contemporary Native American Literary and Political Mobilization* (Seklos, Denmark: University of Aarhus, 1984); Elizabeth Ammons and Annette White-Parks, eds., *Tricksterism in Turn-of-the-Century American Literature* (Hanover, N.H.: University Press of New England, 1994). On the monkey god, see Henry Louis Gates, Jr., *The Signifying Monkey: A Theory of Afro-American Literary Criticism* (New York: Oxford University Press, 1988).

15. Gates, *The Signifying Monkey*, 6–11.

16. Mikhail Bakhtin, *Rabelais and His World*, trans. Hélène Iswolsky (Cambridge, Mass.: MIT Press, 1968), 4–6.

17. Polyglossia is especially pronounced when an oral culture and language compete with a literate culture and language, as in the case of both medieval carnival-goers and modern Deaf Americans.

18. See Ruth Finnegan, *Oral Poetry: Its Nature, Significance, and Social Context* (New York: Cambridge University Press, 1977), 121.

19. Douglas Bullard, *Islay: A Novel* (Silver Spring, Md.: TJ Publishers, 1986); Gilbert C. Eastman, *Sign Me Alice*, intro. George Detmold, pref. Gilbert Eastman (Washington, D.C.: Gallaudet College, 1974); Rex Lowman, *Bitterweed* ([Bentonville, Ark.]: Bella Vista Press, 1964).

20. *My Third Eye*, dir. J Ranelli, written and prod. National Theatre of the Deaf, 1971–72; Bahan and Supalla, *Bird of a Different Feather and For a Decent Living*; Peter Cook, performance at the ASL Literature Conference, Rochester, N.Y., 1996.

Chapter
2

Carnival: Orature and Deaf American Literature

LITERATURE HAS been defined as writings in prose or verse, as a body of written works, and as printed matter.[1] If we look at the ASL component of Deaf American literature and its traditional forms, however, we must either stop calling it literature or reconsider our definition.

Indeed, Deaf American literature, particularly its ASL component, actually transgresses the bounds of conventional discourse, which uses speech or print. The very label "ASL literature"—applied to a work not written down—itself breaks the rules of literature. In breaking the rules this form is doing something new, something different, perhaps something better; it thereby displays the essence of "carnival." As Mikhail Bakhtin points out in *Rabelais and His World*, "Carnival was the true feast of time, the feast of becoming, change, and renewal. It was hostile to all that was immortalized and completed."[2]

Happily, the "immortalized and completed" no longer have the same value they once enjoyed. Literary analysts and others have begun to take stock of the complex and wide-ranging nature of discourse. For one thing, the "literary" has changed, evolved, and metamorphosed through the centuries. For another, our Western "masterpieces" are not so "complete" as they once seemed. Many analysts have veered away from focusing on only the written masterpieces and not-so-minor works of Western civilization. As the previously unassailable literary canon is scrutinized and rehashed, more scholars turn their attention away from the written works of Western civilization long accepted as masterpieces and as major works. Such refocusing and reevaluation has been part of the decentering that has fundamentally changed most areas of study in recent decades.[3]

Consequently, conventional terms of praise—literariness, excellence, universality, and humanism—have lost some of their luster and no longer appear as the be-all and end-all of writing and discourse. Instead, there is growing recognition and acceptance of the different functions and stylistics of other discourse modes, forms, and genres: orature, women's writing and discourse, folklore, minority vernacular traditions, and the like. Orature—that is, productions by an oral culture—is especially effective at overturning preconceptions. Thus, the discourse of Deaf Americans exemplifies with particular aptness the decentering of contemporary literature and literary study.

Orature, Orality, and Literacy

A driving force of our carnivalesque Deaf American literature is its oral characteristics. Though ASL, a visual-kinetic vernacular without a written form, involves no speech, it nevertheless falls into the oral category because it relies on face-to-face communication. All this was pointed out in 1993 by *Oral Tradition*, a periodical specializing in research on orality and orature, when it published an intriguing conversation that took place on an on-line discussion group mediated by the Center for Studies in Oral Tradition. Lois Bragg, a Deaf professor on the English faculty of Gallaudet University, made the point that Deaf culture is definitely, and paradoxically, an oral culture and that ASL literature is "perhaps the only true living 'oral' literature in the Western world." Another participant in this dialogue, Stephanie Hall, a researcher at the American Folklife Center at the Library of Congress, asserted that we need to distinguish oral language (i.e., transmitted via the oral apparatus) from signed language (i.e., conveyed on the hands, face, and body). However, when it comes to oral tradition or rhetoric per se, there is little difference between the signing of Deaf Americans and the speaking of cultures recognized as oral.[4]

Pure oratures went out of existence hundreds if not thousands of years ago, but ASL discourse is close to being pure orature because its visual-kinetic modality resists close-written inscription and resists the usual "contamination" by the written tradition.[5] In fact, it is next to impossible to adequately translate the "communicating body" into spoken or written words. Many Deaf Americans, who depend primarily on their eyes and body for linguistic and other information, prefer communication via the hands, face, and body, setting them apart from most of the world's population (who rely on their ears and on printed material). Therefore, they have continued to use a visual-kinetic vernacular and in the process generated a discourse that is at odds with printed languages and literatures. Because of this divergence, their discourse has played a part in the decentering of Western literary discourse. The general decentering of social science has brought renewed attention to orality and orature.

Scholars have long been intrigued about how people expressed themselves—and what their literature was like—before literacy became widespread. Milman Parry, Walter Ong, Eric A. Havelock, and Albert B. Lord, among others, believe that Western peoples have adjusted so completely to reading and writing that they now think differently, approach interpersonal communication differently, and have a different outlook on life than did peoples who used to rely on face-to-face communication.[6] In the past all cultures had a spoken literature, an orature, which is thought to have been quite unlike the written literature of the present. It may have had a different function—perhaps not so much art for art's sake as art for people's sake. It may have taken forms other than those familiar to us from the short stories and poetry of today. There may have been an aesthetics of "telling a good story" rather than "writing a good story."[7]

In *Orality and Literacy*, Walter Ong describes literacy as a comparatively new development that did not materialize all at once. Writing and the subsequent development of literacy spread very gradually and sporadically. At first, literacy was confined to those such as bookkeepers, monks, and scribes for whom writing had a practical function. Later, as men of the upper classes gained leisure time they became largely literate. Not until the rise of the middle class and the invention of the printing press did literacy truly take off. In addition to becoming literate themselves, middle-class reformers worked energetically, beginning in the eighteenth century, to promote public schooling and thus universal literacy. Aside from Deaf literature, today only a few pockets of orality or semi-orality remain, in more remote corners of the world such as the rain forests of South America and less-developed regions of the former Soviet Union.

For the most part, as literacy has increased through the centuries, orality has decreased correspondingly. As a result of this very gradual process, many early written works exhibit an intermixing of oral and literary elements. At times, in many European cultures the lingering oral vernacular traditions have collided with the soon-to-be-dominant literary tradition of early elites; and even in countries with almost universal literacy, those oral remnants are treasured to this day. As Carol Simpson Stern and Bruce Henderson have observed, folklore and many minority literatures (including Asian American and African American) have retained oral characteristics. These rather recalcitrant discourses of the people have persisted in contrast to the more sophisticated (and more conforming) written literature of the literary elite and canon.[8]

We can thus hardly be surprised that Deaf Americans, with a culture based on a visual vernacular, frequently collide with the larger mainstream culture that prioritizes speech, reading, and writing in English. Although many schools for the deaf accept the use of ASL, their curriculums nevertheless stress competency in English. For the most part, instruction concentrates on English syntax and discourse, with no comparable training in ASL. At Gallaudet

University, for example, two years of English instruction is required; ASL instruction is optional.[9] The logic seems to be that since almost all students must seek to obtain employment within mainstream society, competency in English will be a crucial asset.

The Middle Ages

The situation of Deaf Americans resembles that of medieval Europeans before the invention of the printing press.[10] Then, literacy was largely restricted to the upper classes and the clerical orders; the peasantry, townspeople, and traders in premedieval and medieval Europe were mostly oral peoples. Yet written Latin language was valued over oral vernaculars.[11] In their everyday lives, the medieval populace communicated in the vernacular, but written and spoken Latin was used for "higher" (more sophisticated) functions: church liturgy, written records, correspondence, and so on. Within the culture, language use shifted back and forth between Latin for formal use and the vernacular for informal use—that is, between literacy and orality.

Yet throughout the Middle Ages and Renaissance, the various European vernaculars gradually gained the upper hand. For instance, vernacular Italian, which emerged as a separate language about 1000 C.E., competed vigorously with official written and spoken Latin, incorporating many Latinate features and forms in the process. With the poetry of Dante in the early Renaissance, written Italian could finally be considered on a par with written Latin. By the middle of the sixteenth century, Italian had almost completely replaced Latin in both writing and speaking.[12] Nowadays, this vernacular enjoys a sophisticated written form; Latin is universally known as a "dead" language and is used only rarely.

In the Middle Ages, there was competition among social groups, languages, and rhetorical forms.[13] The competition between and intermixing of social and discourse structures climaxed during carnival or festival time. Despite or perhaps partly because of the social and rhetorical strictures imposed by medieval authorities, festivities and popular rituals were a vital part of the culture of the Middle Ages. Some of the cities, by Bakhtin's reckoning, devoted an average of three months a year to fairs, harvest festivals, market days, popular feasts and wakes, processions, competitions, and other open-air amusements.[14] These often included comic shows, mummery and dance in costumes and sometimes masks, giants, dwarfs, and trained animals. During these festivities, which were also an occasion for opportunistic, creative language use, all the social classes with their diverse modes of communication merrily commingled. Such commingling was a playful competing of two ways of living and communicating, in which the "low" and "common" temporarily got the upper hand.

From the aristocracy to the townspeople to the outlying farmers, all individuals came together during festival for a break from everyday life. During this time, cultural mores and social rules were temporarily loosened. The resulting hiatus was carnival. In *Literature and Liminality: Festive Readings in the Hispanic Tradition*, Gustavo Perez Firmat remarks that "Carnival, an interstitial, transgressive moment in the yearly calendar, ushers in a topsy-turvy world, a mundus inversus where the usual rules and restraints are temporarily suspended."[15] The world is not simply leveled, with the ruling classes, peasantry, and townspeople mingling on a somewhat equal footing, but turned upside down. The members of the ruling classes become the few in the midst of the many, as the people, at other times repressed and subservient, in effect become the temporary rulers.

Carnival as *Mundus Inversus*

Carnival is a time of transgressions and playfulness, filled with festivity and exuberance. For the closest modern equivalent, imagine a state fair with its sprawl of amusement rides, eateries, game booths, coin throws, rifle galleries, livestock barns, craft exhibits, grandstand shows, horse racing, dirt bike sprints, and so on. Authorities may prefer the regular, rational, decorous, homogeneous, conformist, and moderate—what they believe is proper, civilized, and stable—but the fair or carnival is all-out revelry. It dishes out the nonrational, heterogeneous, bizarre, grotesque, exorbitant, and so forth. Perhaps even more comparable are the carnival sideshows of the recent past, featuring the bizarre, the freakish, the unusual, the unexpected: the Woman with Three Arms, the Pregnant Man, the Alligator Girl, and the House of Mirrors. Here the unconventional, the unorthodox, the irregular, and the extraordinary are in full play.

Additionally, at the fair or carnival, rather than the spiritual and abstract (as Christian spirituality seeks) the physical and the earthly are glorified.[16] Every state and county fair in the United States includes displays of blue-ribbon livestock and the choicest baked and canned goods. The Ferris wheel with its revolving, sparkling lights, the sideshows with their exaggerated graphics, and the colorfully costumed carnival performers provide a feast for the eyes. Rather than the decorous harmonies and toned-down hues of everyday society, the fair is a kaleidoscope of the visual and spectacular, enhanced by a cacophony of noise, music, and song.

Implicit in carnival is a challenging of authority(ies) and their social mores and regulations. As Bakhtin observes, "As opposed to the official feast, one might say that carnival celebrated temporary liberation from the prevailing truth and from the established order; it marked the suspension of all hierarchical rank, privileges, norms, and prohibitions."[17] Such transgression and playfulness were and still are typical of festivals, fairs, and carnivals.[18] Witness South American carnival, Mardi Gras, and various gay pride parades and marches. These events are all characterized by male-female reversals, as many celebrants dress up in women's clothes that exaggerate their femininity—including overabundant bra padding, garish makeup, and wobbly high heels. The spectacular and even sensational floats and costumes are anything but moderate and subdued.

During the medieval carnival, as a part of the general liberation, popular folk forms and activities were temporarily tolerated. As Bakhtin explains at length in *Rabelais and His World*, it was an opportunity for the people to participate in rituals, ceremonies, and discourse that were usually unwelcome by the majority or the ruling classes. As many of these activities involved sporting with official forms, an intermixing of the official and the popular ensued.[19] Sometimes the populace would come up with vernacular forms that employed, often very playfully, some features of official forms; sometimes the official was made to take on popular characteristics.

Indeed, the populace often disparaged or mocked these official forms, which stressed respect, restraint, and other conventions of expression and behavior promoted by the ruling classes.

This temporary suspension of the norms led to a frank and free type of communication not usually seen in the highly stratified everyday life of medieval people. Such communication had its own logic or illogic, one often shared by parodies and travesties: what Bakhtin calls the logic of the "inside out." Many verbal compositions and rituals reversed established hierarchical structures, moving what was on top to the bottom and elevating what was on the bottom to the top. For instance, many boisterous songs featured the king's jester on the throne, and the king himself banished to the foot of the table. In effect, the king or slaveholder was unseated and the fool or slave temporarily "ruled."[20]

In fact, in playing with official forms, the populace often got down and dirty. These intermixed, comic forms highlighted the physicality and materiality represented by the lower body and devalued the intellectuality and spirituality represented by the head. Their intent was to take potshots at conventional, "civilized" forms of conduct and discourse: the grotesque or material body and its everyday functions (eating, drinking, scratching, excreting, copulating, etc.) were used against decorous behavior and norms of decorum and spirituality.[21]

Carnivalesque Discourse

Comic verbal compositions, including oral and written parodies, travesties, and vulgar farce, were extremely well-received during the Middle Ages.[22] All these forms of low folk humor—as well as curses, oaths, slang, tricks, jokes, and scatological language—disrupted privileged, polite utterance. Bakhtin explains:

> All these forms of protocol and ritual based on laughter
> and consecrated by tradition existed in all the countries of
> medieval Europe; they were sharply distinct from the seri-
> ous, official, ecclesiastical, feudal, and political cult forms
> and ceremonials. They offered a completely different,
> nonofficial, extraecclesiastical and extrapolitical aspect of

the world, of man, and of human relations; they built a second world and a second life outside officialdom.[23]

This other world is not generally known to us today because it does not include the kind of behavior or "literature" that first the aristocracy and then the middle class have promoted, preserved, or publicized. Additionally, since much of this comic folk literature was oral discourse, it has largely vanished into the mists of time. Most of all, such humor is often subversive and aggressive, for when one laughs, one both laughs with and *at* someone. A sense of superiority is felt by those who tell a joke, poke fun at something or someone, and generally indulge in mirth.[24] In brief, laughing is a way of turning the world upside down, an effect hardly welcomed by the aristocracy or the middle class.

But the comic folk literature of the Middle Ages was important despite its not being high, serious, and aesthetic. Most of the populace participated in it; and at a time when few were literate, this discourse was frequently oral. Whether one had a flair for comic expression or not, anyone could make merry during carnival time. Even priests and lay brothers were known to compose humorous versions of the liturgy and the Psalms.[25] Frequent participants were the traveling bards, minstrels, and jongleurs who were the story-tellers, poets, and performers of the Middle Ages. Court jesters, town fools, and jugglers also regaled the populace with songs, jests, stories, and other popular forms of expression.

For a number of reasons, carnival and carnivalesque discourse provide appropriate paradigms for understanding Deaf culture and discourse. Here again, members of a primarily oral culture and some members of a primarily literate culture gather and interact. Carnival provides a break from schooling and from working in the hearing world, a time when Deaf Americans can rely mainly on (oral) ASL rather than (written) English. It allows them to be themselves, unconstrained in how they act and communicate, and also to make merry with mainstream society in numerous forms of ritual and discourse based on laughter, much as the common people in the Middle Ages did during festival time.

Just as the medieval carnival was one big spectacle, so too the Deaf festival has much to feed the eye. Media are predominately visual; everywhere video screens show signing and captioning. Carnival-goers' arms, hands, and heads are in motion. Faces frown, light up, give emphasis, and look aghast. Such extensive use of the face and body in communicating is the norm within Deaf culture but appears excessive if not indecorous in the context of a mainstream culture that downplays the body in formal discourse. Thus, like the many popular forms that stressed the body—even the lower body—during medieval carnival time, many ASL forms valorize the visual and the use of the body. In the process, these embodied, visual forms overturn the dominant discourse that privileges aural and print communication.

As we have seen, in the Middle Ages the playful intermixing of the literate and the oral often involved laughter, satire, and parody —tools of critique that also permeate Deaf American literature and discourse. As MJ Bienvenu has asserted, "Even though we don't have the sense of hearing as our fifth sense, we have the sense of humor as our fifth sense."[26] Almost every major conference or event focusing on Deaf culture includes a presentation or workshop on the prevalence of humor in Deaf discourse. One need only look to Roy Holcomb's *Hazards of Deafness*, the videotaped narratives by Ben Bahan and Sam Supalla, indigenous Deaf dramatic productions, Literary Night, storytelling, and even social gatherings to find humor.[27] Facilitating the merriment is the Deaf American Jester—ASL storyteller, poet, playwright, or comedian. Just as the minstrels, jesters, and jongleurs were everywhere during carnival time in the Middle Ages, so Jester is frequently in evidence at Deaf affairs, whether in festive apparel or suit and tie.

The Deaf American Jester

Festivals and fairs abound in Deaf culture, and an abundance of Deaf Jesters practice a festive critique in diverse ways. In Elizabethan drama, Olive Mary Busby has pointed out, "the jongleurs combined in varying proportions the qualities of the honored bard of Germanic times and the coarse and licentious buffoons of the later Roman stage, often adding to these acrobatic and other tricks acquired from other strolling entertainers of the Middle Ages."[28]

So too is the Deaf ASL artist a kind of jongleur who playfully combines the qualities of both the bard and the buffoon. In so doing, he or she both brings down the house and strews pearls of wisdom.

Wherever Deaf Americans gather in large numbers, there is carnival, and over it all presides a Deaf American Jester. For instance, at a Mardi Gras event in the mid-1990s Stephen Ryan served as Court Jester par excellence. A Phi Kappa Zeta Literary Night at Gallaudet University in 1994 was emceed by a pledge in clown attire. In announcing each performance, she alternated between clownish behavior and dignified address. *My Third Eye*, a 1971–72 production by the National Theatre of the Deaf, has an important segment called "Side Show," a circus scene with a ringmaster and acrobats. Indeed, the whole play gives the viewers the impression of being at a carnival. The 1982 Fairmount Theatre of the Deaf production *Circus of Signs* used a circus format and "clowns" to demonstrate some of the possibilities of sign language as an art form. *Fingers That Tickle and Delight: Stories by Evelyn Zola* features Ms. Zola in a feathered headdress and a feathered wraparound (boa) much like an entertainer at a carnival might wear.[29]

Clowns, jesters, and fools—the representatives of carnival—are not simply buffoons made the butt of society's jokes. They are instead a source of true wisdom that arises from their peculiar double perspective: they stand both within society looking out, and outside society looking in. From their unique position, they are able to hold up the mirror of truth to society.[30] Thus in Shakespeare's *King Lear*, the court fool is the only one who truly *sees* behind the artifice. Likewise, the Jester sees the true state of affairs in Deaf society and communicates what he or she perceives in an entertaining way. Such truth-revealing humor, according to Susan Rutherford, serves to release aggression and relieve group anxieties.[31] It helps members of the minority and the majority better understand both themselves and one another.

The ABC Story-Poem

The Deaf American Jester can be seen in action with the ABC story-poem, a staple at Deaf gatherings large and small. The ABC story is in the vernacular, that is, in ASL, but it makes use of and indeed plays with the English alphabet. Like an English alphabetical acrostic, an ABC story-poem begins with a word or sign using the A handshape, then one using the B handshape, and so on.[32] In this fashion, the performer puts all the signs together to make a story or poem.

The challenge is to tell and perform a fully plotted story, complete with character(s) and action, that makes the audience forget the constraints of the format. In this way, the English alphabet is employed by our Jester to structure comical and unorthodox stories in very fluent ASL. In hanging these stories on the English alphabet, our Jester is making merry with the English language, turning it and rhetorical tradition topsy-turvy. The alphabet's original function—to represent the consonants and vowels of an aural language—is completely done away with. One point for ASL. In addition, using the alphabet as a structuring or organizing device plays havoc with mainstream genre distinctions; is the result a story or a poem? Or does it blithely deign to fit into either English genre? Two points for ASL. The aurality of the consonants and vowels is entirely eclipsed by the visuality of ASL. Three points. Such intermixing subverts the majority language (English), the generic Western narrative, and the mainstream literary tradition as a whole.

In the ABC story, our Jester indirectly comments on the respective languages and the respective cultures in play. By treating taboo subjects and using the English alphabet to structure a kind of burlesque, Jester seems to be saying that Deaf Americans do not need to be repressed or intimidated by the English language; its importance in American society does not make it the *sole* measure of identity and competency. By using the handshapes of the English alphabet so expressively and eloquently, Jester is implying that ASL is a language just as worthy and beautiful—a visual language of a visually oriented people. The ABC story is not a story or a poem but ASL vernacular art: thus English generic distinctions need not apply. Here ASL gets the better of English much as the wonderfully winning, popular comic forms of the Middle Ages triumphed over formal discourse.

Metadiscourse

Just as the writers and performers of the Middle Ages negotiated between the official and the popular, so our Deaf American Jesters travel the continuum between the rhetorical traditions of English and ASL. The works and productions of Jesters say something about the two traditions—how they function, how they do or do not come together, why they are useful, and how they reflect their cultures. Jesters can see the differences and the similarities and play on them. This sportive double-voicedness as two traditions vie with one another makes possible the carnivalesque aspects of Deaf American literature.

At carnival, Deaf Americans can play around with ASL and English. They scoop up native forms and conventional English forms and cheerfully mix them, adding a spoonful of laughter, several cups of body, and a gallon or two of visuality. Particularly apt at the game is Jester, who takes some elements from the vernacular tradition and others from the mainstream literary tradition, molding them together into something completely new—something merrily at odds with the conventional notion of "literature" set out at the beginning of this chapter.

Notes

1. *Merriam Webster's Collegiate Dictionary*, 10th ed., s.v. "literature."
2. Mikhail Bakhtin, *Rabelais and His World*, trans. Hélène Iswolsky (Cambridge, Mass.: MIT Press, 1968), 10.
3. For works particularly germane to my discussion, see Carol Simpson Stern and Bruce Henderson, *Performance: Texts and Contexts* (New York: Longman, 1993); Dennis Tedlock, *The Spoken Word and the Art of Interpretation* (Philadelphia: University of Pennsylvania Press, 1983); and Bill Ashcroft, Gareth Griffiths, and Helen Tiffin, *The Empire Writes Back: Theory and Practice in Post-Colonial Literatures* (London: Routledge, 1989).
4. "Deafness and Orality: An Electronic Conversation," *Oral Tradition* 8 (2): 416.
5. See Ruth Finnegan, *Literacy and Orality: Studies in the Technology of Communication* (Oxford: Blackwell, 1988), 5.

6. Milman Parry, *The Making of Homeric Verse: The Collected Papers of Milman Parry,* ed. Adam Parry (New York: Oxford University Press, 1987); Walter J. Ong, *Orality and Literacy: The Technologizing of the Word* (London: Methuen, 1982); Eric A. Havelock, *Preface to Plato* (Cambridge, Mass.: Belknap Press of Harvard University Press, 1963); Albert B. Lord, *The Singer of Tales,* Harvard Studies in Comparative Literature, 24 (Cambridge, Mass.: Harvard University Press, 1960).

7. See Carol Simpson Stern and Bruce Henderson, *Performance: Texts and Contexts* (New York: Longman, 1993).

8. Ibid., 72.

9. See Brenda Jo Brueggemann, *Lend Me Your Ear: Rhetorical Constructions of Deafness* (Washington, D.C.: Gallaudet University Press, 1999), 50.

10. Lois Bragg, "ASL Literature's Cultural Milieu: Audience Expectations and Participation," paper presented at the ASL Literature Conference, National Technical Institute for the Deaf, Rochester, N.Y., October 1991.

11. Allon White, *Carnival, Hysteria, and Writing: Collected Essays and Autobiography* (New York: Oxford University Press, 1993), 135–59.

12. Similar stories of language development can be gleaned from any reputable encyclopedia; e.g., the *World Book Encyclopedia* (1998), s.v. "Italian."

13. Such intermixing and competing of social strata (ruling classes vs. general populace) and discourse structures (Latin vs. vernacular) within a single social system were characterized as "carnivalesque" by Bakhtin in *Rabelais and His World,* 15.

14. Ibid., 13.

15. Gustavo Perez Firmat, *Literature and Liminality: Festive Readings in the Hispanic Tradition* (Durham, N.C.: Duke University Press, 1986), xv.

16. Bakhtin, *Rabelais and His World,* 18.

17. Ibid., 10.

18. Peter Stallybrass and Allon White make a similar observation in *The Poetics and Politics of Transgression* (London: Methuen, 1986), 11.

19. Bakhtin, *Rabelais and His World,* 13.

20. Ibid., 10–11.

21. Ibid., 21.

22. Latin parodies or semiparodies were common. *Parodia sacra,* or "sacred parody," extended to liturgies (e.g., "The Liturgy of the

Drunkards"), sacred prayers including the Ave Maria, litanies, hymns, psalms, and Gospel sayings. Similar vernacular parodies took as their starting points prayers, sermons, Christmas carols, and legends of the saints; others parodied epics and dealt with heroic deeds, epic heroes (e.g., the comic Roland), and knightly tales (e.g., "The Mule without a Bridle"). See Bakhtin, *Rabelais and His World*, 13–15.

23. Ibid., 5–6.

24. Christie Davies points out that "a sense of sudden vicarious superiority is felt by those who devise, tell or share a joke" in *Ethnic Humor around the World: A Comparative Analysis* (Bloomington: Indiana University Press, 1990), 7.

25. Bakhtin, *Rabelais and His World*, 13–14.

26. Bienvenu is quoted in E. Lynn Jacobowitz, "Humor and Wit in the Deaf Community," on p. 191 of *Deaf Studies: What's Up?*, proceedings of a conference held in Washington, D.C., October 24–25, 1991.

27. Roy Holcomb, *The Hazards of Deafness* (Northridge, Calif.: Joyce Media, 1977); Ben Bahan and Sam Supalla, *Bird of a Different Feather and For a Decent Living*, ASL Literature Series, prod. Joe Dannis, San Diego, Calif., Dawn Pictures/DawnSignPress, videocassette, 60 min., 1992.

28. Olive Mary Busby, *Studies in the Development of the Fool in the Elizabethan Drama* (Philadelphia: R. West, 1977), 9.

29. *Fingers That Tickle and Delight: Stories by Evelyn Zola*, 32 min., performed by Evelyn Zola, prod. Elizabeth Sher, interpreted by Sharon Neumann Solow (Berkeley, Calif.: I.V. Studios, 1994).

30. Chris Stephenson, e-mail to author, May 1995.

31. Susan R. Rutherford, "A Study of American Deaf Folklore" (Ph.D. diss., University of California at Berkeley, 1987), 14. "Clowning" is also often a vehicle for the expression of powerful social and political ideas, as can be seen in the traditional Punch and Judy puppet shows.

32. The American manual alphabet has exactly twenty-six signs, one for each letter of the English alphabet: the first sign is the A handshape, the next is the B handshape, and so on.

Chapter

3

Deaf Carnivals as Centers of Culture

⤸

CARNIVALS, FESTIVALS, fairs, and conventions are a cornerstone of present-day Deaf culture. These gatherings are essential, for sign language—and thus its art forms—requires face-to-face interaction. Unless people congregate in a fairly substantial group, little ASL literature can materialize. Because Deaf people are scattered all over the country, carnival makes possible the dissemination of vernacular storytelling, recorded works on videotape, and texts in English. At these festive gatherings the culture manifests itself in force, a condition necessary to generate literature and the potential for later literature. Carnival is therefore a prerequisite of a healthy Deaf literature, whether that entails texts in English, sign language adaptations, vernacular art forms, or new ASL creations.

At carnival Deaf Americans feel free to be themselves and to produce and distribute their literature. For this minority culture, usually dispersed throughout the majority culture, carnival is the site of communal celebration and liberation. Similarly, Mikhail Bakhtin notes, fairs in the Middle Ages "were the second life of the people, who for a time entered the utopian realm of community, freedom, equality, and abundance."[1] At other times, the people were answerable to feudal lords and masters; only during fairs, harvest festivals, and other festivities was some degree of latitude possible, both in their behavior and in their production of popular art forms. The medieval populace eagerly awaited and participated in these frequent festivals and the literature that they generated; Deaf Americans, who at other times work and live within mainstream society, look forward just as eagerly to festival time when they can engage in their vernacular discourse and literature.

Indeed, "the festival is at the heart of the culture and communication of deaf communities everywhere."[2] This observation in *On the Green*, the faculty/staff publication at Gallaudet University, was inspired by the wildly popular and successful Deaf Way: An International Festival and Conference on the Language, Culture, and History of Deaf People, which was held July 9–14, 1989, in Washington, D.C. The granddaddy of all festivals, the Deaf Way was both a convention and festival (a "confest"). This chapter focuses in large part on this particular confest because it displays so many different aspects of Deaf American carnival.

Gallaudet University, which sponsored Deaf Way, scheduled over 500 presentations and workshops at the Omni Shoreham Hotel and numerous artistic events and performances on campus. For a week, activities stretched from early morning to late evening; there were films, poster talks, exhibits, dramatic productions, workshops, booths, art displays, fashion, roving mimes and clowns, and more. Dancers, storytellers, mimes, and poets entertained in the evening while fairgoers relaxed, socialized, and lined up for Italian, Mexican, and Chinese food, as well as hot dogs and burgers. The 5,000 registrants included students, scholars, psychologists, researchers, linguists, scientists, sociologists, educators, and parents of deaf children from the United States and seventy-five other countries, with interpreters on hand to facilitate communication.[3] A couple of thousand additional, unofficial participants hung around the lobby of the Omni Shoreham and the Gallaudet campus throughout the festival—chatting, reminiscing, and engaging in extensive storytelling.

After and during the festival, countless informal social gatherings took place as Deaf Americans and international visitors congregated and participated in many rhetorical pleasures such as storytelling.

Festivals: Mobile Centers of Community

Gatherings like the Deaf Way are not simply social events or work-related conferences but have cultural and psychological significance. Deaf gatherings provide a focal point and a cultural center for a widely dispersed people, whose orientation (visual) and mode of communication (sign language) differ from those of mainstream society. Here Deaf Americans find community, ease of communication, and their own rhetorical traditions. Just as the viability of medieval culture was linked to the medieval fair, so too is today's festival crucial to the survival of Deaf culture.[4]

In the Middle Ages, fairs provided occasions for community activities of both town and church, for commerce and trade, and for education. At a time when schooling was not widespread and travel of any distance was rare, the fair was itself an educational experience for the lower classes. It also offered popular art forms, public or official rhetoric, and entertainment. Peter Stallybrass and Allon White describe it as "a kind of educative spectacle: a relay for the diffusion of cosmopolitan values of the centre throughout the provinces."[5] Similarly, Deaf festivals provide cultural (art) forms, political debate and action, educational workshops, new technology, interpreted tours, public services, and so forth. For instance, the biennial National Association of the Deaf (NAD) convention serves an official function for the association. Yet the convention also includes the Miss Deaf America pageant, workshops, lectures, exhibits, and tours. In addition, such festivals play as important a role in commerce as did their medieval predecessors. Many Deaf people who own businesses that are not located in large metropolitan centers rely on these gatherings for exhibiting and advertising their products and services.[6]

Thus, Deaf Americans come together from all over the country for periodic conventions, festivals (regional, national, and international), timberfests, school reunions, and the like. Like the Deaf Way, the flourishing Deaf Expo in California and the popular metropolitan festivals in Washington, D.C., are all eagerly awaited. The many academic conferences are also much anticipated and well-attended.[7] Alumni reunions of schools for the deaf attract former students from near and far. The regional and national bowling tournaments dotting the country draw great numbers of enthusiastic participants, and it is not unusual for Deaf people to plan overseas excursions around meetings of the World Federation of the Deaf and the World Games for the Deaf, which convene in a different country every four years.

At these gatherings, the community reaffirms and celebrates its culture and vernacular. Like the medieval fair, all these conventions, tournaments, and festivals serve to draw a widely dispersed community together. Deaf people, like the peoples of the Middle Ages, greatly value the immediacy of personal experience and the more intensive social interaction that is characteristic of traditional oral cultures.[8] Deaf Americans prefer to get together at clubs, at school reunions, in bowling leagues, and at the kitchen table rather than chatting over the phone or e-mailing. In fact, they often spend as much time socializing at such gatherings as they spend attending the official functions.

Indeed, Deaf Americans from all walks of life, ethnic backgrounds, and races travel considerable distances to attend conventions and festivals, much as the medieval populace traveled from outlying farms and manors to converge on the marketplace and fairs. Before telephones and television became accessible, Deaf Americans *had* to move to communicate, socialize, and seek entertainment. Even today, they go to great lengths to see other Deaf Americans and converse in their native language. When they travel and sightsee, they stop frequently along the way, having contacted in advance old friends and school chums and planned their itinerary accordingly.

The coming together of this widely dispersed community provides an arena for public discourse and literature. Once Deaf Americans get together with friends—on whatever occasion— they gather around the kitchen table, along the bar counter, or in the motel room and talk long into the night. A good deal of time is spent storytelling: relating adventures and misadventures of the trip so far and reporting goings-on in other regions of the country. They may also update one another on cultural developments and pass on—transmit—popular stories and other traditional ASL forms. A people who rely on a visual vernacular must meet face-to-face to preserve and disseminate their culture and literature. Even today's video technology cannot approximate the immediacy of oral storytelling, a point discussed at greater length in chapter 9.

The culture of Deaf Americans has no geographical center, but at the festivities where they gather they find a place of their own. Though it is temporary and transient, it is still worth traveling a long distance to get to and luxuriate in for a short time—to be among "family" and catch up on news and gossip. At the Deaf Way, Sam Sonnenstrahl, one of the attendees, exulted in being part of a "big, international family," a family exemplified by a table of fairgoers at the International Tent one evening. As one of the young men seated at the table stated, "East and West come together. I am from the Middle East, my friend here is from the West, and this young woman here is from the East."[9] This place becomes "home"— where one finds oneself and others like oneself; where one's identity is found or is reinforced and strengthened; where one is comfortable with people who communicate the same way and in the process engage in much informal and formal storytelling. Therefore, traveling to festivals and other large gatherings is part of a quest for "home" and identity.

A Place of One's Own

Because most Deaf Americans are born into mainstream (hearing) society but have little or no hearing, many do not fully identify with members of their family or feel fully at home in mainstream society, with its spoken and written English discourse. Lacking an ascribed identity—the identity stamped on one as a result of being a member of a particular family and community—many deaf people feel the need to "achieve" an identity. They must go out into the world and join together with other deaf people to learn what it means to be a Deaf American. A central state residential school draws young deaf children from what may be a very large area; once enrolled, a large percentage of the children (though less now than in the past) remain there for a good portion of the year, because the trip home is too long to make every day or on weekends. At the school, however, the children find people with whom they can communicate and share stories in ASL; they experience the feeling of being at home and part of one big family.[10]

Don Bangs's *Institution Blues* (1993) reveals how thoroughly the school for the deaf becomes a "home" and how all the children and the houseparents become one big family.[11] More often than not, the children arrive unable to communicate at all and thus not knowing why they have been left at the school. The other children, who probably have had the same experience, must help the new arrivals learn sign language and develop as a "civilized" human being. In Bangs's play, as the children are left to their own devices one evening, they play games together and create group narratives; in one, they portray all the animate and inanimate elements of the Frankenstein tale. As the scene closes, the children one after another join in a chorus, declaring "I have one hundred brothers and sisters! I have one hundred brothers and sisters!" They have come to the school from far and near, and there they have acquired a family and an identity.

Indeed, American literature in general has much to say about achieving identity. The cultural historian Werner Sollars argues that American society places greater emphasis on achieved identity than ascribed identity, for the United States has traditionally valued individualism as embodied in the independent, self-made man or woman going out and making his or her own way.[12] Many members of minority groups, in particular, find that they must achieve an identity: they must discover what it is to be a product of both minority and mainstream society, often discovering in the process that the price of success and acceptance is abandoning their own culture. Such a search for identity—or, more accurately, the evolving of a double identity—is the focus of much minority discourse and literature in the United States.

The *Sign Me Alice* plays of Gil Eastman, staged in 1973 and 1983 respectively, both focus on cultural identity.[13] Drawing on the Pygmalion theme, *Sign Me Alice* and *Sign Me Alice II* were the first full-length theatrical productions at Gallaudet University to deal with deafness. Specifically, they examine Deaf identity in relation to the majority culture. The focus is on Alice who, while working as a maid at a large hotel, meets a learned doctor attending a convention who offers to help her better herself. When she agrees, he instructs her in a kind of manual English and has her learn mainstream p's and q's. Being ambitious, Alice at first is eager to move up the ladder. However, she eventually comes to see that she has an identity in her own right—as a Deaf American—and that ASL, far from being a mongrel discourse, is a legitimate means of communication. Realizing this, she backs away from acculturation and instead chooses a path between the two cultures. She is aware of the mores and values of mainstream society but also takes pride in a Deaf identity and a unique visual vernacular.

Alice is a member of a widely dispersed minority group, many of whose members in effect leave their hearing families to find "home" and identity. This urge to travel and socialize in a quest for home is reflected in Deaf American history and literature (as is this quest in American literature as a whole). A particularly widely known story is that of Abbé de l'Epée's almost legendary efforts in the eighteenth century to seek out deaf children in the towns and country villages of France and bring them to Paris to educate them together. As Carol Padden and Tom Humphries report in *Deaf in America: Voices from a Culture*, "l'Epée's wanderings along a dark road represent each deaf child's wanderings before he or she, like l'Epée, finds home."[14]

In seeking home or identity, many Deaf Americans dream of and desire an empowered and autonomous Deaf culture, a social reality of their own; they desire a place where they belong, can identify with others, and can in turn be identified.[15] Not surprisingly, many Deaf American narratives deal with a homeland or a desire for a homeland. For example, Stephen Ryan's *Planet Way Over Yonder* is an ASL narrative about a young Deaf boy who rockets off the earth and lands on a planet where the majority of inhab-

itants are deaf while a small minority is hearing—a comical reversal
of the familiar two-world condition.[16] Communication media are
predominantly visual, as televisions and video screens dot the land-
scape and sign language is used in all the schools, hospitals, government buildings, theaters, and sports arenas.

Another case in point is Douglas Bullard's *Islay* (examined in
chapter 7), a novel that takes place largely on the road and that provides, along with a panorama of Deaf society, a blueprint for a
modern-day political and economic takeover.[17] Its audacious protagonist is an ordinary American with an extraordinary fantasy: to
establish a homeland for Deaf Americans. By the novel's end, his
dream has become a reality.

When Deaf Americans come together for carnival, for a temporary home, they make quite a diverse group (albeit one with a common purpose and a common characteristic). At this gathering,
numerous ideas are discussed, diverse perspectives are shared,
abundant information is made available, extensive commerce is
conducted, and a carnivalesque literature is able to flourish. By its
nature, the festival—in both its medieval and modern forms—not
only establishes and enhances local identity but also to some degree
unsettles this identity by admitting commerce and traffic from else-
where.[18] Like the medieval fair, the Deaf carnival is both bound-
ed—the center of the community—and the point at which commerce (in the most general sense of the word) and social
intercourse converge.

A Literature of Carnival

Although carnival or festival is the mobile center of the culture,
where Deaf identity is formed and reinforced, that culture is hardly
unitary; and its aggregation is mirrored by a richly diversified literature. Here we find not only the performative or oral forms of the
culture, including its traditional art forms, but also hybrid forms
and a conventional English print literature. Vernacular storytelling
and other ASL performance art take place informally in houses and
hotel rooms, while elaborate group and solo performances are
staged in ASL or manually coded English. Videotapes (often

captioned in English) of modern ASL narratives and poetry are offered for sale. And we must not forget the profusion of mime, farcical skits, magic acts, and general clowning. In this setting, decorous, disembodied print collides with very much embodied, visual ASL performances that hark back to the physicality and spectacle of the medieval fair. Again, as in festivals of the Middle Ages, popular forms of expressions and rituals abound and official forms and rituals are adapted, parodied, or burlesqued.

Deaf Americans come from far and near not simply to watch but to participate in all this literary and not-so-literary outpouring. As Bakhtin points out, in medieval carnivals, too, no one was only a spectator:

> Because of their obvious sensuous character and their strong element of play, carnival images closely resemble certain artistic forms, namely the spectacle. . . . But the basic carnival nucleus of this culture is by no means a purely artistic form nor a spectacle and does not, generally speaking, belong to the sphere of art. It belongs to the borderline between art and life. . . . In fact, carnival does not know footlights, in the sense that it does not acknowledge any distinction between actors and spectators. . . . Carnival is not a spectacle seen by the people; they live in it, and everyone participates because its very idea embraces all the people.[19]

Every Deaf American participates in carnival, in vernacular storytelling at the bar, in ASL art at the fraternity or sorority function, in viewing and critiquing modern ASL literature on videotape during a workshop session, in laughing at and with the strolling mimes and clowns during the Deaf Way banquet. For their part, ASL performers of various kinds often make a distinct effort to include their viewers in decidedly interactive productions.

The Literary Versus the Nonliterary

Deaf American literature, having as it does an "oral" component and being produced by a primarily oral people, contains both elements typically viewed as "literary" and elements typically viewed as "nonliterary." An oral literature does not have the same artistic concerns as written literature. As Bakhtin argues in *Rabelais and His World*, carnival specifically welcomes the literary and nonliterary, the printed and performative alike. Indeed it has fun with such distinctions and encourages their erasure.[20] Therefore, at the Deaf American carnival, various forms and modes exist alongside one another, often intermixing quite subversively.

Deaf American literature, particularly in its performative modes, is generally heterogeneous and inclusive. For instance, during the Deaf Way a personable young man from Taiwan took the stage one night at the International Tent on the Gallaudet campus and presented a medley of languages, rhetorical forms, and performative modes: dialogue with the viewers, storytelling, sign art, and interpretation.[21] He began by joking in serviceable ASL with his spectators about the Americans who were adopting Chinese children right and left. The young man then announced that he would perform some sign art in his native sign language and then interpret it in ASL. Such performances were welcome and enjoyed; one Danish fairgoer interviewed at the International Tent expressed first enjoyment at being exposed to many different sign languages and then hope that the Deaf Way would become a regular event.[22] His hope took the physical form of a (signed) caterpillar undulating up his forearm and developing into a graceful butterfly, wings folding and unfolding as it took off into the early evening sky.

Which was literature and which was not? Should we exclude the dialogue with the viewers, even though it was a kind of storytelling? Should we single out only the Chinese poem or the metamorphosing caterpillar as "literature" because it is artistic? Should the commentary or interpretation be excluded because it is not artistic? In both cases, multifaceted discourse arises out of and is part of a larger context; one cannot simply declare where the "literary" begins and where it ends. Such an interrelationship of teller, context, text, and viewers characterizes all oral literature, including the carnivalesque.

Carnival gatherings are particularly important in promoting oral or vernacular (ASL) art forms and their transmission. Unlike the literary forms of mainstream society, which can readily be reproduced and distributed via print and audiovisual media, these indigenous ASL productions rely primarily on the viewers at Deaf gatherings for their distribution. After these viewers take in storytelling, skits, poetry, and theatrical productions, many go home and try out their favorites in front of friends and other members of the Deaf community. In this way, ASL productions are disseminated. In the process they often change, resulting in many variants of a particular work. The endless reproduction of variants makes the literature constantly mobile and fluid.

Performative art forms predominate in Deaf culture and literature. As the world-renowned Polish deaf mime Miko Machalski commented in an interview during the Deaf Way, "Deaf people are particularly suited for theatrics because of sign language and movement."[23] Literal theatrics were visible at the opening night program of the Deaf Way, "The Night of 100 Stars," presented at George Washington University's Lisner Auditorium. The show was transmitted via satellite TV to conventioneers on the campus of Gallaudet University and to many countries around the world, as national theaters of the deaf assembled in one place for the first time ever. They included companies from the United States, France, Japan, Spain, Italy, China, Finland, Greece, the Soviet Union, Israel, Norway, India, Belgium, Sweden, Czechoslovakia, and the Philippines.[24]

The full spectrum of deaf theatrical productions was in evidence at the Deaf Way, ranging from the more nativist to the conventionally mainstream. Gallaudet's *Telling Stories* was an abstract, segmented presentation that used myths and symbols to explore the long conflict between the deaf and hearing worlds; another American production, the popular *Tales from a Clubroom*, was set in a typical deaf clubroom. More hybrid productions included such adaptations of mainstream plays as the (U.S.) National Theatre of the Deaf's *King of Hearts*, *Oedipus* (Moscow Theatre of Mime and Geste); *Hamlet* (senza Parole—an Italian theater company); and *Phantom of the Opera* (Philippine Theatrical Group). And because Deaf confests are more like medieval carnivals than like mainstream conventions, which are geared only to adults, children's theater productions were staged throughout the week.

Other relatively elaborate productions and performances at the International Tent on the Gallaudet campus during the Deaf Way were presented by performers who go from one festival to another, one college campus to another, and one metropolitan playhouse to another. Their works often display a carnivalesque quality as they zero in on the two-world condition of Deaf Americans, playing ASL off English and the vernacular tradition off the mainstream rhetorical tradition.[25]

The mixed works very characteristic of carnivalesque literature as a whole are equally common at Deaf festivals. Extensive interanimation of mainstream and Deaf American cultures and their respective rhetorical traditions could be seen in the presentations of SignWave, a singing and signing ensemble that headlined one evening at the International Tent. A half-dozen young men and women simultaneously sang and signed the lyrics word for word, in their English order. The signing as well as general body movements approximated the tune and pitch of a particular song. They thus dynamically blended the visual and the aural, the English words and the ASL signs.[26]

Appropriately for carnival, the more physical forms of Deaf discourse appeared side by side with sophisticated drama, ASL poetry, and eloquent storytelling. The jesters and jongleurs during the Middle Ages similarly entered the mix of entertainments.[27] The farcical and physical quality of many Deaf American skits was exemplified at the Deaf Way by a young mime. The mime portrayed his struggle to ingest some melted cheese. Despite his diligent efforts, the melted mess stretched and stretched and would not break off. At last, rather than disengaging, it parted the performer abruptly but effectively from his own teeth.[28] Other modern-day jongleurs included the performers in "Stars of Mime," "It's Cabaret" (Model Secondary School for the Deaf students), "Magic Night and Roving Magician," and "Curious Circus," the last presented by a theater from Singapore that uses fluorescent props that glow in ultraviolet light. (This company relies on the universal format of the circus to show off the talents of its young cast, who use masks, mime, and magic.)[29]

Such festivals are also the best place to find another component of this carnivalesque literature: texts and videotapes (often captioned, or at least with English lettering on the packaging) with English and ASL vying with one another are available at countless booths and exhibits. Outside of college campuses with many Deaf students and various organization headquarters, there are few stores catering primarily to Deaf Americans. Thus registrants at the various conventions and festivals crowd eagerly around the vendors and their wares. Here as well, the literary or artistic performances collide with the vernacular storytelling, art, and mime (not considered literature) in which everyone participates. Regardless of which seems to have the upper hand, the carnival offers a superlative opportunity to handle and purchase these writings and videotaped ASL art forms. For instance, during the homecoming festivities at Gallaudet University in 1998, students, faculty, staff, and visitors alike could browse among the Gallaudet University Press exhibits in the student union building adjacent to the football field. Many Deaf American authors were on hand to chat with browsers and autograph their works. At the 1995 Deaf Studies IV convention in Boston, business at the publishing booths was thriving. Indeed, convention and conference planners purposefully include sessions on cultural art forms both to promote them and to deepen the knowledge of attendees. ASL artists themselves are often on hand to conduct workshops.

Laughter, Satire, and Parody

As the earlier discussion of medieval festivals made clear, mainstream or dominant forms of discourse are often adapted and burlesqued during carnival. The similarly subversive, farcical nature of a great deal of our carnivalesque Deaf literature was much in evidence at the NAD convention in Knoxville, Tennessee, in 1994. *Deafology 101: A Crash Course in Deaf Culture*, a comedy presentation by Ken Glickman, a.k.a. Prof. Glick, was one of the very first events on the convention schedule.[30] This extremely entertaining mock lecture on Deaf culture as seen through the eyes of a Deaf humorist poked fun not only at mainstream society and its expectations of Deaf Americans, from birth onward, but also at Deaf culture itself. Indeed, the videotape version (which was available at the NAD convention) begins by displaying the title and playing upbeat classical music—itself a thrust at the "classical." In brief, the production is a classic of what happens to the classical in carnival.

The action in *Deafology 101* begins when Prof. Glick, sporting baggy shorts, black reading glasses, rumpled lab coat, a big bow tie, and disheveled hair, comes striding onstage smoking a pipe, his appearance obviously satirizing absent-minded professors and the educational system that nurtures them. As the professor introduces the course, he stipulates that there is no required reading but has a recommendation: two colorful paperback texts and the human body itself. He explains that the body is necessary for body language, that is, for "bawdy language" or dirty language (which, he points out, is the "same thing"). Instead of the bourgeois downplaying of the physical, we have here a gleeful affirmation of American Sign Language and its expansive use of the body. In introducing himself, Glick asks rhetorically, "What am I? I am a deafologist. Like a scientist? No. I'm a signtist and we will use the signtific method to study the culture." The performer is understated and underhanded in this apparent salute to science and other mainstream systems of knowledge. "Over many years," he continues, "We've experienced many kinds of situations in our deaf world. Every time I spot a unique situation in the deaf world I ask myself what that is called. I run to that big, thick book. It's called an English dictionary. Nothing there." Its very emptiness is why Glick sees a need to analyze particular situations and "describe those situations more accurately and appropriately." Describing accurately is precisely what he does not do, and in this satirical analysis he is not doing it "appropriately."

Prof. Glick also carnivalesquely describes Deaf culture and the mainstream culture that it is and is not a part of. He asks, "What is Deaf Culture? It is deafined as a wonderful way of life that is unheard of. That will be on your test." Continually pacing back and forth between blackboard and podium, Glick goes on to state that deaf people interact with "those people who can't help but hear," noting that "The world is full of hearing people. Let's shorten that to hearies." He then shortens "deaf people" to "deafies." In between are the "heafies"—deafies who look and act like hearies—and the hearies who act like deafies, or "dearies." "Oh, I love them," he proclaims. "Want an example? Here are two dearies." (He gestures at two interpreters sitting in the first row.) Glick continues, "After this lecture I'll get a piece of paper called an in*voice*. It's for their hearings."

The carnivalesque spirit infuses Ken Glickman's production; his show saw the light of day because of the temporary communal celebration and liberation provided by the NAD convention. As Prof. Glick, he feels free to parody "dumb hearies" and to poke fun at himself and other Deaf Americans as "dumb deafies." Glickman also has free rein to make fun of the majority language and its manifestations: discourse in English, publications in English, and the educational system that relies on English. Glickman mixes writing in English (notes on the blackboard) and ASL discourse (his own signing). His performance is highly skilled yet "low" and entertainingly mocking, as if to get back at the high literature and discourse of mainstream society. Moreover, he draws his viewers into this carnivalesque production: he interacts with them by way of good use of eye contact, rhetorical questions, and asides. He incorporates the viewers' responses into the performance, thereby making them participants in this "oral" discourse. In his fluent use of ASL and masterful grasp of rhetorical practices in the culture—playfully set in contrast to conventional mainstream rhetorical practices—Glickman inspires cultural pride in his viewers.

Such carnivalesque discourse is comic, mocking, and culturally informative, and its proficiency strengthens the cultural ego. It inspires in Deaf Americans the élan and courage to keep working for the things they need and the autonomy they desire. It gets them to laugh at themselves and at mainstream society, and that laughter provides a sense of equality. As its insights give them a better understanding of themselves and of mainstream society, they gain more self-esteem and more motivation—more "political" momentum and more hope.

Carnival, by drawing together Deaf Americans from all over the country, showcasing their culture, and inspiring them to greater accomplishments, is a phenomenon of the body politic. As Deaf Americans gather, they determine how best to present their needs to mainstream society and how best to nourish and disseminate their culture. Just as the latitude of the common people during medieval festivals supported popular rituals and forms of expression, so Deaf Americans at their festivals take advantage of their freedom to engage in their own rhetorical forms and poke fun at mainstream rhetorical traditions. Such discourse is an expression of the body politic.

Against Bakhtin's view that carnival represents opposition to hierarchy, Stallybrass and White argue that "One could even mount the precise contrary argument . . . : that the fair, far from being the privileged site of popular symbolic opposition to hierarchies was in fact a kind of educative spectacle, a relay for the diffusion of the cosmopolitan values of the 'center' (particularly the capital and the new urban centres of production) throughout the provinces and the lower orders."[31] However, the Deaf carnival simultaneously grounds symbolic opposition and provides the center for the diffusion of Deaf culture. The Deaf Way, for instance, attracted men and women of all ages with a common purpose: to preserve their culture (and deaf cultures in other countries) and to improve the situation of deaf people around the world. That goal was reflected by Deaf American literature—symbolic opposition—created and disseminated during the festival.

Mircea Eliade, Mary Douglas, Victor Turner, and other anthropologists see the archetypal festival as beneficially transforming for both the minority and majority groups involved.[32] Since Deaf Americans are a minority, they constantly struggle for recognition from the majority of their status as a unique group with their own needs. Most festivals are somewhat tame occasions that nevertheless lead to promising changes. At other times, the festival can become very charged. At its most political—for example, the 1988 Deaf President Now (DPN) movement—the festival can be a revolt that leads to major upheaval (whose aftereffects included, in the case of DPN, the Deaf Way). Festival or carnival has historically been an agent of transformation, to whatever degree, and Stallybrass and White would undoubtedly see late-twentieth-century Deaf culture as similar to other contemporary cultures that "still have a strong repertoire of carnivalesque practices such as Latin America or literatures in colonial/neo-colonial context where the political difference between the dominant and subordinate cultures is very charged."[33]

Carnival leads to social, economic, cultural, and political opportunities and advances, whether small or large. One Deaf Way attendee saw the effect of the Deaf Way confest as having "the potential to change the lives of deaf people around the globe."[34] Indeed, Deaf Americans generally see themselves as having experienced an improvement (despite some setbacks) in their quality of life and a growing freedom to be themselves, to celebrate their culture, and to use their vernacular. Their gatherings and literature reflect both this progress and the need for more improvement and empowerment.

Coming into the Light

The optimism of carnival corresponds to a theme pervasive in Deaf culture and discourse, that of "coming into the light." Historically, it is linked to the coming together of deaf people and the development of a means of communication—sign language—in France in the late eighteenth century, when the Abbé de l'Epée came upon two young deaf sisters, became interested in sign language and deaf education, and subsequently established a deaf school in Paris. It attracted deaf adults as well as children, and soon a small deaf community blossomed around it.[35] When a deaf person finally finds the community so lacking in mainstream society, and with it an ease of communication and fellowship, she or he comes into the light. Particularly when coming together for carnival, deaf people find light: fellowship, communication, laughter, and hope. As Bakhtin tells us, "Light [not darkness] characterizes folk grotesque [i.e., the carnival]. It is a festival of spring, of sunrise, of morning."[36]

This theme has manifestations from the commercial to the artistic: witness the frequent images of rays of lights in various kinds of advertising circulars and businesses aimed at Deaf Americans. For instance, the logo for Deaf Way II incorporates the image of the sun's rays. The logo of Nationwide Flashing Signal Systems, a company specializing in environmental assistive technologies, is an abstracted light bulb, and Starlite CyberBusiness Services provides Internet assistance to deaf clients. Optimism prevails as more and more Deaf businesses—with or without a "light" theme—spring up across the country. DawnSignPress is an important Deaf press and videotape distributor; SignRise Cultural Arts was once a leading community theater in the Washington, D.C., area (producing *Institution Blues* and *A Deaf Family Diary*).

In literature, the theme of light takes many forms. In Clayton Valli's "Windy Bright Morning," sunshine seems to refer to the possibilities of a new day:

> *Through the open window*
> *with its shade swinging, sunshine, playful*
> *taps my sleepy eyes.*[37]

In Ben Bahan's well-known, humorous videotaped ASL narrative "Bird of a Different Feather" (discussed at greater length in chapter 9), the absence of light plays an important role.[38] A young eaglet who lacks the physical capability to hunt and survive as an eagle, having instead more in common with songbirds, is convinced by his family to undergo an operation. Unfortunately, it makes him only slightly more eagle-like, and it takes away what he had in common with the song birds. Thus, not fully belonging to either species, the much-maligned creature flies off alone into the sunset—going out of the light, bereft of community and communication.

One of the most widely reproduced images of the National Theatre of the Deaf is the photograph of a dynamic ASL tableau from the company's production of *My Third Eye*.[39] This group narrative tells of a helicopter rescue during a violent storm at sea. As the victim is rescued, the storm abates and the sun rises over the horizon. In the closing image, all the performers come together and their outspread hands manifest the rays of the rising sun. Where there is community and communication, there is light and ongoing hope. Such light and hope is provided by carnival—and by the culture that it celebrates and nourishes.

Notes

1. Mikhail Bakhtin, *Rabelais and His World*, trans. Hélène Iswolsky (Cambridge, Mass.: MIT Press, 1968), 9.
2. "Festival Reflects Heart of Deaf Community," *On the Green*, July 24, 1989, p. 4.

3. See Merv Garretson, foreword to *The Deaf Way: Perspectives from the International Conference on Deaf Cultures*, ed. Carol J. Erting, Robert C. Johnson, Dorothy L. Smith, and Bruce D. Snyder (Washington, D.C.: Gallaudet University Press, 1994), xvii–xix. See also Erting's introduction, xxiii–xxxi.

4. Peter Stallybrass and Allon White, *The Politics and Poetics of Transgression* (London: Methuen, 1986), 38.

5. Ibid.

6. Ibid., 61.

7. To date, there have been five national Deaf Studies conferences and two ASL Literature conferences; many smaller meetings (e.g., of state affiliates of the NAD) are also held.

8. Bill Ashcroft, Gareth Griffiths, and Helen Tiffin, *The Empire Writes Back: Theory and Practice in Post-Colonial Literatures* (London: Routledge, 1989), 81.

9. *The Deaf Way*, prod. Department of Television, Film, and Photography, Gallaudet University, videocassettes, July 10–14, 1989.

10. Carol Padden and Tom Humphries, *Deaf in America: Voices from a Culture* (Cambridge, Mass.: Harvard University Press, 1988), 30.

11. *Institution Blues*, scripted by Don Bangs and Jan DeLap, dir. Don Bangs, SignRise Cultural Arts Production, Publick Playhouse, Cheverly, Md., June 6, 1993.

12. Werner Sollars, *Beyond Ethnicity: Consent and Descent in American Culture* (New York: Oxford University Press, 1986), 5.

13. Gilbert C. Eastman, *Sign Me Alice*, intro. George Detmold, pref. Gilbert Eastman (Washington, D.C.: Gallaudet University, 1974); *Sign Me Alice II*, written and dir. Gilbert C. Eastman, Washington, D.C., Gallaudet College TV Studio, three videocassettes, 60 min. each, 1983.

14. Padden and Humphries, *Deaf in America*, 31.

15. Wolfgang Karrer and Hartmut Lutz, "Minority Literatures in North America: From Cultural Nationalism to Liminality," in *Minority Literatures in North America: Contemporary Perspectives,* ed. Karrer and Lutz (New York: Lang, 1990), 11–64.

16. Stephen M. Ryan, *Planet Way Over Yonder*, vol. 5 of *ASL Storytime*, prod. Department of Communication, Gallaudet University, videocassette, 30 min., 1991.

17. Douglas Bullard, *Islay: A Novel* (Silver Spring, Md.: TJ Publishers, 1986).

18. Stallybrass and White, *The Politics and Poetics of Transgression*, 20.

19. Bakhtin, *Rabelais and His World*, 7.

20. Ibid., 6.

21. *The Deaf Way*, July 14, 1989, videocassette, 30 min.

22. Ibid.

23. Machalski is quoted in "The Deaf Way: Creating a World Community," *On the Green*, July 24, 1989, p. 4.

24. *The Deaf Way Conference and Festival Program* (Washington, D.C.: Gallaudet University, 1989).

25. See, for example, CHALB (Charlie McKinney and Alan Barwiolek), *Live at SMI!*, Burtonsville, Md.: Sign Media, videocassette, 60 min., 1993; Bob Daniels, "Am I Paranoid?" unpublished manuscript, 1992.

26. *The Deaf Way*, July 10, 1989, videocassette, 30 min..

27. Stallybrass and White, *The Politics and Poetics of Transgression*, 35.

28. *The Deaf Way*, July 14, 1989, videocassette, 30 min.

29. *The Deaf Way Conference and Festival Program*, 46.

30. Ken Glickman, *Deafology 101: Deaf Culture as Seen through the Eyes of a Deaf Humorist*, Silver Spring, Md., DEAFinitely Yours Studio, videocassette, 60 min., 1993.

31. Stallybrass and White, *The Politics and Poetics of Transgression*, 38.

32. Mircea Eliade, *Rites and Symbols of Initiation: The Mysteries of Birth and Rebirth*, trans. Willard R. Trask (New York: Harper Torchbooks, 1965); Mary Douglas, *Purity and Danger: An Analysis of Concepts of Pollution and Taboo* (London: Routledge, 1966); and Victor Turner, *From Ritual to Theatre: The Human Seriousness of Play* (New York: Performing Arts Journal Publications, 1982).

33. Stallybrass and White, *The Politics and Poetics of Transgression*, 11.

34. Quoted in "The Deaf Way," 1.

35. Padden and Humphries, *Deaf in America*, 29–31.

36. Bakhtin, *Rabelais and His World*, 41.

37. Clayton Valli, "Windy Bright Morning," trans. Karen Willis and Clayton Valli, in *Deaf in America*, ed. Padden and Humphries, 83. See *Poetry in Motion: Original Works in ASL*, Burtonsville, Md., Sign Media, videocassette, 60 min., 1990.

38. Ben Bahan and Sam Supalla, *Bird of a Different Feather and For a Decent Living*, ASL Literature Series, prod. Joe Dannis, San Diego, Calif., Dawn Pictures/DawnSignPress, videocassette, 60 min., 1992.

39. For example, see the cover of Stephen C. Baldwin's *Pictures in the Air: The Story of the National Theatre of the Deaf* (Washington, D.C.: Gallaudet University Press, 1993).

Chapter

4

The Oral Tradition: Deaf American Storytellers as Tricksters

IN THE 1960s American Sign Language finally achieved recognition as a legitimate language, after more than one hundred years of relegation to the realm of gestures. During that time the vernacular had gone underground, its more indigenous form preserved and perpetuated primarily by Deaf families with hereditary deafness. These family members passed on not only the vernacular itself but also the culture's rhetorical tradition, including traditional narratives and other forms now termed "ASL art" (many of which do not correspond to mainstream literary art forms). They, as well as a number of others exposed to ASL from an early age, have since provided the culture's storytellers and artists: Bernard Bragg, Pat Graybill, Bill Ennis, Mary Beth Miller, Ella Mae Lentz, Ben Bahan, Sam Supalla, and others, with more appearing every day.

Now that ASL has come up from the underground, its users desire to showcase the vernacular and its properties. Frequently, this is accomplished—in a very carnivalesque fashion—in relation to and at the expense of English and the mainstream literary tradition. As a whole, this language play often has an instrumental purpose that shows relatively little concern for meaning: that is, *how* something is communicated has more importance than *what* is communicated. To be sure, ASL art has content—but how the language is used and that it is used at all has much cultural meaning or value. The emphasis on form is particularly strong in more vernacular productions, which thereby challenge conventions of Western literature that traditionally have put less stress on the medium itself. (Yet in response to the concept of the "artistic" in the Western literary sense, some ASL artists now strive for more layered meanings in their productions.) For most Deaf Americans, whose visual vernacular has so recently gained legitimacy, the use of ASL continues to take precedence over what is being said.[1]

Such play is not entirely new, but it is newly visible. Because Deaf Americans have often grown up relatively isolated from one another—spread across the country, born into hearing families, and often mainstreamed—few use ASL as their first language. Many instead mix sign language and English to create a kind of manually coded English. Thus, they are not fully aware of the vernacular's distinctive properties. Even fewer have the facility with the language needed to become storytellers and performers. It is hardly surprising that they are often most interested in the fluent *use* of the language and the values thereby conveyed and pay little attention to precisely what is being said.

Delivery over Content

As we have already seen, as possessors of an "oral" culture, Deaf Americans have not a literature but an orature, a form with somewhat different properties than written literature. For instance, in the ASL vernacular tradition, a storyteller often draws on a stock of well-known stories, modifying the standard version to a greater or lesser extent. Moreover, as a storyteller tells and retells any particular story to different groups, it always changes because the context of each telling changes.[2] Many scholars of traditional oral literatures have argued that formal oral discourse was rather formulaic, allowing the speaker to memorize and use phrases, themes, episodes, and even whole stories in different ways to reflect different circumstances.[3] Very often, after a storyteller or performer has moved on, one of the bolder audience members will try out some of the stories and art forms, taking certain parts, certain themes, certain phrases, and remolding them to make the product his or her own. So too the ASL narrative emphasizes not the content of the story but its delivery, that is, a "procedural aesthetics"—how a storyteller proceeds with his or her story. The ASL storyteller or performer engages his or her spectators in the *process* of story-telling, in taking note of formal qualities that include the properties of the language itself and the way the story is delivered. As Dennis Tedlock has stressed, the result is a performance-based event, not a text-based art form.[4]

We can see an analogous form in African American culture in the practice of "playing the dozens," a kind of discourse utilizing an almost endless string of tropes.[5] The process of change is vastly accelerated, but the core is the same: an individual's skillful manipulation of the vernacular, here Black English, is often of paramount importance. For example, someone in a group of youths may begin by belittling another's family member or close friend. After that opening sally, the whole point becomes not mounting a defense against insult but the verbal contest itself: the best metaphor, the best analogy, the most cutting words, the most daring linguistic play. At its height, the initial challenge is all but forgotten in the pleasure and challenge of the verbal sparring. The artistry and originality lie in the use of the language, not in the subject matter.[6] Each performer pays close attention to context—to his or her "sparring partner" and audience, who are undoubtedly all ears and eyes, and how they respond. Such a preoccupation with felicitous expression contrasts sharply with the romantic emphasis on literary originality.

ASL artists have a similar desire to show off the language and what it—and they—can do. Often their triumph comes at the expense of English and mainstream literature. Because these "joke-sters," as Mikhail Bakhtin calls them, enjoy a perspectival advantage, they are able to play off ASL against English in a double-voiced discourse full of nuance and double meanings.[7] Many comic ASL productions play off against the "official forms," either explicitly or implicitly. As we saw in chapter 2, this is very much like what Bakhtin so clearly describes in *Rabelais and His World*: the comic interplay in the Middle Ages when vernacular forms and rituals played with the official forms.[8] The interanimation of ASL and English, often with one burlesquing the other, has something comically telling to say about the two-world condition of Deaf Americans; for how we think about and see the world is closely tied to the language we use.

ABC Stories

The playing with English and mainstream literature is particularly evident in the ABC story, a staple of the culture mentioned briefly in chapter 2. This quick narrative or poem has a rigid structure—only twenty-six signs—provided by the handshapes of the fingerspelled English alphabet.[9] A given handshape is used in many signs: for instance, to knock on a door one uses the A handshape as if knocking on a door; an A used on the chest in a circular motion can say one is sorry; or one can use both hands, each hand forming A and miming the washing of a car. The handshape for any of the English letters can be held in any position and with any orientation; it can also be moved in any way and doubled (i.e., made by both hands). Being tied to the English alphabet as a structuring device is a considerable handicap, but one that can be effectively overcome by the versatility of the language and the dexterity of a skillful signer. Displaying dexterity in using the handshapes is more important than telling a profoundly meaningful story.

Consider Bill Ennis's "Drag Racing" (available on a 1993 videocassette).[10] Ennis begins the story with the thumbs-up sign, using the A handshape (both hands) as if he is the starter signaling to two drag racers, one on each side. He then portrays the two cars using the B handshape (both hands side by side, palm-side down, flat and parallel to the ground). The B handshape then becomes the C handshape as Ennis depicts the two cars with their engines roaring and frames shaking, each barely restrained by the driver's foot on the brake (each hand held to the side with the open part of the C facing backward). Next, the two racers spurt forward, the C handshape changing into the D handshape plunging ahead, as if the cars are careening and veering from one side to the other as their engine power surges. As they roar ahead, the overstressed wheels (or is it the engines?) emit an "e-e-e-e-e-" sound.

Ennis, the master storyteller, pauses at this moment, ensuring that the narration does not get out of hand. Rather than letting it surge ahead at a breakneck pace, Ennis slows it down so that it becomes more than a vignette about a short drag race. He displays the F handshape in an "all's fine" manner, as if enacting a spectator—someone other than the starter? This character—definitely not one of the two drag racers who just took off—uses the G handshape to sign the two cars speeding off into the distance. Turning to the side, as if talking to still another person, he uses the H handshape to say "I'd beat you." Following this little boast, Ennis goes quickly from I to Y, indulging in a little more braggadocio with each sign. But then, on getting a good look at his competitor, Ennis makes the "Oh nooooo" Z handshape, as common sense gets the better of competitiveness.

Ennis has created, individualized, and performed this story-poem. He has chosen (or modified) the signs for each of the letters and determined how to manipulate them to add dimension and depth to the narrative. He takes on the role of each character and yet never completely becomes any of them. Throughout his performance he maintains eye contact with his supposed audience (my description is drawn from the videotape), thus maintaining an interactive relationship with his viewers. Most important, he achieves the main objective of any ABC story-poem: he displays, despite formal constraints, his dexterity—that is, his creativity—with the language.

In "Drag Racing," Ennis skillfully chooses signs that are appropriate for the actions and dialogue. His pacing and precision in their use make the narrative easy to follow. The signs are further manipulated in such a way as to indicate the intensity, the quality, and the speed of the actions. When Ennis uses D handshapes to show the two cars careening down the track, he orients them downward, with his index fingers plowing ahead and angled to the side in a tight balancing action. He also adds drama with nonmanual signals: his eyes and face convey excitement, effort, a gung ho attitude, and the eventual realization, "I'm way outclassed here." Moreover, Ennis adroitly shifts from one character to another, using facial expression and body posture to indicate which role he is taking on, never ceasing his movement to show what that individual feels, says, or does. More than just a story or poem, "Drag Racing" is a small play going on before one's eyes.

As we saw in chapter 2, the ABC story-poem is a kind of parodic, subversive thrust at English and its all-important alphabet of twenty-six vowels and consonants. The vaunted English alphabet is deprived of any meaning in itself; it merely provides the framework of the story-poem. More radically, the alphabet is put to a use for which it was never intended, as letters are emptied of their aurality and become instead fully visual and fully animated elements in a semiplay, semipoem, seminarrative—an all-in-one presentation. ABC story-poems also typically deal with subjects considered somewhat inappropriate or taboo in formal English discourse, such as sex, ghosts, and quasi-legal activities, which adds to the mischief.[11] The haunted house story, whose main character enters a haunted house and encounters ghosts and other strange things that go bump in the night, is especially common. Other ABC stories deal with carnal relations, with the performer delightedly going into the most intimate and minute detail. Even Ennis's "Drag Racing" focuses on an activity hardly welcome in the most formal circles (or by law enforcement officials).

As "Drag Racing" clearly shows, this art form plays with and subverts not only the English language but also generic distinctions. Ennis's piece is a "story," and yet no comparable form exists in the mainstream Western literary tradition, where such a rigid structuring framework is characteristic not of narrative (which traditionally has tried to escape constraints) but of poetry. Indeed, it is both something of a poem and something of a story—but such generic distinctions are actually of little importance. The objective here is not to render either a story or a poem but to showcase ASL and its properties to the fullest degree. In that process, a very important part of the majority language is being used artistically and dexterously—and quite unlike it is "supposed" to be used. This format is a challenge to ASL users, and Deaf Americans of all ages have come up with hundreds of variants of popular tales. Everyone appreciates a good haunted house story; and what older teenager doesn't enjoy either performing or viewing variants of the ABC story-poem detailing intimate relations? The ABC story-poem thus provides useful training for budding young ASL artists and story-tellers, who then go on to compose more sophisticated works.

Jabberwocky

Another example of delivery over content is the ASL adaptation of Lewis Carroll's "Jabberwocky," especially the adaptations done by Eric Malzkuhn.[12] "Jabberwocky" is itself an unusual example in English of delivery/language-over-content. The nineteenth-century poem was composed to focus attention on the English language and how it is habitually used. Its author, a logician now best known for his *Alice* books written under the pen name Carroll, wished to show that syntax and narrative structure can provide some meaningful content even when many of the words of a poem individually cannot be understood (or can be understood only by association with words that they resemble). Indeed, despite the nonsensical words, a reader clearly perceives that something (a heroic figure with some kind of sword) battles and defeats something else, the Jabberwock.

Similarly, Malzkuhn created an ASL "Jabberwocky" that is full of nonsensical signs but that enables a viewer to grasp, relying on the syntax and narrative structure, that a group of something is competing against or battling something else. But in several regards, Malzkuhn's creation outdoes Carroll's. No longer a poem highlighting the English language and conventional Western poetic forms, the main point of the work has become ASL—a visual-kinetic vernacular—and ASL art themselves. Moreover, this adaptation is not simply a poem but a performance, which is open to multiple reworkings to suit the viewers and the context. For example, for young children Malzkuhn depicted strange creatures battling other strange creatures. Before an adult group in Detroit, he replaced the creatures battling one another with vehicles racing one another. While Carroll created just one "Jabberwocky," Malzkuhn produced several "Jabberwockies" and the diverse groups enjoyed the play of the language and the one-upmanship.

The Advantages of ASL

As we have already seen in Ennis's performance, Deaf Americans can communicate with two hands, whereas hearing people can use only one voice. The Deaf storyteller has the advantage in that she or he can have both hands talking at once, like the Harlequin figure of old. Northrop Frye tells us, "Of the various things Harlequin does, one is to divide himself into two people and hold dialogues with himself."[13]

For example, at the beginning of *Mary Beth Miller: Live at SMI!*, Miller splits into two separate identities, one hand signing to/conversing with the other one.[14] The left hand has rebelled, causing havoc because ordinarily both hands are needed to communicate in ASL:

> R: It's time to go on with the show.
> L: I don't care.
> R: Finished! (Stop it!)
> L: Don't care.
> R: Why not? I can't go on without you.

The two hands fight and Miller is comically aghast. "My left hand is jealous of my right."

> L: Yes. I want to sign and receive attention. You understand?
> R: Why don't you go ahead and perform?
> L: With people staring at me?
> R: Yes.

The left hand freezes in uncertainty, not sure how to proceed. It starts signing "Three blind mice. Three blind mice. See how, how . . ." (and must stop, because HOW is a two-handed sign). Subsequent signing also falters, since many signs are two-handed. The left hand admits, "We need to work together I guess." The left hand prods the right shoulder—"I made a mistake"—whereupon the right hand answers irascibly, "I told you. I told you. You always foul up my show. You know-it-all." Eventually, Miller gets both hands to make amends by promising to favor one hand or the other at different times.

The use of two hands gives ASL discourse many other advantages. A signer can fingerspell a different word on each hand simultaneously. Many young Deaf children enjoy this practice as a kind of juvenile ASL art; a common starting point is to fingerspell "cat" with one hand and "dog" with the other. A real challenge is to fingerspell "supracalifragelistic," half of Mary Poppins's favorite word, with both hands simultaneously. Obviously one can't use the voice to say two different things at once. In addition, there is a kind of built-in redundancy to the hands, making possible adjustments both for convenience (e.g., to compensate for position or posture, the fingerspeller can switch to the more visible hand) and for necessity: one can lose one hand and still fingerspell with the other, but the loss of one's voice is absolute.

Multifunctionality and Multidimensionality

A signer using fingerspelling can convey at the same time a word and an image of that word. For example, the fingerspelling of "reflection" enacts the concept when both hands fingerspell the letters one on top of the other, as if one hand is mirroring the other. Debbie Rennie provides a heart-wrenching fingerspelled manifestation of a calf on the way to becoming veal in her videocassette *Poetry in Motion: Original Works in ASL.*[15] The C handshapes are the round, velvety eyes of the young calf, and the A handshapes image the calf chewing hay. L is the knife striking down, and F is the meat on the dinner plate. Another performer might simultaneously fingerspell "leaf" and—using his or her fingers, hand, arm, and (to a lesser degree) torso—depict a falling leaf. One begins with L as the leaf becomes detached from a branch at a height a bit above one's head, then fingerspells the E and the A as the leaf drifts in the breeze to the ground. Finally, the hand moves into the F handshape as it comes to a rest on the ground.

Such iconicity and drama highlight the contrast between ASL and English, which, as "only" an aural language, is limited to one dimension: sound. Moreover, while English stories are "just" narratives, ASL stories roll narrative, visual art, and drama into one. Many ASL artists exult in this multidimensionality and seem to be saying in their performances, "Try that, English!" They know that an aural language such as English cannot match ASL's graphic, cinematic, and "architectural" properties.

The contrast between the two modalities is evident in a popular set piece: the story (or is it a poem?) of the high diver. MJ Bienvenu, a well-known Deaf ASL artist, has created a particularly masterful variant.[16] In it, a diver at a swimming meet walks along the side of a pool lined with bleachers crammed with spectators. After climbing the ladder to the diving board, the athlete executes a graceful dive, earning a "10" from the judges and much applause from the spectators. Bienvenu conveys all this in ASL without moving one inch backward or forward—but she presents her viewers with a multidimensional art form that almost becomes a play. Conventionally, "to narrate" means to tell a story using words, and "to dramatize" typically involves both action and dialogue, yet Bienvenu does both without using words, action, or dialogue.

Bienvenu's success at narrating and dramatizing in this fashion illustrates the multidimensional properties of ASL. Like any language, it convey concepts; but it can also illustrate them visually—indicating space, placement, direction, and motion. For this reason, it is intrinsically dramatic. The viewer of Bienvenu's diver narrative not only receives concepts but also observes the scene and takes in the performance of the storyteller. To be sure, a person using English can get up on a stage and act out some scenes; but in acting, he or she is going beyond the everyday qualities of aural English discourse. In contrast, to a greater or lesser extent everyday ASL discourse is multidimensional as a matter of course.

As a part of this multidimensionality, an ASL story is often structured with close-ups, distant shots, flashbacks, and scenes presented in fast-forward or slow motion, making it more like an edited film than a written narrative. Oliver Sacks has noted that an ASL story is architectural in its placement of characters and objects—we can "see" where everything is—and cinematic in the camera-like focusing on imaged people and action.[17] Both signer and spectators are aware of the signer's visual orientation to what is being related. For example, a performer may enact a woman standing at a street corner. The performer's facial expressions show very clearly this woman's impatience and nervousness. Using the right index finger, the same performer depicts another person approaching from the far right side, crossing the street, and coming face to face with the woman, with arms outstretched. The performer then switches the view to enact the two of them embracing. The focus then moves from the two of them embracing to the performer's face, expressing relief and joy. We are in effect shown a medium shot, a close-up, a long shot, a medium shot, and a final close-up.

Such skillful enactment, which relies on semi-mimicry, is considered "high" artistic ASL discourse; in contrast, mime and even acting itself are not regarded highly in Western culture.[18] Mary Beth Miller provides an excellent example in "The Mouth Story" from *Live at SMI!*. This ASL "narrative" opens with a woman driving along a country road. She rolls along without concern until one of her tires suddenly goes flat. At a loss, as the night is coming on and only empty road stretches ahead, she goes for help. After going through some underbrush, she comes to a house; but the man who opens the door shrugs his shoulders when she explains her predicament. She asks if she can call for assistance, but learns there's no phone and no electricity. "I use candles," he tells her. "Can I sleep here?" asks the distressed woman. The man offers hospitality and leads her upstairs to a spare bedroom. In this bedroom, he leaves a candle that flickers and flickers, effectively preventing the woman from sleeping. But alas, she cannot blow it out—nor can her host. Three neighbors get involved, as one by one each enters the house, goes up to the candle, and then exits the house. The last, a sexy woman, simply uses her thumb and finger to snuff out the flame.

Miller differentiates each character simply by varying her gait, posture, facial expression, and manner of signing. For instance, to enact the host she walks slowly and arthritically, sucks in her cheeks, and puts her hands on her hips. For one male neighbor, Miller hunches her shoulders a bit more, adds a lopsided mouth, and moves with a limp. For another, she makes her mouth lopsided on the other side. For the female character, Miller tosses her hair, gestures gracefully with her hand, and glides across the stage. Such simple but very effective variations provide a sharp contrast to the very detailed and finely drawn characterizations we have learned to expect from "literary" English narratives.

Playing with the low status of mimicry, ASL storytellers frequently add farcical elements to their characterizations. Their portrayals of authority figures in mainstream society are often caricatures. Bill Ennis's enactment of a heavy-set houseparent, too large for her chair and with only her index finger in motion, is a hilarious, "low" spoof of the typical dorm supervisor.[19] Miller provides another good example of such broad characterization in her *Live at SMI!* narrative "Sign Language Class." She begins by asking rhetorically if any of her viewers teach sign language classes at the beginning, intermediate, and advanced levels. Then for each of these three levels, Miller enacts a student entering the classroom with a card. She shows how, typically, the beginner wants to talk a lot but cannot even form the ABCs properly. When this beginner signs I, she sticks herself in the chest. She next inadvertently hits someone when she tries to sign. Frustrated by it all, she announces that she has to leave, admitting "This is hard." As the intermediate student, Miller signs less, her hand moving up and down like a yo-yo, and jiggles her head a good deal. In contrast, the advanced student signs fluently but can barely understand others. To bring home this failure of communication, Miller signs RECEPTION on the eyes, with one hand dropping down to indicate a "collapse" in those particular skills. At each level, Miller zeros in on a characteristic weakness—the overeager beginner who does not realize that the hands are means of communication, the overactive intermediate student, and the advanced student who can send but not receive—and caricatures it with great glee. In this "low" vernacular storytelling, she displays as much artistry and skill as do writers in printed English, but in a different, visual way.

As if deliberately demonstrating that the ASL vernacular is as legitimate as the official language, such use of high ASL draws on many properties not available in English. Whereas high English discourse does not encourage low humor and exaggeration, high ASL discourse is replete with the low and down-to-earth. In this way, the artists show that the conventional distinction between "high" and "low" discourse does not hold in ASL. Thus, another common jester strategy is the use of fluent, aesthetic ASL in comic, vulgar, subversive pieces. High language is used in detailing "lowly" physical description, actions, and circumstances.

Collaboration

ASL artists sometimes join together in pairs or small groups. While Western culture makes much of the single author who creates a discrete work, Deaf culture has many short, collaborative, and interactive forms that often have a number of purposes besides telling a story. For instance, we already saw in chapter 3 that in Don Bangs's *Institution Blues*, produced by SignRise Cultural Arts in 1993, the actors play children collaborating on a visual retelling of the Frankenstein story.[20] The children enact not only all the characters—the doctor, his wife, his assistant, and the creature—but also inanimate objects; particularly ingenious is their rendition of the main lever controlling the lab machinery. As one of the children raises clasped hands to mime a lever, the assistant pulls down on this lever, thereby "turning on" the apparatus (three children surrounding the creature, their fingers serving as electrical connections to the creature's body). Deaf children often undertake such collaborations with no advance planning; instead, individuals take turns adding to an impromptu group narrative.

In another common collaborative genre, two people work together as a united whole, merging their two bodies into one. Well-known examples are the makeup skit and the mirror skit. In the former, one performer sits with arms behind her back; as another performer stands behind her, his arms and hands ostensibly become hers. Only his arms and hands are seen, and the humor is in these masculine hands erratically applying makeup to a girl's face. Not only do the two performers go through the motions of applying makeup, but "they" drop a sign here and there. It takes more than the usual dexterity for two performers to sign as one in this way. In the mirror skit, one performer mirrors the body movements of another. In its most familiar mainstream form (perhaps most memorably portrayed by the Marx Brothers in *Duck Soup* [1933]), this kind of number does not extend to forming spoken words. In the ASL version, however, verbal communication can be added because the body is an integral part of such communication, which becomes yet another element to mirror.

Rhythm, Music, and Song in ASL

Deaf culture and language have an indigenous rhythm, music, and song. That is, they possess a visual way of incorporating musicality to which nothing in any other culture and language can be compared and which belies the notion that Deaf Americans have little interest in music, song, and rhythm. Many Deaf Americans can hear to some extent, play music, and sing (or sign) songs; and more important, even deaf performers with little or no hearing make use of rhythm, rhyme, and tempo in numerous vernacular pieces. This section explores the function of those tools in vernacular performances, rather than discussing the many Deaf American performances of singing and dancing.

Rhythm and tempo arose long ago out of the movement and manipulation of the body. In centuries past, making music often involved human hands and feet; people would bang drums with their hands, vigorously shake gourds, and lift their feet up and down while chanting and calling out in song. The body was an integral part of song and music.[21] Only relatively recently has music become increasingly divorced from the body in a manner that parallels the divorce of word from body in everyday discourse. Aside from the more exuberant musicals and performers, many songs performed today entail a stationary person making love to a microphone, and a great deal of modern music is instrumental, not vocal.

ASL speakers, however, have continued to use the body to communicate in rhythmic ways. Either the whole body or just part of the body, such as the arms and hands moving in a rhythmic way, can be used to convey visual-kinetic rhythm and tempo. For instance, a person can sign "Row, row, row your boat," repeating the sign for ROW BOAT three times, from side to side slowly (to approximate "row, row, row"), and two times quickly (to approximate "your boat"), with a tighter, narrower swing.

Moreover, Deaf Americans have retained an oral culture. In traditional oral cultures, song was an integral part of many people's lives. Written communication had not yet developed and there was little formal expression or "art"; in their place was much use of the voice and spoken words (as well as the body) in some patterned, musical way. From these songs poetry has developed; it thus traditionally has had a lyrical (literally, "suitable for singing to a lyre") quality, as early chants and ballads clearly show. Up to the twentieth century the lyricism produced by rhythm and rhyme persisted in poetry even in print; and still today, most people prefer poems and songs that they can recognize as "poetry," with strict meter and rhyme.[22] Therefore, it should be no surprise that this lyricism persists in the more "oral" vernacular of Deaf Americans.

Visual rhythm, rhyme, and tempo can be seen in Deaf culture's numerous "ASL songs," some of which are adaptations and some of which are original. One example of the art form that is an adaptation of a hearing song appears in *Charles Krauel: A Profile of a Deaf Filmmaker*, a documentary profiling a Deaf American who filmed the lives and culture of Deaf Americans for half a century.[23] During a picnic, one of the guests (named George Kannapell) amuses the others with a drinking song, probably adapted from a traditional English tune. He does each sign from one side to the other to a one-two, one-two-three beat, as his torso leans accordingly:

> *boat-boat*
> *boat-boat-boat*
>
> *drink-drink*
> *drink-drink-drink*
>
> *fun-fun*
> *fun-fun-fun*
>
> *enjoy-enjoy*
> *enjoy-enjoy-enjoy*

In the video, the spectators clap along with the signer, creating an interanimation of the aural and the visual. It is very obvious to any viewer that Deaf Americans enjoy, with visual modifications, rhythmic and rhyming songs.

Many Deaf vernacular forms take their cue from the beat of a drum. "The Bison Song," the college song of Gallaudet University, is the best example of a slow one-two, fast one-two-three beat. This distinctive rhythm came about because the members of the football team needed a way to communicate, whether signaling the handoff of the ball from the center to the quarterback, or announcing specific plays. Therefore, a big band drum was brought to the sideline; when struck at appropriate times by an assistant manager, the players could hear it or feel its vibrations.

These rhythms are common in ASL songs. For instance, Mary Beth Miller's "Cowboy Story" in her *Live at SMI!* videocassette is based on a slow one-two-three-four drum beat, and it frequently repeats signs/phrases.

boom boom
ride ride
ride ride
handkerchief, handkerchief   [Handkerchief around the neck
   lifting in the wind]
strings strings   [Hat strings sway in cowboy's face]
hat hat
pistol pistol
gallop gallop
dust dust   [Dust piles stirred up by horse's hoofs]
gallop gallop
rise rise   [Rider rises off saddle]
pistol pistol
strings strings
handkerchief, handkerchief
hat hat
town town
town recede
ride ride
gallop, gallop

string string
dust dust

ride ride
pistol pistol
handkerchief handkerchief
hat hat
strings strings
see b-a-r
halt horse
get off——walk——go into saloon
go to counter
hit counter
hat hat
beer slides down
gurgle gurgle
wipe mouth   [switches sides]   *wipe mouth*

man playing piano
woman with lashes
la la
la la
cowboy with hat
heart flutters
woman's eyelashes flutter
man plays piano
girl dances
cowboy falls in love
cowboy goes up to girl
hat hat
hi
lashes flutter

you and me
ride ride
arms around girl
take girl out
mount horse

lift girl onto horse
braids fly
ride ride
pistol pistol
handkerchief handkerchief
strings strings
braids braids
lashes flutter

ride ride
gallop gallop
dust dust
sun sets
gallop into distance
dust recedes into the distance
close out
t-h-e e-n-d   [Signed slowly]

"The Cowboy Story" is similar to premodern mainstream vernacular forms that relied heavily on meter and rhyme to aid the performer's memory. In this case the mnemonic devices are the visual beat, the very basic story line, and the visual rhyme. Often one scene uses the same handshape in many signs; for example, the V handshape is incorporated into the handkerchief flying, the hat strings lifting, the riding, and the rising on the horse. At the bar, the 5 handshape recurs in the piano playing and the girl's flirty lashes. The O handshape is used for the dust balls and the hands holding the reins. Finally, the B handshape is used for both the town and its receding into the distance.

The visual fluency and dexterity that incorporate rhythm and rhyme in these productions play against the aural musicality of English and mainstream society. Clearly, deaf people appreciate music, rhythm, and song: these artworks show that rhythm, music, and song can be conveyed visually, by the tempo of the performer's signing and the movement of his or her body, as well as aurally. A tactile dimension is often added through drumming. The repetition of signs or the repetitions of any aspect of a sign—its orientation, handshape, or movement—visually conveys rhyme.

Motion also has an aesthetic value in ASL that has no equivalent in aural English. The rate of signing, or of the motion of an individual sign, can be varied, sometimes to indicate an emotional quality. Also, to heighten the impression of speeding up or slowing down the motion, an outside light source can be employed. For instance, a strobe light seems to slow and add a rhythmic quality to signing. In one ASL performance presented during Deaf Literature Week at Gallaudet University in 1994, a strobe light flashed and revolved as the performer signed the poem. The effect was not only to slow the rhythm but also to change the orientation of light and dark. The whole presentation was akin to a carnival light show where time and space seem to merge. Once again, the significance of the performance lay not so much in the poem's content as in how it was rendered (indeed, one could not quite grasp what was being signed).

Humor and Burlesque

Varying the speed and intensity of signing can control excitement and suspense or give a performance a slightly burlesque quality.[24] It is particularly common for ASL artists to burlesque American song classics by producing faster- or slower-paced ASL versions. Charlie McKinney and Alan Barliowek, for example, render "My Country 'Tis of Thee" in three different modes. The first version is done in grand opera style and features impressive, sweeping signs. The second, in Signing Exact English, is delightfully nonsensical. The version that follows uses fingerspelled words marching along briskly.[25]

Quite a few ASL artists take particular pleasure in "playing" with the national anthem. In her three renditions of "The Star-Spangled Banner" in *Live at SMI!*, Mary Beth Miller burlesques the various approaches taken over the years to signing this song, effectively and comically conveying in a nutshell the main phases that the anthem has passed through. Miller begins her presentation by suggesting an impromptu language study. She points out that in the 1940s and 1950s, Deaf Americans did their own thing when adapting songs, using signing and rhythm that largely disregarded the original musical score. In the 1960s and the 1970s, however, they endeavored to adhere to the words and tempo of the original. According to Miller, this change was a sign of oppression: Deaf Americans wanted to be like hearing people, so they signed the words and attempted to approximate the meter and pitch. She uses "The Star-Spangled Banner" to make her point because in the past, whenever Deaf Americans gathered, everyone was asked to stand up and pledge to the flag. The anthem was signed so inspiringly that it could bring tears to the eyes—but also, according to Miller, at such length that younger viewers sometimes wished the singer would make haste. Miller believes that renditions of the anthem have become shorter and that the trend will continue in the future.

Miller's first version, typical of the 1940s and 1950s, is inspiringly and beautifully signed but completely ignores the original music. The performer enacts a broad-shouldered, dignified woman with complete confidence in her ability to sign the anthem. The opening "Oh" goes on and on and on, followed by a small "say." "All of you" is repeated with alternating hands, and an expansive "see" is again repeated with alternating hands. "The star-spangled banner" is a phrase of just three words in the original text, but in this version Miller images the entire flag: red and white stripes, a square blue field in the corner, and stars spangling this field from top to bottom. As a whole, this rendition has its own tempo, with visual enhancements to add appropriate emphasis and drama; throughout the song, Miller keeps time with her foot (in an aside to the viewers, she explains that such foot-tapping was customary in the past). The anthem comes to a close with a very prolonged and thrice raised—but dignified—"brave." Staying in character, Miller signs "Thank you, thank you. If you would like to invite me to your next gathering, I will come and sign for you."

In her next version, typical of the 1960s and 1970s, Miller does a well-signed rendition that retains much of the original score. It attempts to approximate the tempo and pitch, but an approximation is the best that it can achieve. It is vague and less visually "flowing" than the previous version, with expansive, dramatic signing at those times when a singer's voice would rise or intone dramatically. On the tape, spectators appear quite unimpressed with this shorter and less facile adaptation. Miller rhetorically queries,

"Me, a deaf Whitney Houston? Remember the Astrodome?" She parodically enacts Houston singing, putting heart, body, and soul into her voice, and points out, "I'm like a Whitney Houston in the way I just signed the anthem."

Miller concludes with a version that simply gives the facts: "As we come to the end of the millennium and on to 2025, 2400—will we be on our backs with feet up in the air?—Deaf Americans won't understand what the anthem is all about. You don't understand? OK, I will explain it to you. You know in the past, before the atom bomb, before World War II, before, before, before, when ships sailed" (she shows how the sails react to wind), "the British were warring with the United States, using cannons on the fort. . . . There was a lot of smoke and it was difficult to see. People weren't sure what was going on. Have the British captured the country? Are we free? But then was espied a tattered flag waving, barely waving. Wheww, it's still waving. It's the home of brave and free still." The whole tongue-in-cheek presentation is quite factual and informative, as Miller moves along a bit cursorily, but her comic prediction is clear: Deaf Americans will have little understanding of or interest in an anthem about a long-ago historical event.

In the same performance, Miller burlesques the limitations of relying on the voice and the spoken language. At one point she asks during a "break," "Do you mind if I have some water?" (She inserts her hands into a glass of water and spectators titter.) "My hand is thirsty." (She does the THIRSTY sign down the palm.) "Deaf is different." Miller is here drawing attention to "problems" inherent in communicating with the voice. An oral speaker who goes on at length needs the lubricating action of water or coffee. In focusing on this "deficiency" of oral discourse, Miller shines a light on the other culture—the culture of people using their voices. She spotlights how those in the other culture tend to talk and thus need to drink periodically. In so doing, she parodies these beverage breaks in a double-voiced playfulness. In contrast to people who use their vocal cords, people who sign take breaks in a different way. Indeed, because facility in ASL consists of an economy of movement and because native signers can vary the pace and size of signs as well as make signs flow into one another, Deaf Americans never suffer from "hoarseness" in the hands.

The reach for water or some other liquid to dampen an oral speaker's lips is sometimes just a discourse marker signaling a change of topic or the need for a break. There may be no coffee in the coffee cup and the person may just be going through the motions. At other times, the lubrication ritual helps cover up pregnant pauses. Such stratagems are characteristic of oral-aural discourse, in which the conversationalists need not maintain eye contact and keep at least one hand free of encumbrances. ASL discourse, however, precludes the breaking of eye contact and participants rarely converse while holding objects in their hands. Again, Miller is playing one culture off another, one language off another, using humor to challenge boundaries and what is considered the "norm." In this assault, she is provoking Deaf Americans to reconsider how the ways they use language are different from the ways used by English speakers: she makes them think about how they divide up discourse, how they handle pregnant pauses, and how they handle topic changes.

Miller is like a traditional trickster or jester in juxtaposing the two cultures in ways that go beyond superficial comparisons. As C. W. Spinks explains, "Wherever the culture has drawn a line of demarcation, Trickster is there to probe the line and test the limits. . . . [H]e reminds us that the cultural boundaries are arbitrary, and he releases the desire, at least vicariously, to challenge those boundaries. He both exercises and exorcises the negation of the Cultural Other."[26] Just as a speaker focuses attention on the voice or the speaking apparatus, Miller focuses attention on the hands, the "voice" of the Deaf American. She shows the difference between the two cultures in a way that demonstrates that "other" is not a negation; here "different" has a positive sense.

Bill Ennis's "Mississippi Squirrel Revival" provides an appropriate conclusion to this chapter. With its comic synthesis of song, narrative, and drama, the "narrative" stars Ennis himself as a young boy on a trip down south—or rather it stars a feisty little squirrel who turns the mainstream ecclesiastical ritual of a Sunday revival meeting topsy-turvy.[27]

> When I was a little boy, my parents and I drove south to visit Grandmother. She was my favorite person in the whole wide world. What did I do when we got there? I went without shoes all day and climbed trees. One time I saw a squirrel in a tree I was climbing. I caught it and put it in a shoe box. I punched holes in the box so it could breathe. The next day was Sunday and I took the box to church with me. I joined some boys and a cute little girl in the back rows. I sat down and straightaway the boys wanted to see what was in the box. I took the lid off the box and the squirrel leaped out and scampered all the way to the front where parishioners were singing a hymn in chorus. The squirrel scooted into the trousers of a dozing old man who leaped up, startled, from his pew. Everyone was amazed at the old man's religious enthusiasm. The squirrel circled around inside the old man's trousers, causing him to hop around agitatedly. The other parishioners picked up on this and sang even more spiritedly. Finally, the squirrel escaped and scampered further up to the very front of the church. A holier-than-thou woman was the squirrel's next victim. It leaped up into the woman's skirt, causing her to hop up and down and run around inside the church. Thinking she was possessed, she poured out confession after confession, admitting to all the men she'd slept with. Each of these seven men rushed to the altar to ask for forgiveness. Caught up in the revivalist spirit, fifty parishioners gathered in front to volunteer for missionary work in Africa. Many others made additional offerings. It was all a miracle and a very spirited revival. Thanks to whom? The feisty little squirrel!

In this ASL production, Ennis uses his face, body, and arms to indicate pitch, intensity, duration, and beat in a kind of parody of the conventional hymn. As he signs, he conveys the sense of music as the high ritual of a Sunday church service is brought low—to the living, material earth—by a feisty little squirrel. Whereas the stress in aural singing is on the voice and some facial expressiveness, this signed vernacular form emphasizes the moving hands and body.

Usually rhythm and tempo are conveyed aurally, yet in "Mississippi Squirrel Revival" they are conveyed visually-kinetically. It is a kind of song and yet nothing is heard. And whereas a narrative is usually a story told via print or a human voice, this "narrative" is told in ASL, a language that uses movements of the body to convey meaningful information. So it is not solely narrative or solely song—it is, more accurately, ASL burlesque.

In the Middle Ages, low comic rituals and art forms played against the high official rituals and art forms in ways that brought down to earth the high and the official. Similarly, Deaf Americans have rituals and art forms that play up against the official English art forms of majority society. In the interanimation of the two, the characteristic features of these ASL art forms provide certain advantages over written language (the official, the conventional, and the traditional): the end result is the creation of very playful hybrid forms that are both subversive and comically down-to-earth.

Notes

1. See Carol Padden and Tom Humphries, *Deaf in America: Voices from a Culture* (Cambridge, Mass.: Harvard University Press, 1988), 76–77.
2. Viv Edwards and Thomas J. Sienkewicz, *Oral Cultures Past and Present: Rappin' and Homer* (Oxford: Blackwell, 1991), 26.
3. See especially Ruth Finnegan, *Literacy and Orality: Studies in the Technology of Communication* (Oxford: Blackwell, 1988); Albert B. Lord, *The Singer of Tales*, Harvard Studies in Comparative Literature, 24 (Cambridge, Mass.: Harvard University Press, 1960); and Walter Ong, *Orality and Literacy: The Technologizing of the Word* (London: Methuen, 1982).
4. Dennis Tedlock, *The Spoken Word and the Art of Interpretation* (Philadelphia: University of Pennsylvania Press, 1983), 4.
5. Though somewhat outdated, *playing the dozens* is still the best-known term for this kind of verbal duel. Slang, of course, changes quickly; more recent names include *capping*, *snapping*, and *joning*.
6. Cf. Lord, *The Singer of Tales*, 44.

7. M. M. Bakhtin, *The Dialogic Imagination: Four Essays*, ed. Michael Holquist, trans. Caryl Emerson and Michael Holquist (Austin: University of Texas Press, 1981), 401.

8. Mikhail Bakhtin, *Rabelais and His World*, trans. Hélène Iswolsky (Cambridge, Mass.: Harvard University Press, 1968), 5–15.

9. Although fingerspelling is considered part of ASL, it consists of hand-shapes representing the English alphabet.

10. Bill Ennis, *Bill Ennis: Live at SMI!*, Burtonsville, Md., produced by Sign Media, videocassette, 60 min., 1993.

11. Sherman Wilcox and Phyllis Wilcox, *Learning to See: American Sign Language as a Second Language* (Englewood Cliffs, N.J.: Prentice Hall/Regents, 1991), 71.

12. Padden and Humphries, *Deaf in America*, 84-86.

13. Northrop Frye, *The Secular Scripture: A Study of the Structure of Romance* (Cambridge, Mass.: Harvard University Press, 1976), 111.

14. Mary Beth Miller, *Mary Beth Miller: Live at SMI!*, Burtonsville, Md., Sign Media, videocassette, 60 min., 1991.

15. Debbie Rennie, "Veal Boycott," in *Poetry in Motion: Original Works in ASL*, Burtonsville, Md., Sign Media, videocassette, 60 min., 1990.

16. MJ Bienvenu, "Tales from the Green Books," in *American Sign Language*, dir. Dennis Cokely, Falls Church, Va., Sign Media, videocassette, 60 min., 1981.

17. Oliver Sacks, *Seeing Voices: A Journey into the World of the Deaf* (Berkeley: University of California Press, 1989), 74, 89.

18. Mime has been in the repertoire of trickster/fool figures since Roman times, when the *mimus* was a player of farce. See Olive Mary Busby, *Studies in the Development of the Fool in the Elizabethan Drama* (Philadelphia: R. West, 1977), 11.

19. In ASL works, such narrative mimicry of the houseparent, teacher, policeman, and employer, as inhumane people of bulk and self-importance, is often used to personalize and personify power relations; see Wolfgang Karrer and Harmut Lutz, "Minority Literatures in North America: From Cultural Nationalism to Liminality," in *Minority Literatures in North America: Contemporary Perspectives*, ed. Karrer and Lutz (New York: Lang, 1990), 11–64.

20. *Institution Blues*, scripted by Don Bangs and Jan DeLap, dir. Don Bangs, SignRise Cultural Arts Production, Cheverly, Md., June 6, 1993.

21. See William Haviland, *Cultural Anthropology*, 4th ed. (New York: Holt, Rinehart, and Winston, 1983); Alexander Alland, *To Be*

Human: An Introduction to Cultural Anthropology (New York: Wiley, 1981); Ong, *Orality and Literacy*, 34; and Finnegan, *Literacy and Orality*, 153.

22. Free verse is the modernist—elitist and literary, rather than popular and oral—break from the lyric form, reflecting the modern quest to open up new forms. See P. J. Laska, "Poetry at the Periphery," in *A Gift of Tongues: Critical Challenges in Contemporary American Poetry*, ed. Marie Harris and Kathleen Agueros (Athens, Ga.: University of Georgia Press, 1987), 327–28.

23. *Charles Krauel: A Profile of a Deaf Filmmaker*, prod. Joe Dannis, San Diego, Calif., Dawn Pictures, videocassette, 30 min., 1994.

24. Ella Mae Lentz, "Sign Poetry," in *Gallaudet Encyclopedia of Deaf People and Deafness*, vol. 3, ed. John Van Cleve (New York: McGraw-Hill, 1987), 125.

25. Charlie McKinney and Alan Barwiolek, *CHALB: Live at SMI!*, Burtonsville, Md., Sign Media, videocassette, 60 min., 1993.

26. C. W. Spinks, *Semiosis, Marginal Signs, and Trickster: A Dagger of the Mind* (New York: Macmillan, 1991), 178.

27. Ennis, *Live at SMI!*

Chapter

5

Literary Night: The Restorative Power of Comedic and Grotesque Literature

‿⟶

ONE TRADITIONAL ASL production that clearly displays the carnivalesque nature of Deaf American literature is "Literary Night." This cultural staple, presented by literary societies at residential schools or by adult organizations, is a heterogeneous mix of news, storytelling, skits, one-act plays, poetry/song, art sign, and mimicry. These diverse forms and performance styles are assembled into a kind of variety or talent show, but here the accent is (or is supposed to be) on the "literary."

Before the 1960s there were comparatively few residential schools, and they were widely scattered across the country; thus many of the children had little opportunity to go home during the school year, and the faculty and staff tried to promote various organizations and weekend activities. One of these organizations was usually a literary society for the older students. Because the term "literary" was interpreted very loosely, the literary framework was capacious and flexible enough to accommodate almost anything from nativist ASL art to signed English readings, although it usually contained works that were originally literary.

Because their education has been modeled as much as possible on that in the public schools, deaf schoolchildren have always been exposed to literature in English. As they have read short stories, novels, and poetry, they have learned to analyze plots, themes, and symbolism. In absorbing details about the backgrounds of the writers themselves, they have become more knowledgeable about British and American culture and society as a whole. Some of them—perhaps fascinated by the adventures of Jack London's characters, or drawn into the trials and tribulations of heroines created by women writers—have taken the next step: using their favorite authors as models, they have come up with their own poetry and narratives in English, with varying degrees of success. In addition, students in schools that permitted sign language in class were also encouraged by their English instructors to sign English stories and poems, thereby demonstrating that they understood all the English words and, it was hoped, the work as a whole. Such adaptations were expressly intended to promote an appreciation of literature in English, both by the performers and by the other students in the audience.

Many of the English teachers at residential schools were graduates of Gallaudet College (now Gallaudet University). They were generally fluent in spoken English because they were likely to be among the many deaf people in the nineteenth and early twentieth centuries who were (to use a term disliked by most of today's Deaf Americans) "postlingually" deaf: that is, they became deaf after they had already acquired language (i.e., English). Many of them enrolled at schools for the deaf and then the only college for deaf students, Gallaudet, where the more enterprising adapted English works to sign language, often under the aegis of the Ballard Literary Society.[1] Upon graduation, they took up posts at schools around the country, where they may well have helped promote or establish literary societies modeled on the one they had known in college. They were then undoubtedly the most likely candidates to serve as faculty sponsors for such societies.

Because ASL was not recognized as a legitimate language, teachers and students alike signed English works using a kind of manually coded English, without entirely translating them or adapting them. But we can see in this "signing" of English works and in Literary Night a linguistic phenomenon known as *polyglossia*: that is, "the simultaneous presence of two or more national languages interacting within a single cultural system."[2] In this case, we have not just two languages but two modalities: an aural language (with a written form) and a visual language. Moreover, this intertwining reflects not the mixing of equals but the jockeying for position of two languages of very different statuses. English is the "majority language," ever trying to extend its control; ASL is the "minority language," relegated at the time to being a supplementary means of communication. Yet ASL, a language with its own morphological, phonological, and semantic complexity, attempts to avoid, negotiate, or subvert that control.[3] Despite being devalued, the minority language asserts itself in this intermixing; the result is an ongoing tug-of-war.

No full-length Literary Night program is commercially available on video, but a few works have provided some idea of its nature. For example, Don Bangs's *Institution Blues* depicts a Literary Night adaptation of "The Midnight Ride of Paul Revere" by two performers, one narrating and one acting out the story. This production-within-the-play also includes an ASL tableau, whose four signers inform the viewers that they are doing the haiku "Seasons" by Dorothy Miles, and a poem rendered by a young lady to the "Bison Song" beat.[4] A more striking example of the interanimation between Deaf and mainstream cultures and literatures, and of the carnivalesque quality of Deaf American literature, appears in *The World According to Pat: Reflections of Residential School Days*, a videotape of Patrick Graybill's performance originally done at a regional convention in 1984.[5]

In *World*, Graybill reminisces about his experiences at the Kansas School for the Deaf in the 1950s. One of his more memorable recollections concerns the literary society and its eagerly awaited productions. At Graybill's school, every third Sunday was Literary Night, which the older students took turns (by class) staging for the edification and entertainment of all. In *World*, Graybill simulates part of a Literary Night production by presenting a remarkably faithful ASL adaptation of "Yankee Doodle Dandy" as well as a version of "The Black Cat," an 1843 short story by Edgar Allan Poe.

"The Black Cat"

In his version of "The Black Cat," Patrick Graybill imitates a signed rendition previously done by a Deaf instructor at his school. He goes beyond signing the story word for word to enact the characters, alternating between Poe's narrator and the cat and conveying their appearances, personalities, and emotional states. He additionally sets the scene—the dimly lit room lined with brick walls—to give spectators the sense that they are there. In the process, he adapts the English story to ASL and its rhetorical requirements. In this interplay the majority language is made to appear not so important after all.

Graybill's performance provides a specific example of a more general phenomenon: the subversion of English by Deaf Americans at Literary Night productions and other occasions of the interanimation of the two languages. Graybill uses this classic narrative in a way at odds with its original intention, ignoring the literary requirements of mainstream society. His starting point is a printed English narrative; although Poe's first-person narrators seem to be talking to a listener, they are *written* stories, meant to be consumed by a solitary reader who is expected to mentally visualize the action. Moreover, the generic status of Poe's "Black Cat" is clear: it is a tale of terror, meant to be considered in isolation from other works.

On every count, Graybill's version departs from Poe's, underscoring the negotiation between two languages. To be sure, "The Black Cat" first appeared not on its own but in a newspaper, and today's reader is most likely to encounter it in some kind of collection (of Poe's works, of short stories, or of American literature generally); but in these contemporary anthologies, all the selections have some recognized literary value. In contrast, the Literary Night version might have been preceded by a group act of two signers dexterously mirroring each other as the viewers applauded enthusiastically. It might have been followed by another signer, pigtails flying, vivaciously signing and lip-synching "The Star-Spangled Banner" to a recording by Kate Smith. Despite its name, this particular Literary Night production is an irreverent assemblage of the literary and the nonliterary, bound together solely by their performative nature.

In his performance of Poe's classic short story, Graybill does not scrimp in any way. He becomes every character in turn, displaying their mannerisms, appearances, attitudes, utterances, and actions. Enacting the main character, Graybill walks, talks, and anguishes like a man in great fear. As the cat, he is all animal, down to the swishing tail and the hidden claws. The result is both narrative and drama, a spectacle that is a semiplay. Therefore, although conveyed within the "literary" framing, Graybill's adaptation of "The Black Cat" is performance. He has taken a written English story, meant to be read (or perhaps heard), and transformed it into a hybrid English/ASL art form, meant to be performed and viewed.

It is certainly possible to read aloud a written story; but the speaker generally puts all effort into animating the author's precise words, for it is the words themselves that are important. The speaker tries to approximate what the author had in mind when he or she set pen to paper: the proper tone, intonation, pacing, volume, pitch, and pronunciation. A reader might sit alone with her book, or someone hearing a story being read might close his eyes and listen; but a good deal of the time, the ASL storyteller keeps his or her eyes on the viewers during the performance, often as part of whatever eye behavior is required at the linguistic level. The "literary"—solitary, private, imagining—is thus subverted by the visual, the performative, and the interactive. The emphasis on eye contact is felt even in the videotape of Graybill's performance; in close-up, he appears to be talking directly to the viewer rather than across a distance of miles and years.

Modalities of Storytelling

ASL is a visual vernacular, and ASL storytelling makes much use of visualizing a narrative, printed or otherwise. Unlike the writer, who leaves it to the reader to mentally visualize what is going on, the ASL storyteller both tells and shows what is happening. To be effective, acclaimed storyteller Stephen Ryan explains, the performer must mentally visualize and plan the story well in advance, coordinating gestures, mime, language, facial expressions, and any appropriate props. The ASL performer "imagine[s] that [he or she is] an illustrator bringing the most important visual moments to life. . . . Non-manual signals, such as facial expression, provide important information in ASL storytelling. The exaggeration of facial expression is very significant . . . By changing [the] body position so that each character faces a different direction, [the performer] help[s] the audience understand which character is doing the action."[6] The storyteller thus goes beyond conveying, say, angry words to acting like an angry person, with appropriate face, mouth, and eye movements, as well as larger-scale body movements such as shoulder angle, body tilt, and foot placement. Such movements are not merely mimicry or acting but draw on features inherent to ASL at lexical, morphological, syntactic, and discourse levels.

Thus, these linguistic principles incorporate the whole body. Whereas spoken English employs sounds to create meaningful units (words), ASL relies on the body (particularly the hands) moving through space to form meaningful units. Sign languages don't rely heavily on word endings and word order but modify the movements of signs themselves.[7] Consider, for example, how a person speaking English expresses the progressive stages of anger in a changing series of phrases: "I'm irritated," "I'm annoyed," "I'm fuming," "I'm seething," and then "I'm enraged." A Deaf American communicating in ASL not only signs these phrases but also uses body movements and facial expressions to convey the internal physical state. "Irritation" is conveyed with its appropriate sign (the middle finger twisting against the forehead) along with narrowed eyes, a slight grimace, and a 40 degree turn of the head. "Annoyance" is STOP

BOTHERING ME with widening, threatening eyes and an angling toward and shaking of the head at the offending person. "Fuming" and "seething" can be signed as BOILING INSIDE THE BODY, the latter with more intensity, speed, and movement, along with an angry (and slightly exaggerated) facial expression and body stance. "Rage" is a POW—the fist of the right hand erupting from the enclosing left hand—in simulation of a lid blowing off a pot and cracking the ceiling.

It is therefore not too surprising that many Deaf readers find printed English—an abstract representation of an aural language—rather meaningless, impersonal, and lifeless. Since ASL does not have a corresponding written form, those accustomed to using unmediated sign language often find it difficult to relate to written English. For instance, Graybill in *World* comments that he was so enthralled with his instructor's performance of "The Black Cat" that he raced to the library to get Poe's original only to find black marks on a white page. Many Deaf Americans are indifferent to English poems, stories, or plays on paper; but when these works are adapted to ASL, interest immediately perks up—the ASL adaptation in effect "revives" the printed word.

For example, Leon Auerbach, former chair of the Department of Mathematics at Gallaudet, recalls his schooldays: "We also had monthly literary club meetings where we would sit and tell stories and recite poems; but it was mostly stories, sometimes more like pantomime, acting it out. Signing straight or 'cold' wasn't very interesting, but using a lot of expression, a bit of hamming it up, made it very interesting for people to watch."[8] Auerbach and his schoolmates didn't just sign the written words but transformed them into ASL by making much use of the body (and hence adding visual appeal). This bodying forth is integral to ASL discourse; indeed, according to noted storyteller Ben Bahan, the ASL signer is not just signing a story, he or she *is* the story.[9] We can separate the English words from the writer or the English utterances from the speaker but we cannot separate the signs from the signer.

Therefore, when English forms or works are adapted to sign language we see what Bakhtin in *Rabelais and His World* terms a "degradation," that is, a transfer to the material level.[10] This fundamental principle of many comic activities and a great deal of comic folk literature is much in evidence in Literary Night—the lowering of all that is high, spiritual, ideal, and abstract to the material level of earth and body. For instance, a "vulgar" variant of the dignified, spiritual Psalm 23 (". . . he leadeth me beside the still waters") that begins "I snuggle close to a voluptuous bottom beside still waters" comically brings the high and spiritual back down to earth—in a way that is literally productive, as these two lovers may very well end up with a child. As Bakhtin explains, earth is "an element that swallows up and gives birth at the same time"; to degrade something—to bring it down to earth—is to bury and sow it (in the earth) in order to bring forth something more, or something better. Degradation affirms the lower body, the belly and the reproductive organs.[11] In this fruitful destruction lies regeneration.

English words that are reinfused with the body are in a sense brought down to the level of the body. Words per se are aural or printed abstractions lacking materiality or physical substance; but when translated into ASL, the words are necessarily materialized and embodied. This transference of the high, spiritual, ideal, and abstract to the material level is especially visible (in varying degrees) during Literary Night productions, when the disparity between a written English original and its visual-kinetic ASL adaptation is unavoidable. Consider the ASL adaptation of Longfellow's "Midnight Ride of Paul Revere" performed in the Literary Night segment of Bangs's *Institution Blues*. Blending literature and performance, English and ASL, the aural and the visual, two performers in period costume convey the poem; one does most of the reciting, the other most of the enacting. The alternation between reciting and acting out combines English and ASL with a slight exaggeration in tone and movement that gives the work a comical, irreverent, and parodic quality; the synthesis is dynamic, vivid, visually appealing, and in many ways an improvement on the original.

Let us return to the ASL adaptation of "The Black Cat." Instead of writing or simply saying that it is frightening to come face to face with terror in a dimly illuminated basement, Patrick Graybill enacts an actual person trembling and perspiring alone in a brick-walled room. As he images it, the small damp room is dreadfully dark except for a single lantern in one shadowy corner. The English words "frightening," "solitude," and "adequate" are abstractions, not things we can see, hear, touch, feel, or smell, and "illumination" is a high-sounding synonym for "light" that conveys little of the essence and energy of light itself. In contrast, Graybill puts the body back into these words by showing a person frantic and alone, with beads of perspiration on his forehead. He cowers, talking fearfully to himself. His eyes are wild and grotesquely protruding with terror.

By reinserting the body, Graybill is also administering an "earthy" corrective to the classical or literary, which rejects the physical, emotional, and excessively graphic. This move, according to Stuart Hall, is typical of the carnivalesque, whereby "the grotesque image of the body and its functions subvert the models of decorous behavior and classical ideals."[12] Graybill's use of the body to communicate, like that of a modern dancer, is very sensuous and graphic, and not at all classically restrained. Indeed, his material rendition displays a grotesque, indecorous quality, probably going well beyond the presumably fairly dignified version by his English teacher. He changes quickly from enacting the protagonist, heart beating wildly and eyes wide, to becoming the black cat, snarling and baring its fangs. Graybill makes good use of his body to make all the action very sensuous, dramatic, and vivid.

Graybill's rendition is almost a burlesque of Poe's story. The dark, terrifying tale becomes rather comical in the ASL adaptation—the by-product of a high-status language and a low-status language interacting and playing off one another. Even though the narrative is terrifying, Graybill's subtle exaggerations of body movements and facial expressions are entertaining. When a low discourse takes on the dominant high discourse, the result is subversive yet dynamic.[13] Such mixing of high and low often shines a bright light on the shortcomings of high discourse and the merits of low discourse.

Signed adaptations of English stories and poems are thus a double-edged form of expression that seems to "degrade" English (in Bakhtin's sense of the word). On the one hand, English discourse is brought down from its abstract, refined perch to the physical and impure material world. On the other hand, when "body" is reinserted into English discourse, it reinvigorates a language that seems to have largely lost its capacity to communicate fully using more than one sense. It is especially restorative to use the body in all its physicality as Graybill does. After all, performance and mimicry, which are two ways of employing the body, are fundamental modes of human behavior.[14]

The Dematerializing of the Word

As early as the nineteenth century, Ralph Waldo Emerson was concerned that the English language was becoming divorced from real, lived experience.[15] As an accomplished lecturer, Emerson was very attuned to the growing desiccation of the language in both its spoken and written forms. Oratory, which was then still a vital part of American culture, engaged audiences more deeply than most public speaking does today. In a number of his writings, especially "Nature" (1836), Emerson bemoaned the increasing corruption of language and the need to maintain the correspondence between visible (and material) things and discourse.[16] His message was not lost on other American poets and writers, including Walt Whitman, whose *Leaves of Grass* notoriously sang of the bodily and the sensuous.[17]

This increasing "lifelessness" in the English language is a result of worldwide cultural and sociolinguistic developments. The general shift from orality to literacy changed the way that people communicate, altering their outlook on life as well as their arts, literature, and modes of performance. Carol Simpson Stern and Bruce Henderson argue that the performative styles of today's more print-oriented cultures aspire to "abstract, mystical height" while oral cultures favored performances focused on the lower strata: that is, performances in which the supernatural emerges from the body itself.[18] Such an emphasis on the lower strata is, as we have seen, associated with the comic, and Bakhtin believes that the comic aspects of the world and the gods were once as "official" as the serious. But early in recorded Western history, "in the definitely consolidated state and class structure," the comic became first nonofficial and later an expression of folk culture—the carnivalesque.[19]

So, for a millennium, the comic manifestations of popular folk culture—including Roman saturnalias, medieval carnivals, and especially verbal compositions with their positive and reviving laughter linked to the material and low—existed alongside but sharply differentiated from the official political and aesthetic forms of late antiquity and later ecclesiastical and feudal culture. As we saw in chapter 2, medieval feast days had their fairs and other open-air amusements with giants, dwarfs, monsters, and trained animals. Alongside civil and social ceremonies and rituals such as the initiation of a knight were clowns and fools mimicking and mocking those rituals and ceremonies. Similarly, as official "classical" discourse developed so did comic literature, which Bakhtin calls "the entire recreational literature of the Middle Ages."[20] As we have seen, this literature included countless parodies, both written and oral, in Latin as well as the vernacular. Even the mystery, miracle, and morality plays of medieval theater often had a carnivalesque quality.

Bakhtin laments the tendency, begun in the Enlightenment and reinforced by the Romantics, to overlook the comic:

> The element of laughter was accorded the least place of all in the vast literature devoted to myth, to folk lyrics, and to epics. . . . And yet, the scope and the importance of this culture were immense in the Renaissance and the Middle Ages. A boundless world of humorous forms and manifestations opposed the official and serious tone of medieval ecclesiastical and feudal culture. In spite of their variety, folk festivities of the carnival type, the comic rites and cults, the clowns and fools, giants, dwarfs, and jugglers, the vast and manifold literature of parody—all these forms have one style in common: they belong to one culture of folk carnival humor.[21]

Comic discourse still receives far less critical attention and respect than does more serious, high-minded discourse. But such comic and popular discourse had and continues to have immense scope and importance, particularly in Deaf American literature.

Grotesque Bodies Versus Bourgeois Bodies

Bakhtin discovered that inherent in these comic forms and manifestations was a concept of the body as multiple, vigorous, and part of the swelling crowd. This "grotesque body," as opposed to the atomized, individual body, is one with the earth. Flesh is emphasized and in excess, representing all aspects of the cosmos. The body as a whole, particularly the mouth and the lower body, is a subject of pleasure and never removed from its social and physical environment. The body is fertile, procreative, and regenerating. Furthermore, this body indulges in degrading laughter—which, as discussed above, reinvigorates through contact with the material, the earth.[22]

However, the late Middle Ages and Renaissance saw the rise of the middle class, which clasped to its heart humanism (that is, individualism) and classical aesthetics. Peter Stallybrass and Allon White believe that the middle class gradually distanced itself from popular culture and its materialistic metaphysics, and even sought to repress this other world.[23] This emergent class wished to distance itself from the decadent nobility and the unmannered peasantry and seek an identity as a civilized social rank. Such "civilization" was thought to reside in a restrained mode of behavior and communication; and such restraint and decorum seemed inherent in classical aesthetics.

The middle class's embrace of this metaphorical body, and rejection of that represented in the materialistic folk tradition of medieval popular culture, can be seen in literal bodies: in the statuary of the Renaissance and of later periods of neoclassical revivals. The classical statue—such as that of Thomas Jefferson at the Jefferson Memorial in Washington, D.C.—is mounted "above" (above the common people) and evokes passive admiration. It also evokes the transcendent, individual, static, and universal, and it intimates the epic, the tragic, and nostalgia for a lost past. Smooth and without openings, the statue is a finished product that reveals no evidence of process, growth, or change. It thus disavows any incomplete or potentially disturbing aspects of the human body such as birth and death. The classical statue often features a single individual—isolated and cut off from all other bodies. This feature appealed to the middle class, which was in favor of bodies and objects acquiring a private, individual nature.[24] During the Renaissance and Enlightenment, "private" bodies became atomized, individualized, and divided from the collectivity represented by the grotesque body of folk culture, with its links to the all-embracing, fertile earth. The individual members of the middle class, after all, have risen on their own and made their own way; unlike the aristocrats, they have not inherited their status.

Classical aesthetics were also adopted for official discourse, the high language of statecraft, literature, and religion. Such dictates emphasized the closed, homogeneous, monumental, and symmetrical in public discourse. Discourse that was excessive, open-ended, asymmetrical, and vulgar—such as the writings of Rabelais, which provided the occasion of Bakhtin's theorizing on the carnivalesque—were deemed of less value. As Stallybrass and White explain, "[The bourgeoisie] put discourse that is transcendent, civilized, rational, related to 'spirit' and the mind/imagination, above the low, popular, vulgar discourse of popular culture. The very sign of rationality, wit, judgement was the suppression and distancing of the physical (grotesque) body."[25] In this way official speech and writing avoided the features or faults of the "grotesque" body, with its excesses, openings, physical needs, and sensuality. High writing and rhetoric were to be "clean," polite, and unemotional and were to avoid unnecessary references to the body, especially its grosser aspects.

With the rise of the middle class, the principle of constructive degradation and its corollary concept of the body—perpetuated in the best tradition of the culture of folk humor—was weakened and narrowed. As Bakhtin points out, traces of it can still be found in many of the great Renaissance writers, including Rabelais, Dante, Cervantes, Boccaccio, and Shakespeare; they all to some extent manifest a "coming down to earth." Each disobeyed the classical dictates to some extent, with Rabelais going the furthest in retaining elements of the materialistic ethos: *Pantagruel and Gargantua* in particular contains many images of the human body—eating, imbibing, defecating, and engaging in sexual life, often in an exaggerated way.[26] To the rising middle class, however, the physicality of the body was gross and uncivilized; they preferred an *aesthetics of the beautiful*, which cleaned up and even did away with the hideous and formless body. At the same time, literacy was spreading and the text was taking on a new importance. To give the appearance of rationality, moderation, and objectivity—that is, greater civilization and progress—communications relied less on the subjectivity of the speaker and the use of the body; the message, not the messenger, was central. This trend only continued with the invention of the printing press, the proliferation of printed text, and modern communications media such as the telegraph and radio. In effect, the body disappeared.

The Deaf Concept of the Body

Members of mainstream (middle-class) Western culture generally have a constrained, "civilized" body image as part of their sense of self or cultural identity—but the cultural identity of Deaf Americans has bodily communication at its core. In ASL, the body is text and articulation. When signing narratives and other art forms, Deaf Americans assert the body as text. In this manner, they affirm a language that incorporates the body. They also contrast their wonderfully visual-kinetic vernacular with a language that is merely rational, disembodied speech or text.

Because deafness is not a conspicuous physical difference, deafness and the Deaf culture are largely invisible. Making deafness, deaf people, and sign language visible—making the body visible as a matter of pride and difference—has thus become a political objective. The various productions of professional theater groups such as the National Theatre of the Deaf and the increased availability of ASL videotapes are part of a deliberate effort to bring Deaf Americans and their visual vernacular into view. Signing stories and poems in public, rather than putting pen to paper, is Deaf Americans' metaphor for self-determination.

By adapting English stories, poems, and plays to ASL in playful forms that reinsert the body, Deaf American literature administers a reinvigorating corrective to the English language. A "high" discourse can become ossified when overly elevated and artificially divorced from everyday life.[27] It needs interanimation with the "low," with the everyday found in the common people's vernacular forms—such as the visual vernacular of Deaf Americans.

Thus Literary Night reflects a two-world condition similar to that which existed during the Middle Ages. In the official world, a restrained middle class (mainstream society) privileges literacy and the civilized body; in the nonofficial world, Deaf culture keeps alive its embodied vernacular and performative tradition.

Literary Night is the carnivalesque intermingling of the two, setting canonical short stories and poems alongside taboo-busting ABC story-poems, Poe's "The Black Cat" alongside Graybill's slyly humorous version of the tale, Longfellow's "Midnight Ride of Paul Revere" alongside its dynamic ASL adaptation in *Institution Blues*. Literary Night turns what was originally aural, represented by black marks on a white page, into a visual, interactive performance that materializes in front of us. Just as during carnival the high and the low, the official and the nonofficial, are playfully intermixed and inverted, so here the usual hierarchies—including the placement of the English language "above" ASL—are turned upside down and inside out. As Gustavo Perez Firmat asserts in his study of liminality in the Hispanic tradition, such is the nature of carnival, which "operates by destabilizing oppositions, by inverting hierarchies."[28]

In the case of "The Black Cat," the opposition between the "official"—aural or literate—and the "nonofficial"—visual or oral—is destabilized and the hierarchy upended, as the ASL performance in many ways outdoes communication that is printed or aural. Literary Night thus functions as a Bakhtinian polyglossic festival, when, in Allon White's words:

> carnival languages of the common people "pla[y] up"
> against the tragic pathos and high seriousness of the domi-
> nant artistic, moral, and political discourses of the period.
> In this view the "earthy" folk word—scatological, irrever-
> ent, humorous, and contradictory—becomes both a cri-
> tique of, and corrective to, the lie of pathos. The lofty
> word of authority is "brought down a peg or two." In
> polyglossia, the focus of interest for Bakhtin is not merely
> the interanimation of "equal" languages, but the interani-

mation of high with low, the conflicts engendered when the dominant, centralizing and unifying language of a hegemonic group is contested by the low language of sub-ordinated classes.[29]

Even though English teachers and their students were just trying to sign English works in Literary Night, they produced some unprecedented new forms, for they were combining the aural and the visual, the hearing and the deaf, the oral and the literate. In these hybrid forms, English sometimes dominated; at other times, ASL dominated. But all were intriguing and all were happening along the lines of the carnivalesque, whose function, Bakhtin tells us, is always "to consecrate inventive freedom, to permit the combination of a variety of different elements and their rapprochement, to liberate from the prevailing point of view of the world, from conventions and established truths, from clichés, from all that is humdrum and universally accepted."[30] The carnival spirit and its laughter in Literary Night free both participants and viewers from dogmatism, piety, and uniformity. The carnival spirit is gay, triumphant, and slightly derisive. It buries and revives—generating something new—as it brings the lofty down to earth. In this degrading of English forms—that is, the mixing up of English and ASL—something different and perhaps better can emerge.

Notes

1. On this dramatic organization, see Shanny Mow, "Theater, Community," in *Gallaudet Encyclopedia of Deaf People and Deafness*, vol. 3, ed. John Van Cleve (New York: McGraw-Hill, 1987), 288.
2. This definition is offered by the editor of M. M. Bakhtin, *The Dialogic Imagination: Four Essays*, ed. Michael Holquist, trans. Caryl Emerson and Michael Holquist (Austin, Tex.: University of Texas Press, 1981), 431.
3. See Allon White, *Carnival, Hysteria, and Writing: Collected Essays and Autobiography* (New York: Oxford University Press, 1993), 137.
4. *Institution Blues*, scripted by Don Bangs and Jan DeLap, dir. Don Bangs, SignRise Cultural Arts Production, Publick Playhouse, Cheverly, Md., June 6, 1993.

5. *The World According to Pat: Reflections of Residential School Days*, performed and dir. Patrick Graybill, Silver Spring, Md., Sign Media and TJ Publishers, videocassette, 60 min., 1986.

6. Stephen Ryan, "Let's Tell an ASL Story," in *Deaf Studies III: Bridging Cultures in the Twenty-first Century*, conference proceedings, April 22–25, 1993, ed. Jackie Mann (Washington, D.C.: Gallaudet University, College for Continuing Education, 1993), 147.

7. Carol Padden, "Sign Languages," in Van Cleve, *Gallaudet Encyclopedia of Deaf People and Deafness*, vol. 3, 43–53.

8. Leon Auerbach and Hortense Auerbach, "The Good Old Days," *Deaf American* 38 (4): 13.

9. Ben Bahan, e-mail correspondence with author, February 1995.

10. Mikhail Bakhtin, *Rabelais and His World*, trans. Hélène Iswolsky (Cambridge, Mass.: MIT Press, 1968), 19–21.

11. Ibid., 21.

12. Stuart Hall, "Metaphors of Transformation," introduction to White, *Carnival, Hysteria, and Writing*, 7.

13. White, *Carnival, Hysteria, and Writing*, 145.

14. Carol Simpson Stern and Bruce Henderson, *Performance: Texts and Contexts* (New York: Longman, 1993), 10. See also Johan Huizinga, *Homo Ludens: A Study of the Play-Element in Culture* (Boston: Beacon Press, 1955).

15. Gene Bluestein, *The Voice of the Folk: Folklore and American Literary History* (Amherst, Mass.: University of Massachusetts Press, 1972), 17.

16. Ralph Waldo Emerson, "Nature," in *Selections from Ralph Waldo Emerson: An Organic Anthology*, ed. Stephen E. Whicher (Boston: Houghton Mifflin, 1960), 21–56, esp. 31–36.

17. Walt Whitman, *Leaves of Grass* (Philadelphia: David McKay, 1888).

18. Samuel Kinser, *Carnival, American Style: Mardi Gras at New Orleans and Mobile* (Chicago: University of Chicago Press, 1990), 171; cited in Stern and Henderson, *Performance*, 158.

19. Bakhtin, *Rabelais and His World*, 6.

20. Ibid., 13.

21. Ibid., 4; on miracle plays, see 15.

22. Ibid., 20–21. Preindustrial societies stressed this interconnection in their worship of fertility goddesses identified with mother earth, represented in ancient sculptures that have endured to the present.

23. Peter Stallybrass and Allon White, *The Politics and Poetics of Transgression* (London: Methuen, 1986), 21.

24. Ibid., 22–24.
25. Ibid., 21.
26. Bakhtin, *Rabelais and His World*, 18, 22.
27. Stallybrass and White, *The Politics and Poetics of Transgression*, 8.
28. Gustavo Perez Firmat, *Literature and Liminality: Festive Readings in the Hispanic Tradition* (Durham, N.C.: Duke University Press, 1986), 14.
29. White, *Carnival, Hysteria, and Writing*, 145.
30. Bakhtin, *Rabelais and His World*, 34.

Chapter

6

Deaf American Theater

In 1993, Institution Blues *enjoyed full houses during its two-day run at a Deaf community theater in Washington, D.C.[1] The three-hour play about the imminent closing of a state residential school struck very close to home, for at the time increasing numbers of deaf schools were shutting down across the nation. Outside the Deaf family, the school for the deaf is the primary breeding ground of Deaf culture and thus its closure is tantamount to gutting the Deaf community. Theatergoers were immediately drawn into this dramatic production; indeed, as the lights dimmed and actors/protesters entered from the back, marched down the aisles waving their placards, and ascended the stage, many viewers joined in the protest. They left their seats and, with arms and hands pumping, signed "Keep the institution open! Keep the institution open!" They stopped only when one of the protest rally leaders moved to the front of the stage and began speaking passionately and eloquently to the energized house.*

DEAF AMERICANS stage numerous productions every year, ranging from mainstream plays, such as Gallaudet University's fall 1997 production of *Dr. Jekyll and Mr. Hyde,* to vaudeville-like productions, such as the National Theatre of the Deaf's *My Third Eye* and *Parade*.[2] In between are both original but conventional plays focusing on Deaf culture, such as *Sign Me Alice, Tales from a Clubroom*, and *A Deaf Family Diary*,[3] and hybrid productions that mix classical and indigenous theater, such as *Institution Blues*. Most are mainstream plays or faithful adaptations; only a handful of original Deaf productions see the light of day. In the 1990s playgoers could see Willy Conley's *The Water Falls, The Hearing Test*, and *Falling on Hearing Eyes*; Bob Daniels's *I Didn't Hear That Color* and *Hand in Hand, Foot in Mouth: An Unmusical*; Michele Verhoosky's *Middle of Nowhere* and *I See the Moon*; and Shanny Mow's *Counterfeits, Cat Spanking Machine*, and *Letters from Heaven*. *Deafywood*, compiled by John Maucere, toured the country for three years in the late 1990s.[4] A few other original productions have been written and produced by theater departments at Gallaudet University, the National Technical Institute for the Deaf, and California State University at Northridge over the past few years. Undoubtedly many unstaged scripts are composed by would-be playwrights working on their own or in creative writing classes or workshops.[5]

Despite their diversity, original scripts by Deaf American playwrights share some general characteristics. Like minority drama in general, these plays draw in varying degrees both on indigenous (i.e., unique to Deaf culture) and conventional (i.e., mainstream) elements. Because of this dual nature, each counters mainstream literary and dramatic conventions in one way or another. In many instances, plays (like *Alice*) are conventional in form, but original in subject.

Modern Conventional Theater as High Art

Michael Bristol, a drama historian, argues that today's conventional mainstream theater as a whole is a fairly formal affair that helps support the status quo.[6] Most municipalities of any size have at least one separate building—the "theater"—just for dramatic productions. On the infrequent occasions that the building is in use, theatergoers make dinner reservations, dress up, and head out for a night on the town. Once they arrive and get ensconced in their plush seats, the lights dim and the action begins, apart from and above them on a raised stage. Theatergoers stay in their seats, players stay on the stage, and the two groups interact very little. The audience, mostly upper class and college educated, has come to see what the playwright and director have crafted and how the stars interpret what has been given them. The theatergoers have come to be passively entertained, and the privilege rarely comes cheaply.

Manifesting the alienation and differentiation of social structure that Henri Lefebvre finds characteristic of modernity, mainstream theater often has the quality of a high art.[7] Rather than being engaged with everyday life, it usually aims at the transcendent and serious; even its comedy is of a sophisticated sort. As an artistic enterprise, it is carefully crafted and orchestrated for aesthetic ends.[8] Most plays observe the conventional (neoclassical) unities of time, place, and action; in three to five acts, replete with dialogue mouthed by actors all over the stage, they move linearly from start to middle to denouement to end.

Typical Broadway dramas and musicals possess scintillating songs or tragic, brooding story lines, marvelous stage scenery, and tightly structured movement. They are high theater that seeks to entertain rather than to accentuate cultural identity (a viewer's sense of self) or to guide an audience through difficult economic and political realities.[9] Rather than addressing critical issues they usually offer momentary escape: for two to three hours in a darkened hall, the theatergoer is caught up in a completely different, artificial world.

This kind of theater bears little resemblance to the earliest Western drama, which was incorporated into religious festivities and rituals. As part of the general "progress" of Western civilization and art, plays have been made to conform with "classical" conventions derived from Greek drama, whose characteristics were then "improved on."[10] In contrast, folk or popular manifestations—including vaudeville and its various, sometimes physical, acts—are often perceived to be simple or juvenile forms, worthy of interest only insofar as they have the potential to evolve toward more complex and sophisticated literary or dramatic art.

However, in becoming more "developed," modern theater has traded in its original social and political impulse for an aesthetics of the beautiful. Bristol observes of the older forms, "Because of its capacity to create and sustain a briefly intensified social life, the theater is festive and political as well as literary—a privileged site for the celebration and critique of the needs and concerns of the polis."[11] Theater in this sense is an opportunity for people to gather for a heightened experience that has to do with matters of interest to the community. It may rely on artifice and exaggeration, but not nearly so much as the conventional theater of today. It still partakes of everyday life with an eye to social, civic, religious, and economic conditions.

In the past, dramatics were a more lively and communal affair, as well as an integral part of the social, civic, religious, and economic fabric of local life.[12] People flocked to plays, processions, and various ceremonials and rituals. In classical Greece, the tragedies and comedies viewed in outdoor amphitheaters were an essential part of community life. As we saw in earlier chapters, during festival times in the Middle Ages and Renaissance—such as market days, fairs, parish feasts, and so on—dramatic performances both serious and comic were customary. People gathered to see miracle plays, which depicted the lives of the saints; mystery plays, whose cycles covered history from the fall of Satan to the Resurrection (and which often interpolated comic material); and morality plays, allegorical dramas whose characters were abstract personifications struggling to achieve salvation. Such forms addressed the deep concerns of their audiences, as well as playing an important social role in their lives.

A Theater of Two Worlds

Like the theatricals of the Middle Ages, indigenous Deaf American theater remains close to the everyday lives of its viewers. When Deaf playwrights create original scripts, they tend to focus on immediate social and political matters. Thus, as it focused on the closing of residential schools for the deaf, *Institution Blues* dramatized related issues in ways that highlighted Deaf culture and strengthened theatergoers in their resolve to take some action. They were caught up during and after the play, lingering on the sidewalk outside the theater and debating the issues that the play had raised.

This socially engaged theater arises in part from Deaf Americans' position as a smaller culture within mainstream culture, part of it and yet simultaneously apart from it. Almost all original scripts, stage productions, and films are concerned in some way with this two-world condition, either explicitly or implicitly. As we saw in chapter 2, the two-world condition of medieval Europe underlays the serious laughter of carnival and the theatricals interwoven with the people's social and religious life. The experience of living in two worlds is just as important in shaping Deaf American theater. For example:

- *A Deaf Family Diary* depicts a young Deaf couple endeavoring to get their respective Deaf and hearing families to coexist
- *Sign Me Alice* portrays a young woman's struggle to be herself and not something mainstream society wants her to be
- *Tales from a Clubroom* takes place entirely and focuses wholly on members' relationships within a Deaf club, but one is always aware that outside this oasis is hearing society
- *Deafula*, one of the first original Deaf American films, is permeated by the double and conflicted identity of the protagonist even though deafness is barely mentioned.[13]

This two-world condition is quite explicitly a subject of the National Theatre of the Deaf's *My Third Eye* (1971–72). Interspersed through its segments of diverse formats are short narratives by individual performers. One performer relates his experience of entering a residential school for the first time: "We walked into the building, and once inside I was immediately struck by a medicinal, institutional smell. This did not look like a hospital, or like any other building I had ever seen before. My mother bent down, turned me toward her, and said: 'This is where you will get all your education. You will live here for a while. Don't worry, I will see you again later.' "[14] This typical story of a deaf child born into a Deaf family is emblematic of the clash between two cul-

tures. In many of these accounts of childhood, hearing people—
the other culture—are initially shadowy, background figures.
Then, suddenly, they break into the child's world. In *My Third
Eye*, a young boy becomes disoriented when he encounters the
alien organization of the school with its aural perspective and its
hierarchical structure. School is the place where he comes to realize that others—people in mainstream society—have a different
view of reality, a different way of thinking, that in fact is authoritative.[15]

For the most part, those within the mainstream are blithely
unaware of any world outside their own. They tend toward a uniform and univocal view of deaf people, relying on neat stereotypes
to make sense of things. For instance, the popular 1994 TV mini-
series *The Stand* presented deaf people as saintly speechreaders who
integrate amazingly well into mainstream society,[16] while the truth
is that most deaf people are not very good speechreaders, ground
themselves in Deaf communities, and are no more saintly than anyone else.

Bakhtin's festive critique—which does not allow one way of
looking at things, one established truth, one established reality—
emerges when the official and dominant is mixed with the popular
and subordinate. Many indigenous Deaf productions work diligently to demystify pervasive universal and univocal outlooks, relying on a double-voicedness that highlights the relationship
between the reality constructed by aural authority and a Deaf reality whose perspectives, needs, and values—frequently ignored or
overlooked—are quite different from those of mainstream society.
Such double-voicedness sets the one point of view against the
other, contrasts one evaluation or tone with the other. Thus in the
"Side Show" segment of *My Third Eye*, the assertive, self-assured
ringmaster—a woman—rebuts the feminization of Deaf culture by
mainstream culture and media; in this drama it is the voice readers—those who interpret for the hearing audience—who are inar-
ticulate, limited, and passive (i.e., exhibit the majority culture's
view of deaf behavior).[17] In every production, the dominant
assumption that sign language is "mere gestures" is countered by
the reality: a legitimate, vibrant, complex language.

Moreover, the conventional position is often revealed to be rooted in ignorance. In *A Deaf Family Diary*, the Deaf family of the bride finds themselves dealing with the groom's hearing parents, who simply do not know how to raise and treat their deaf children and future daughter-in-law. These parents so thoroughly fail to relate to the Deaf family that the play descends into a comedy of errors.

In *Institution Blues*, the state clearly errs in closing the residential state school for the deaf: the authorities—the blockheads!—simply do not understand. The reporter covering the protest rally is equally lacking in comprehension, and the whole play concerns his learning enough to pass on the true state of affairs to general readers. To show him how a school for the deaf that segregates Deaf Americans can be beneficial, two alumni take the clueless reporter in hand and back through the years to their own student days. In play-within-a-play flashbacks, they and others act out various scenes that look at the assigning of sign names, the teaching of social conventions such as table manners, the efficacy of peer instruction in the classroom, a Literary Night, a suicide, a prom, and a graduation. As the play's action progresses, it continues to move back and forth in time from the present-day rally aimed at saving the school to the past experiences of the alumni.

A Mundus Inversus

Like many popular rituals of the Middle Ages, these Deaf American plays festively and carnivalesquely turn upside down the usual relations between minority and majority, upending the dominant and focusing on those who are usually marginalized. As we have seen, this is typical of carnival, which, as Carol Simpson Stern and Bruce Henderson explain, "inverts the normal hierarchical order, turning everything upside down and inviting laughter. The laughter destabilizes authority, not allowing any one view of the world to rule. [Carnival] gives expression to multiple voices and ways of seeing the world, liberating people through the socially acceptable mechanism of laughter."[18]

We see this inversion particularly clearly if we turn once again to the "Side Show" segment of *My Third Eye*, a circus scene with a ringmaster and acrobats. The videotape version shows a red-and-white striped tent in the background and in the foreground a large enclosure—akin to a large, old-fashioned birdcage—with two voice readers inside. Suddenly, the ringmaster appears and strikes the ground with an imaginary whip. In top hat and black leather boots, she promises to tell about "strange things . . . a strange people"—the two voice readers caged as if they were an exhibit. At her behest, various acrobats go through their acts, while the voice readers stand virtually motionless (while speaking the performers' words for those in the audience who can only hear). As the acrobats perform onstage, the ringmaster extols the interaction, expressiveness, and freedom of ASL, which utilizes the face and the whole body. At the same time, she dismisses the poker faces, small mouth movements, and limp body appendages of the voice readers (representing mainstream society). The advantages of the visual language and culture contrast with the stiffness (unnaturalness) and impersonality of the aural-oral language and culture. In effect, Deaf culture is depicted as fluid and free—a little three-ring circus within an aural majority culture shown as sadly limited, inflexible, and authoritarian.

Much of the world today puts a priority on aural communication, whereas Deaf Americans valorize visual/tactile communication and believe they have the best of it. In "Side Show" the distinction between the two modalities is comically drawn. Various acrobats aptly demonstrate how people talk without looking at one another and how one person is hesitant to touch another to get his or her attention. On a train, a woman jumps when another passenger, unable to get her attention aurally, gingerly taps her on the shoulder. A second woman caught up in her own thoughts plays with a pencil in her mouth, moving it with clockwork precision from one side to the other without touching it with her hands. In another vignette, a mother attempts to get her affectionate young son to vocalize "mother," making him touch her throat (and preventing him from signing MOTHER); when he finally does utter an approximation of the word, she beams proudly and shows off the obviously frustrated and miserable little boy. All these portrayals have a slightly parodic quality, and their deft presentation is uplifting for their Deaf viewers.

Cultural Encyclopedias

In Deaf American theater, the creation of and delight in a feeling of collectivity takes precedence over the more narrow assessment of literary and artistic values.[19] The aim is not to put on a well-made, classical, three- to five-act comedy or tragedy but to bring together and foster cultural pride and identity in a widely scattered people. In its more indigenous form, the Deaf American play is cultural performance, uniting the community (including its marginal members) and facilitating a bonding and defining of the culture's identity and viability. By participating in this production (by staging, acting, or simply viewing it), Deaf Americans construct and revel in their identity.[20]

In this respect, nativist Deaf American drama resembles the ancient Greek epics, described by the cultural historian Werner Sollars as the "cultural encyclopedias" of their times. As cultural encyclopedias, they attempted to appeal to and bring together a widely dispersed people.[21] In classical times, the Greeks were scattered about in small communities, which sometimes fought among themselves; but they were at greater risk from outside forces and cultural systems. By fostering a cultural identity and thus a shared loyalty, the epics gave the Greek peoples a common history and helped enlarge their sense of a homeland. Drawing on this cultural identity encouraged them to join together to resist foreign expansionist empires.

As cultural encyclopedias, *Institution Blues*, *My Third Eye*, and other more nativist Deaf dramas make available to a heterogeneous and widely scattered people essential knowledge of both Deaf culture and mainstream culture.[22] Using both vernacular Deaf and mainstream languages and genres, both artistic and extra-artistic, the nativist drama helps Deaf Americans better understand and connect to their own culture, and also helps them learn how to deal with hearing society.

Indeed, Deaf performances often include too much cultural information. In response to audience feedback at its first staging, *Institution Blues*, which originally ran almost four hours, was whittled down. Even in its shortened form, the play is a big, sprawling production that encompasses a large part of Deaf culture and spans some twenty years, presenting what Peter Stallybrass and Allon

White call "a world of topsy-turvy, of heteroglot exuberance, of ceaseless overrunning and excess where all is mixed, hybrid, ritually degraded and defiled."[23]

A Comprehensive Form

The inclusiveness of indigenous Deaf American theater represents another break with mainstream dramatic conventions—here, those of unity and linearity. On its surface, *Institution Blues* is a traditional play of three acts and a single theme. But underneath, it is a cultural treasure trove of ASL poetry, ASL art, biography, eulogy, oratory, fairy tales, games, skits, jokes, and satire, framed as a kind of Literary Night. Sollars argues that more popular, festive productions—in contrast with those that adhere to conventions of high literary and dramatic art—characteristically include such miscellanies of genres and forms.[24] In such heterogeneity art and life are intertwined, not constructed as separate realms, and the more indigenous Deaf productions unite the two.[25]

The structure of many of these vaudeville-like productions is decentered and eccentric, for the producers are less concerned with generic distinctions or with creating a homogeneous, "complete," aesthetic product than with reflecting Deaf culture in all its multifacetedness and building a community of laughter. In the process, the producers have fun with the exaggerated, the disproportioned, the abundant, and the diverse. It is carnivalesque: an "experience . . . opposed to all that [is] ready-made and completed, to all pretense of immutability, [seeking] a dynamic expression; it demand[s] ever changing, playful, undefined forms."[26] The spirit of carnival plays, experiments, and mixes things up, rather than adhering to dramatic stipulations, classical or otherwise. Such inclusive theatricals are an image-ideal of and for a community as a heterogeneous and boundless totality (Bakhtin's teeming "grotesque body").[27]

Not surprisingly, as Don Bangs documents in his study of practices and principles in Deaf American theater, many original dramatic productions are explicitly vaudeville-like and festive, along the lines of *My Third Eye*.[28] Indeed, many display nonrigid structures and generic diversity. For instance, the theater program at the National Technical Institute for the Deaf (NTID) in Rochester,

New York, got its start in 1969 when students under Robert Panara organized a variety show as the first half of "An Experiment in Dramatics." When the NTID Drama Club was established in 1970, its first production was *Footlight Fever*, which contained a number of comedy sketches and routines.[29] In Ohio, not too far away, the first production of the Fairmount Theatre of the Deaf (FTD) was *My Eyes Are My Ears*, a theatrical collage based on popular entertainment forms used by Deaf Americans. FTD's *Story Theatre* (1970), although an adaptation, featured mime, improvisation, visual signplay, and general horsing around. In FTD's *Alice in Deafinity* (1975), Alice traveled in a deaf world in which each deaf person signed in his or her own way.[30]

Productions in New York and California in the 1980s and 1990s have also featured a large number of nativist or adapted plays with an inherently heterogeneous quality.[31] *Telling Stories*, Gallaudet University's original offering during the Deaf Way confest, was anything but a conventional dramatic production.[32] In their focus on parts rather than a polished whole, these theatricals connect to carnival; Gustavo Perez Firmat reminds us that "carnival is partial to *parts*. Carnival is part time. During carnival every part aspires to the condition of wholeness."[33]

Vaudeville in Deaf culture goes back to the nineteenth century, when it was a vital and popular form of entertainment for deaf and hearing people alike.[34] According to Don Bangs, however, the hearing tradition influenced the Deaf tradition only indirectly, and relatively late. Both the acting method and the melodramatic intertitles in the silent films of the 1910s and 1920s drew on vaudeville styles, and these films in turn influenced Deaf American vaudeville by supplying plots and other material. (The silent films were accessible; the talkies that superseded them were not.) When sound was successfully meshed with motion pictures, vaudeville began to die out in mainstream society—but it took on even greater importance in Deaf culture.

With the advent of the talkies, many Deaf Americans turned to vaudeville-like entertainment. Emerson Romero, a famous Deaf star of silent films, organized programs of playlets and skits that combined sign language with pantomime and acting.[35] Wolf Bragg established a New York amateur theater company that put on adaptations of short plays or short stories. The Chicago Silent Dramatic Club did skits and sign language adaptations of one-act plays, all within a vaudeville format. Other similar community groups and indigenous theater companies around the country produced traditional ASL-based entertainment for Deaf Americans: that is, short comedies and variety acts.

Even Gallaudet University, a stronghold of academe, put on vaudeville productions. The vaudeville tradition at Gallaudet in fact began in the 1880s, when college thespians performed shadow and open pantomime and produced spoofs of college life. Men had their Saturday Night Dramatics Club, founded in 1886, with an accent on the amusing; women joined together to form the Jollity Club. Even the Ballard Literary Society, which emphasized the literary, was inclined to present "shorties" such as skits, farce, and sketches. The college's drama department, despite generally favoring conventional theater, at first promoted vaudeville, farce, comedy, melodrama, costume drama, and classical tragedy. It later changed its focus from practical theater to the academic study of drama, leaving various student organizations on campus to carry on the performance tradition.[36]

The National Theatre of the Deaf

The National Theatre of the Deaf (NTD), funded by the federal government and geared to mainstream audiences, has also gone in for the medley, although in a modernist (i.e., symbolic, artistic, layered) way. Usually the company presents several short works adapted to sign language in accordance with its philosophy of "See the sign, hear the word."[37] Most NTD productions are simultaneously presented in spoken and sign language, and the company generally avoids Deaf forms and approaches or material specifically related to the deafness of the actors. Aiming at making both the hearing public more aware of deaf people and the deaf people more aware of highly artistic and sophisticated theater, it attempts to present "hearing theater" in a visual form and to enhance the theater experience by using material inherently rich in visually dramatic components. Thus, it often showcases haiku and other short poems that have strong visual imagery and lend themselves well to the creative use of sign language.[38]

NTD's *Under Milkwood*, for example, is not a conventional three- to five-act play.[39] Based on Dylan Thomas's radio play that offers vignettes of a day in the life of the residents of a Welsh village, the play switches focus from one group of people to another (with some of the players taking on multiple roles). This emphasis on characterization and dialogue makes it possible for the audience to pay attention to a few individuals at a time. As the dialogue is translated into artistic sign language—as much as possible, given that the voice readers are simultaneously reading the original words—the performers concentrate on the ASL/English translation. In doing so, they showcase the visual imagery of sign language and make beautiful pictures in the air.

NTD has staged three indigenous productions: *My Third Eye* (1971–71), *Parade* (1975–76), and *Parzival* (1982–83).[40] *Parzival*, though not vaudeville-like in tone or approach, is a medley. Personal quest stories told by individual performers—several of whom took part in creating those stories—are woven into an epic tale about a questing Arthurian knight. *Parade* has many more characteristics of vaudeville. On its title's framework is hung a number of demonstrations on the part of a group of Deaf protesters who want to establish their own political state, "New Deaf Dominion."[41] It also offers a number of comic vignettes: one features a Deaf American Columbus who discovers a new land, and another one provides a glimpse of a Deaf soap opera titled *As the Hand Turns*. Still another stars a Deaf Superman who does amazing feats and accomplishes daring rescues.[42]

My Third Eye is the most miscellaneous of the three. The videotape version begins by providing a view of the stage through shadowy bars; luminescent globes resembling three balloons hang suspended in the background. This opening segues into a birthing sequence, "Promenade," during which one player after another emerges from under a woman's immense skirt. As the sequence draws to an end, two of the players begin to reminisce about their respective childhoods, either conversing with a fellow performer or speaking directly to the audience. "Side Show," the circus scene discussed above, follows. Later segments, "Manifest" and "Curtain Raiser," include choreographed chorus numbers, "The Quick Brown Fox" and "Three Blind Mice." Other presentations highlight the iconic qualities of ASL. For instance, in "Manifest" several performers showcase ASL's capacity to convey different kinds of light: the breaking of day, fireflies, a flashlight, streetlights, lightning, and so on. In "A Little Dictionary of Slang," the actors depict emotional states, such as the different degrees of love. Frequently, they line up and perform a kind of revue, each doing a brief turn and then going off to the side.

Many nativist Deaf dramatic productions defy classical unity and linearity, as well as ignoring classical decorum. In other words, they disregard the conventional separation of the high genres from the low genres, high behavior from low behavior, tragedy from comedy. To be sure, such generic boundary crossing has a history as long as that of these respective genres; perhaps the playwright best known for nonconformity is Shakespeare, whose tragedies feature rustics and fools and whose "problem plays" and "tragicomedies" famously defy categorization. To this day some object to these liberties; but Shakespeare's refusal to obey the classical canons may also have contributed to his popularity, especially among the common people in his audience, the groundlings.

My Third Eye, like many other vaudeville-like Deaf American productions, is a hodgepodge of the high, serious, and artistic and the low, vulgar, and jokey. Right after the wrenching story of a small boy having to leave home and family to study at a residential school is the rambunctious, bouncy "Side Show." As one critic commented, "The play might best be described as a bittersweet adventure, often depicting incidents that are at once joyous and defeating."[43] *My Third Eye* combines the serious, high "Biography" with the low, comic "Sideshow"; the poignant narratives with the musically visual and amusing group performance of "Three Blind Mice"; and the entertaining ASL signplay with the highly artistic ASL tableau. It is a miscellany structured without regard for classical decorum.

Such mixing comes naturally to Deaf American theater, which exists in two worlds, negotiating two modalities of language and two belief systems. Indeed, some ASL art has no counterpart in any other literature, and thus no label. For example, is the ABC story a narrative, a poem, or performance? Is the ASL tableau a poem, a story, or performance? Transgression is inevitable when conventional distinctions do not apply.

Graybill's *A Deaf Family Diary* is a more conventional play, from the standpoint of classical stipulations. Yet it also depicts more of the vulgarities of life than one would expect in a mainstream comedy. In one scene, the bride's father, who has just undergone an operation, tells the full story to his hearing, soon-to-be relatives. The groom's uptight family is scandalized and set reeling by the gory details—the slicing of the stomach area, the probing to locate the cancerous part, the cutting away of the malignancy, and the sewing up of the incision—but the bride's family relishes the father's artistic use of ASL, including the excellent, if very graphic, visual imagery.

Collaborative Theater

The more indigenous Deaf American vaudeville productions also differ from conventional plays in the degree of collaboration involved, both in the work as a whole and in its numerous constitutive elements (the individual acts). The ASL tableau, which is structured by visual images and scenes, rather than thematically, is especially dependent on the performers' interaction. In this sequence of images composed of form and movement, which produces an imagic narrative, Deaf Americans relate to the world visually and develop it rhetorically. Rather than presenting oral discourse arranged in a more or less logical progression, the tableau fuses painting, drama (or cinema), and narrative or poetry. The form both exists independently and appears often within dramatic productions, including *Institution Blues* and *My Third Eye*.

The Collective as Creator

Deaf American theater often breaks with the rigid and hierarchical divisions of labor in Western theater tradition.[44] Despite the large number of participants in a conventional modern play, only a few are seen to be ultimately responsible for the enterprise: the playwright, the director (and sometimes the producer), and the head-liners. After a playwright hammers a story into a script, the director stages that script more or less as given; and the leading actors usually work within the constraints set by the director. Every entity and nonentity, from the director and leading lady and man down to the lowliest stagehand, has his or her separate function. Everyone's job is compartmentalized—including that of the theatergoers, who have come to be entertained.

In particular, the mainstream playwright is seen to be a highly creative individual, who receives the bulk of the accolades or condemnation drawn by the play. Even on those occasions when an actor or director draws much attention in a particular production, the play remains the author's—Eugene O'Neill's work, not that of Jason Robards or José Quintero. The Deaf dramatist, in contrast, is more of a skilled cultural worker. He or she is not innately more creative or important than the others involved. Don Bangs, for example, was a jack-of-all-trades at SignRise Cultural Arts: he often wrote (that is, guided all the brainstorming and structuring of one or more scripts), directed, acted, and handled public relations. He was also heavily involved in fund-raising, reviewing, and attending to the company's correspondence. Many other Deaf American intellectuals are at once playwrights, public relations agents, producers, fund-raisers, political activists, and teachers.

Moreover, this de-emphasis of specialized labor applies to the audience as well. As has already been noted in chapter 3, Bakhtin observes that everyone participates during carnival. The distinction between actors and spectators disappears: the clowns and fools of the festivals "remained clowns and fools always," representing "the carnival spirit in everyday life out of carnival season."[45] Productions such as the mystery plays involved large segments of the community; in England, different plays came to be performed by local guilds. Likewise in Deaf American theater, the local populace comes together to create, improvise, and dramatize. So few scripts exist that original text must be created first, a task that is often undertaken collectively.

NTD's *My Third Eye* is a case in point: to come up with the opening sequence, company members were asked to share their individual and collective aspirations in several improvisational planning sessions. J Ranelli, the director, made selections from these and then unified them all by having the actors emerge from under a huge blue cloth, in an approximation of a multiple birthing. One company member, Dorothy Miles, encouraged her fellow thespians to discuss their stories about aspects of the two-world condition that they found most disturbing or memorable, and from these reminiscences "Side Show" was born.[46] Thus, the director acts more as a facilitator than a taskmaster; and this collective effort extends to producing the play. *My Third Eye*, writes Stephen Baldwin in his history of the National Theatre of the Deaf, "marked the first time that deaf company members had assumed responsibility for directing and designing sets and costumes."[47]

In a typical Deaf American theatrical production, therefore, this process of creating a script is as important as the end product. As those involved in drawing up the script share ideas, buried knowledge and cultural codes come to light. For instance, when company members searched for examples of differences between Deaf and hearing culture, they thought of the famous balcony scene between Romeo and Juliet: such a fervent address to one at a window high above has no place in Deaf culture, where closer proximity and interaction are preferred. Thus this scene was chosen for the "Side Show" segment. Such recollection and discovery of cultural values makes theater in Deaf culture both a forum for playmakers' concerns and a cultural encyclopedia for viewers.

Parade also was a collaborative effort; the actors were heavily involved in determining the content and structure of the play, contributing some ideas and suggestions and objecting to and discarding others.[48] Even what might appear at first to be Pat Graybill's one-man show, the collage of vignettes about the residential school experience that constitutes *The World According to Pat*, was created through improvisations and storytelling sessions. The creators of *A Deaf Family Diary* even went on the Internet to solicit ideas and suggestions. According to Don Bangs, the guiding spirit of Sign-Rise Cultural Arts, it took a year to develop the play: "Countless hours of interviews, meetings, and rehearsals and 304 pages of writes and rewrites later, *Diary* . . . finally leaped upon the stage."

The ongoing creative, collaborative process continued even during rehearsals. Graybill, the director, explains, "When rehearsals began, we had no inkling as to how the play would come together. A brief promise and the preliminary draft of the first four scenes were all we received from the playwright a few days in advance. . . . It is the first time for me to direct a play which is being written and rewritten during rehearsal."[49]

The Collective as Hero

In the hierarchy of mainstream theater, leading men and ladies are near the top. Popular theater and movie stars are often sought to "carry a play," and theatergoers are attracted more by these famous actors than by the play itself or by the idea of being part of a community. In contrast, Deaf American theater has a foundation in ensemble acting, a practice that reflects the communal nature of the culture. Productions are created or selected to showcase the performers as a whole rather than one or two stars. Accordingly, we have not just one hero or heroine but a *collective as hero*. This pattern is typical of many minority works and performances, in which a whole community is the protagonist and a blurry collective (mainstream society) serves as the antagonist.[50]

When a production does feature a solo performance or spotlight one leading character, that performer is singled out not as an individual but as representative: the spotlight is on *the* Deaf American, the culture, or the language, rather than *a* Deaf American. In comparable memorable mainstream plays, the focus is on one person (usually a man): think of Shakespeare's *Hamlet* or Andrew Lloyd Webber's *Phantom of the Opera*. Vacillating prince and disfigured denizen of the opera house—both are created to be unique individuals. Yet just about the only heroines or heroes in Deaf American theater history are the famous Alice of the two *Sign Me Alice* plays and Sarah of *Children of a Lesser God*, and they are hardly unusual characters; Alices and Sarahs can be found across the United States.[51] Most of the other renowned Deaf American plays examined in this chapter—including *My Third Eye*, *Institution Blues*, and *A Deaf Family Diary*—are ensemble presentations. Many are vaudeville-like productions with many performers.

Interaction and Viewer Participation

Another aspect of the collective ethos in Deaf culture and theater is the expectation of an intimate connection between actors and spectators. Mainstream theater generally involves carefully orchestrated action and dialogue taking place on a raised stage apart from the audience. In contrast, traditional Deaf American theater is typically interactive, with much less separation between play and viewers. Because they are addressing the playgoers in ASL, an "oral" vernacular that itself is naturally interactive, many Deaf actors and playwrights seek collaboration not only within their productions but also with the viewers.

Patrick Graybill is among those who rely largely on an interactive format in their productions, ensuring that the spectators can relate to the players and even contribute their own material.[52] In this way, Deaf American theater resembles the mainstream theatricals of the past, which were more thoroughly integrated into everyday life. In his *Critique of Everyday Life*, Henri Lefebvre expresses concern about modern passivity: "The discreteness of the elements of the everyday (work—family and 'private' life—leisure activities) implies an alienation. . . . On a higher level, leisure involves passive attitudes, someone sitting in front of a cinema or screen."[53] Leisure in the past was more likely to involve active, communal festivities rather than solitary sitting, listening, and viewing.

In part, such alienation can be addressed by making sure that theatergoers are physically close to the performers and onstage action. Indeed, in any sign language theater such closeness is necessary: actors in a mainstream production can project their voices or even use artificial amplification, but there is no practical way to magnify the face and hands. Therefore, Graybill is in favor of much of the action occurring on an apron extending outward at floor level into a steeply inclined house with only 250 to 300 seats. Also, Deaf viewers are most comfortable when one or two performers or a compact group is onstage; it is visually difficult to follow actors carrying on a conversation as they move around all over the stage. Customarily, performers in a Deaf American dramatic production face and approach viewers, interacting with them as much as is humanly possible.

Don Bangs and his SignRise Cultural Arts team also worked to facilitate increased intimacy and interaction in their productions. In the 1990s, SignRise Cultural Arts produced "DeafTheatre Showcase," three short comedy acts sharing the same bill. Two were original works with Deaf themes, and the other was an adaptation of a Chekhov story. The use of short forms itself made the production feel "small" and more intimate. Bangs also had the players move from one small theater to another in the Washington, D.C., vicinity, rather like medieval players who pulled their sets on wheels to various locations in a town to bring drama to the people. This production was staged at five different sites; in one instance just the upper part of a clubroom floor was set apart for the stage, and ten or so rows of chairs filled the rest.

SignRise Cultural Arts had additional strategies for increasing the immediacy and intimacy of its productions. The protest rally that begins *Institution Blues* started not on the stage but in the aisles—and in fact, as already noted at the start of this chapter, the viewers were made to feel so personally involved that they joined in. Similarly, in *A Deaf Family Diary* the processional wedding march proceeded from the back of the auditorium down through the aisle and up onto the stage. Such techniques, says Graybill, put the viewers "in the thick of a visual feast."[54] Deaf dramatists thus resist the idea of theater as passive spectacle, seeking instead participatory, interactive, embodied communication. They put vision to use in sensuous rather than abstract communication. Deaf performers use their eyes to maintain rapport with the spectators and ensure comprehension. The ringmaster in *My Third Eye* snaps her invisible whip, takes in the assembled viewers with her eyes, and bids them "Look, and you will see."

The Carnivalesque Eye

The close interaction, heterogeneity, and engaging physicality of vaudeville-like productions are appropriate for a visually oriented community. The eye enjoys visual stimuli—*variable* visual stimuli—and is inherently restless, in continual motion. The eye revels in color, shape, movement, and gradations of light and dark. The heterogeneity, physicality, and visuality of the vaudeville-like format is therefore more appropriate for Deaf viewers, for it holds the attention of the eye and thus of the theatergoer much longer than the typical, word-centered, five-act play.

Because the highly verbal quality of modern plays is hard on the eyes, it is not surprising that Deaf Americans go in for the popular and physical over the "high art" of the intellectual, abstract, and serious. Deaf Americans prefer action over verbal/poetic drama, the simple and clear over the abstract, and the humorous (often physical farce) over the serious and heavy.[55] They favor skits, songs, mimicry, melodrama, farce, and thrillers.[56] Thus, as Baldwin points out in his study of Deaf American theater, the two original episodic, physical, and vaudeville-like NTD productions that focused on deafness, *My Third Eye* and *Parade*, were more popular with Deaf viewers than the company's adaptation of Dylan Thomas's *Under Milkwood*. Many bilingual Deaf Americans find that sitting through a college production of *Othello* or *Dr. Jekyll and Mr. Hyde* is more labor than pleasure. Long before intermission comes along they are squirming in their seats, experiencing eye strain and temporary attention deficit disorder. Not surprisingly, directors putting on mainstream plays for Deaf Americans take their viewers into consideration: they add visual elements, cut down on the talk, and exhort players to sign full body or in profile to the audience—and they remind minor characters not to move an eyebrow when another actor is signing.

Such reminders are not needed in indigenous Deaf American theater, which has an immediacy and relevance for its viewers that goes far beyond what plays meeting the classical conventions of Western drama might hope for. As we have seen, such conventions promote the aesthetic, the individual, and the ideal rather than the sociopolitical, communal, and real. In contrast, the dynamic, polyvocal, hybrid, and heterogeneous forms of Deaf American theater provide lively entertainment in the commedia dell'arte style— political, comic, and parodic, consciously or subconsciously, of "high" mainstream genres and conventions. They thereby epitomize the transformation of the spirit of carnival festivities into art. Each production contains a repertoire of festive and popular elements intermixing with and countering the serious high languages and forms of mainstream culture.[57]

Most Deaf dramatists are highly educated and very much aware of theatrical conventions; theirs is thus a metadiscourse. They bear in mind that their culture utilizes an "oral" and visual mode of communication very different from that used by hearing playwrights. In selecting suitable elements and rejecting others, they show us something not just about the drama of Deaf Americans but also about modern conventional drama. Give us a Deaf playwright or actor, and we'll give you a Jester facilitating the theatric metadiscourse.

Notes

1. *Institution Blues*, scripted by Don Bangs and Jan DeLap, dir. Don Bangs, prod. SignRise Cultural Arts, Publick Playhouse, Cheverly, Md., October 1 and 2, 1993.

2. *Dr. Jekyll and Mr. Hyde*, prod. Theater Arts Department, Gallaudet University, Washington, D.C., fall 1997; *My Third Eye*, dir. J Ranelli, written and prod. National Theatre of the Deaf, 1971–72, video-recording shown on WTTW-TV, Chicago, 58 min., 1973; *Parade*, scripted by Jeff Wanshell, dir. Larry Amick, prod. National Theatre of the Deaf, 1975–76.

3. *Sign Me Alice*, scripted and dir. Gilbert C. Eastman, prod. Theater Arts Department, Gallaudet University, Washington, D.C., 1973; Bernard Bragg and Eugene Bergman, *Tales from a Clubroom* (Washington, D.C.: Gallaudet University Press, 1981); *A Deaf Family Diary*, scripted Don Bangs, dir. Patrick Graybill, prod. SignRise Cultural Arts, Publick Playhouse, Cheverly, Md., February–March 1994.

4. Willy Conley and Bob Daniels, e-mail to author, fall 1998.

5. Stephen C. Baldwin, *Pictures in the Air: The Story of the National Theatre of the Deaf* (Washington D.C.: Gallaudet University Press, 1993), 81.

6. Michael Bristol, *Carnival and Theater: Plebian Culture and the Structure of Authority in Renaissance England* (London: Methuen, 1985), 24.

7. Henri Lefebvre, *Critique of Everyday Life*, vol. 1, trans. John Moore (London: Verso, 1991), 32.

8. Bristol, *Carnival and Theater*, 46.

9. Ibid., 3.
10. Ibid., 46.
11. Ibid., 3.
12. Lefebvre, *Critique of Everyday Life*, 23.
13. *Deafula*, written and dir. Peter Wechsberg, prod. Gary Holstrom, Signscope, 1975.
14. Quoted in Carol Padden and Tom Humphries, *Deaf in America: Voices from a Culture* (Cambridge, Mass.: Harvard University Press, 1988), 18.
15. Padden and Humphreys, *Deaf in America*, 18–19.
16. *Stephen King's The Stand*, dir. Mick Garris, ABC-TV, May 1994; based on the novel *The Stand* by Stephen King (Garden City, N.Y.: Doubleday, 1978).
17. Indeed, in Deaf American drama "Everyman" is often a woman. Like other minority literatures, it often runs counter to conventional expectation by featuring women as leading characters and political activists.
18. Carol Simpson Stern and Bruce Henderson, *Performance: Texts and Contexts* (New York: Longman, 1993), 89.
19. Bristol, *Carnival and Theater*, 5.
20. Ibid., 4.
21. Werner Sollars, *Beyond Ethnicity: Consent and Descent in American Culture* (New York: Oxford University Press, 1986), 239.
22. See John Fiske, "Cultural Studies and the Culture of Everyday Life," in *Cultural Studies*, ed. Lawrence Grossberg, Cary Nelson, and Paula A. Treichler (New York: Routledge, 1992), 157–58.
23. Peter Stallybrass and Allon White, *The Politics and Poetics of Transgression* (London: Methuen, 1986), 8.
24. Sollars, *Beyond Ethnicity*, 239.
25. E.g., see also *The World According to Pat: Reflections of Residential School Days*, scripted and dir. Patrick Graybill, Silver Spring, Md., Sign Media and TJ Publishers, videocassette, 80 min., [1986].
26. Mikhail Bakhtin, *Rabelais and His World*, trans. Hélène Iswolsky (Cambridge, Mass.: MIT Press, 1968), 11–12.
27. Ibid., 19.
28. Donald Richard Bangs, "Deaf Theatre in America: Practices and Principles" (Ph.D. diss., University of California at Berkeley, 1989). Bangs was specifically concerned with how drama as a whole can be promoted for both Deaf Americans and mainstream society.
29. Ibid., 196–98.
30. Ibid., 269, 293, 270.

31. Gleaned from issues of the *Silent News* (New York) from the late 1980s and the 1990s.

32. *Telling Stories*, scripted and dir. William Moses, prod. Theater Arts Department, Gallaudet University, Washington, D.C., 1989.

33. Gustavo Perez Firmat, *Literature and Liminality: Festive Readings in the Hispanic Tradition* (Durham, N.C.: Duke University Press, 1986), 14.

34. Shanny Mow, "Theater, Community," in *Gallaudet Encyclopedia of Deaf People and Deafness*, vol. 3, ed. John Van Cleve (New York: McGraw-Hill, 1987), 288.

35. The following discussion draws on Bangs, "Deaf Theatre in America," 30–40.

36. Gallaudet's first course in sign language theater in 1940 was primarily aimed at fostering an appreciation for theatrical works from the mainstream stage; the courses in play production were dropped in 1953, when Gallaudet was seeking accreditation. The Gallaudet College Theatre, established in 1963, adapted mainstream plays until 1973, when it put on *Sign Me Alice*, its first full-length original Deaf American play.

37. Bangs, "Deaf Theatre in America," 71, 108.

38. Ibid., 68.

39. *Under Milkwood*, based on the 1954 radio play by Dylan Thomas, prod. National Theatre of the Deaf, 1993–94.

40. *Parzival: From the Horse's Mouth*, scripted Shanny Mow and David Hays, prod. National Theatre of the Deaf, 1982–83. See Bangs, "Deaf Theatre in America," 153–54.

41. Bangs, "Deaf Theatre in America," 105.

42. Baldwin, *Pictures in the Air*, 51.

43. John M. Heidger, "The History of the Deaf in America: The Silent Stage" (master's thesis, Southern Illinois University, 1979), 35.

44. Honor Ford-Smith, "Notes toward a New Aesthetic," *MELUS* 16 (3): 27–34.

45. Bakhtin, *Rabelais and His World*, 7, 8.

46. Dorothy Miles, "A History of Theatre Activities in the Deaf Community of the United States" (master's thesis, Connecticut College, 1974), 62; quoted in Baldwin, *Pictures in the Air*, 48.

47. Baldwin, *Pictures in the Air*, 48.

48. Bangs, "Deaf Theatre in America," 153.

49. Bangs and Graybill are quoted in the program for *A Deaf Family Diary*, 9.

50. Wolfgang Karrer and Hartmut Lutz, "Minority Literatures in North America: From Cultural Nationalism to Liminality," in *Minority Literatures in North America: Contemporary Perspectives*, ed. Karrer and Lutz (New York: Lang, 1990), 11–64. Deaf Americans affirm tradition, culture, and community and thus run contrary to the dominant discourse of this country, which puts individualism before tradition and community.

51. *Sign Me Alice* and *Sign Me Alice II*, written and dir. Gilbert C. Eastman, Gallaudet College TV Studio, Washington, D.C., 3 videocassettes, 60 min. each, 1983; Mark H. Medoff, *Children of a Lesser God: A Play in Two Acts* (Clifton, N.J.: J. T. White, 1980).

52. Bangs, "Deaf Theatre in America," 233.

53. Lefebvre, *Critique of Everyday Life*, 32.

54. Graybill is quoted in Bangs, "Deaf Theatre in America," 258–59.

55. George D. McClendon, "The Unique Contribution of the National Theatre of the Deaf to the American Theatre" (Ph.D. diss., Catholic University of America, 1972), 89–90; cited in Bangs, "Deaf Theatre in America," 87. But Bangs (40) observes that despite the developments at Gallaudet University (what I'd call the "institutionalization" of drama), Deaf community theaters continue to use traditional entertainment media such as variety acts and short comedies.

56. Dorothy S. Miles and Louie J. Fant, *Sign Language Theatre and Deaf Theatre: New Definitions and Directions* (Northridge, Calif.: California State University at Northridge, Center on Deafness, 1975). See also Baldwin, *Pictures in the Air*, 48–49.

57. Stuart Hall, "Metaphors of Transformation," introduction to *Carnival, Hysteria, and Writing: Collected Essays and Autobiography*, by Allon White (New York: Oxford University Press, 1993), 1.

Chapter

7

Islay: *The Deaf American Novel*

THE CARNIVALESQUE quality of Deaf American literature is not limited to productions and presentations in ASL. It also can be found in text-based stories, poems, and plays published in English. In these texts, Deaf writers may reveal their roots in ASL by highlighting the visual—focusing more on the shapes and movements of things than on sounds—even as they rely on the written form of an aural language, English. More important, they deliberately draw on not just two languages but two cultures, two worlds. In this interplay they capture the spirit of carnival in ways both subtle and overt. For example, a Deaf American writing in English about the sunrise might focus on the scene's visual glory. The writer would detail the shining orb peeping over the horizon, then its blazing rays of light awakening the denizens of the air who, swooping and gliding, welcome in the new day. Missing or getting only a passing mention would be the environmental sounds likely to accompany the breaking of day: birdcalls, train whistles, and doors opening and closing. Yet despite all this visual detail so crucial in ASL and

Deaf culture, the author's vehicle is the written form of an aural language, English.

The first and possibly the only novel by a Deaf American to focus on Deaf culture is *Islay* (1986) by Douglas Bullard.[1] The book therefore provides a fascinating case in point; it is a commingling of two different rhetorical traditions: mainstream literature and ASL literature. Bullard had acquired a good command of English before he became deaf, and he learned ASL in his four years at Gallaudet University during the 1960s. As an avid reader, he was familiar with the mainstream literary tradition; as a Gallaudet student, he was exposed to the vernacular or storytelling tradition in ASL. In *Islay* these two traditions jostle and play off one other. The novel (the first in a planned but unfinished trilogy) was published to great fanfare.

The Interplay of ASL and English

One formidable challenge facing a novelist wishing to fully portray Deaf culture is how to convey a visual-kinetic language that has no written form in a way that distinguishes it from both English speech and TTY (teletypewriter) text in English. In the foreword to Bullard's novel, Dr. Dennis Cokely explains that as a spoken language with a "linear disposition," English is not suited to describing visually perceived material, such as dialogue in ASL, in a visual-kinetic language (ix–x).

To some extent, Bullard surmounts this obstacle by using distinctive syntax and font styles. Bullard transcribes ASL discourse in italics in a glossed English that is neither truly English nor ASL. For instance, the protagonist, Lyson Sulla, says of the desire for a homeland,

> *You know that Laurent Clerc had same dream. Himself greatest deaf in history, started Golden Age for deaf there France. Then brought sign here America; almost started new Golden Age for us deaf, but hearing oralism frustrated him, broke up deaf cooperation and almost destroyed Sign Language. That why Clerc liked idea for deaf gathering into one state where deaf itself normal!* (6–7)

Many Deaf Americans, who take much pride in using a visual vernacular and believe that no written approximation can do it justice, may have disliked this approach; there is little sense here of facile hands and mobile facial expressions. However, it serves its immediate purpose.

Bullard similarly relies on typography to convey TTY text, which is set in big, bold capital letters that fairly leap off the page at the reader. When Sulla uses a TTY to phone his wife from Islay, for example, the conversation is rendered like this:

> [Sulla] sat down on the chair and prepared to dial the telephone. . . . The lamp flickered with just one ring before Mary started typing. Lyson never failed to marvel at the green letters streaming across the display board of the teletype-writer.

MARY HERE GA.

HI. LYSON HERE ISLAY HOTEL ROOM 628. HOW ARE YOU Q GA

LYSON WHY YOU CALL ME Q GA

STOP MAD AT ME PLEASE—

SORRY CANT HELP IT WORRY AND WAIT AND WAIT FOR HOURS GA.

FORGIVE ME BUT CANT HELP VERY BUSY DAY. VISITED THE GOVERNOR AND THEN HAD IMPORTANT DINNER AND THEN CRAZY BATH . . . (32–33)

Bullard is thus careful to distinguish among modalities, when many writers would simply translate and convey everything in grammatically correct English. He thereby sets the two languages at play, bouncing one off the other in a carnivalesque fashion. ASL discourse, although it technically cannot be conveyed in print, is transliterated into a kind of pidgin English that does neither language proud. ASL loses all its visual beauty as it becomes simply black marks on a white page. That the pared-down-English translit-eration is quite understandable makes the reader realize that the language usually is full of redundancies and unnecessary syntactical markers and stipulations. Similarly, the TTY text, which is not grammatically correct English, is nevertheless perfectly serviceable. Bullard is underscoring that when a people with a visual-kinetic vernacular do not have a handy, inexpensive means of communicat-ing at a distance—practical videophones, for instance—they must resort to printed English; and at the same time, they use the lan-guage in nonofficial ways.

Indeed, the title itself manifests the interanimation of two lan-guages. When *Islay* first came out, it attracted great attention in the Deaf community, and both those who had read it and those who had only heard of it speculated about the origin and significance of the title. Bullard was much in demand to talk about the genesis and history of his magnum opus, and he responded to questions about the book's themes, plotting, characterization, and style—as well as its title. One popular hypothesis was that the title was an anagram of the fingerspelled acronyms for "I Love You" (ILY) and Ameri-can Sign Language (ASL). According to another theory, "Islay" was derived from "island." Bullard actually came across the word in the dictionary, liked how it sounded, and decided to use it—then later flew to the island of Islay off the coast of Scotland only to dis-cover that the real island closely resembled his fictional one.

The plot could hardly feature the conflict between the two cultures more prominently. In the novel's prologue, Lyson Sulla fantasizes about creating a Deaf homeland. He is in his den, envisaging an army of Deaf Americans invading Islay with himself a knight on a white horse leading the charge. By taking over this island, which we are told is a separate state, they would create a haven for Deaf Americans and thereby fulfill a century-old dream. With such a homeland of their own, they could have their own culture and utilize visual communication. It is a variant of the great American dream of personal and cultural liberation, and Sulla and his merry band do manage to take over Islay with aston-ishing swiftness.

In the first of three sections, "Strings," Sulla summons up the nerve to solicit his prosperous in-laws for the financial backing to move to Islay. He succeeds, and their financial largesse includes a new Lincoln in which Sulla makes his first, bumbling trip to the island. On the way he runs out of fuel because he is unable to hear the "talking" car warn him that the gas tank is almost empty. Eventually Sulla arrives in Islay and spends a week essaying the possibilities and meeting with unconcerned and dismissive public officials. Things look promising; he and his wife move into a castle-like residence and throw a big party to which they invite one and all.

"Drums" covers Sulla's cross-country travels to persuade Deaf Americans to move to and help establish this new homeland. As he journeys clear across the country and back, he pulls in a doctor, a minister, a bowling alley owner, and an insurance underwriter (an officer of the National Fraternal Society of the Deaf, or NFSD). Along the way, his identity and his mission are often misconstrued. For instance, in Iowa, where he visits a Deaf club, the members take him for a peddler and nearly ride him out of town on a rail. In Salt Lake City he confuses a genealogist when he states that Deaf Americans are true brothers and sisters; forced to backtrack, he clarifies by explaining his mission to draw as many Deaf Americans to Islay as he can to form one big family there. Despite such misunderstandings, Sulla returns to Islay having largely succeeded in his recruiting efforts.

In the final section, "Cymbals," increasing numbers of Deaf Americans surge into Islay. They take up residence, establish businesses, and register to vote. This is all to the good, but Sulla's mishaps continue. When he comes home to Islay, now booming with new Deaf businesses and residents, he immediately finds himself accused of real estate fraud. He is brought low—but then is able to prove that someone else has been impersonating him. When he goes to a bandstand to make known his gubernatorial ambitions, he and his supporters are driven away by a horde of wasps; and before the election results are made known, his Deaf opponent attempts to physically assault him. Yet he does win, both defeating the old governor and getting the better of the oral school superintendent. The comic happy ending prevails: the Deaf world is triumphant.

The Two-World Milieu

Islay not only portrays but also hilariously spoofs the two-world condition discussed so often in earlier chapters, as Deaf and hearing Americans wrestle over a poor excuse of a state. In the best tradition of carnivalesque laughter, *Islay* makes fun of everything and everyone—mainstream society and Deaf culture alike. By translating ASL into a kind of broken English, it pokes fun at both languages. It satirizes both hearing authority figures and Deaf entrepreneurs. It scoffs at vaunted American technology (witness the talking car) and efficiency (not much in evidence in decaying Islay). It even good-naturedly mocks the overall mission, which the blurb on the book's cover describes as "the Great American Dream": the desire to establish a Deaf homeland. Though they might yearn for a close-knit collective, Deaf Americans also have their internal differences and squabbles. All this Bullard depicts with comic delight.

Yet there is a point to his spoofing. Just as the medieval populace upended the feudal hierarchy—if only rhetorically and temporarily—during carnival times, so Bullard and his Deaf characters rhetorically upend the majority society in the United States. In a plethora of interactions between Deaf and mainstream Islay residents, including the island's administrators and civil servants, the usual outcome is reversed. For instance, Lyson Sulla's meeting with the governor and his two minions in many ways typifies that of any Deaf American with any hearing executive; and the public school principal's encounter with Deaf mothers has been played out all over the country, usually with the former getting the upper hand—but not in this story. In the end, the Deaf Americans are firmly in control of the state of Islay, to the consternation and confoundment of the Islay authorities.

Upending the Mainstream Narrative Tradition

Islay begins undermining the idea of authority before the novel even begins. The short foreword by Dennis Cokely, a well-known researcher in ASL and novelist (who currently owns an American company that distributes ASL videotapes and other cultural materials) is apparently designed to authorize the text that follows. Much as nineteenth-century abolitionists provided forewords to slave narratives and other works by African Americans, testifying to the writer's credibility and identity, so Cokely is confirming that Bullard actually wrote this novel, ASL is a bona fide language, and Deaf culture really exists. The big difference here is that both the author and the authorizer are aware of the paternalism behind such framing and turn it into a satiric device. Bullard has no need for the authorization or approval of mainstream culture—which indeed his novel renounces, for his hero turns mainstream society itself on its head.

At the same time, the foreword also makes fun of narrative authority. Indeed *Islay* as a whole plays with the rhetorical conventions of the novel in particular, principally by mixing the Deaf American storytelling tradition, which has more "oral" requirements, with the mainstream high narrative tradition, which heeds literary conventions. In effect, Bullard's novel interanimates the low and the high. To be sure, the novel itself has a history of playing against the high narrative tradition. It has a reputation for being eclectic and frolicsome—combining anything and everything—and for resisting pigeonholes and "decorum." In *The Dialogic Imagination*, Bakhtin argues that unlike other genres, "the novel has no canon of its own."[2] Thus critics place into the category *novel* everything from *The Tale of Genji*, a vast Japanese fictional chronicle from the early tenth century, to yesterday's formulaic Harlequin paperback original; from the dense and highly mannered prose of Henry James to the spare understatement of the novels of Ernest Hemingway. Just about anything goes when it comes to the novel, which is something of a catch-all art form, ever ready to take on something new: after all, "novel" means "new." Its subcategories are legion and often overlapping, and for every high-minded, grave novel of ideals (e.g., Samuel Richardson's epistolary *Pamela* [1740–42] and *Clarissa* [1747–48]) there is a debunking novel of the down-to-earth, comic, and realistic (e.g., Henry Fielding's *Joseph Andrews* [1742] and *Tom Jones* [1749]).

If anything, the novel's tendency to debunk and undercut its own "rules" is stronger than any tendency to formulate those rules. One of the earliest novels in English, Lawrence Sterne's *Tristram Shandy* (1759–67), is as self-referential and resistant to convention as any postmodern fiction of the late twentieth century; some of the greatest novels of all time, including Rabelais's *Gargantua and Pantagruel* (1532–64) and James Joyce's *Ulysses* (1922), are heterogeneous, vulgar, seemingly illogical, and yet profound. As Bakhtin points out, the novel pays little lip service to separating high discourse from low discourse. It has little liking for separating high, decorous behavior from low behavior and confining them to specified genres and other forms of discourse.[3]

Nevertheless, the average reader has come to expect novels to have certain typical features. The conventional novel is a story with a main plot and often some ancillary subplots, dealing with the trials, tribulations, and triumphs of human existence on earth in a real-life, everyday manner. Its plausible events occur with a clear cause-and-effect linkage, progressing to a logical end; and what happens would happen to just about anyone. The main characters are like the people we bump into every day: they are, to use E. M. Forster's famous description, usually "round"—that is, they are complex, with some psychological depth, as opposed to being "flat" (one-dimensional and predictable). The dialogue is the kind of conversation we hear in daily use and not the high rhetoric of inaugural addresses or eulogies. Yet the novel often has a high-minded albeit somewhat reductive theme or moral (e.g., pride goeth before a fall, love is star-crossed, or war is hell). The author is trying to tell the reader something, trying to help the reader gain insight into another world that the reader is then invited to experience.

But *Islay* makes fun of these stipulations of the novel's ingredients. Like Cervantes's *Don Quixote* (1605, 1615) and Mark Twain's *Adventures of Huckleberry Finn* (1884), it is in the tradition of novels debunking high-minded ideals and high-minded writing.[4] It cares little for conventional plotting, characterization, and moral themes except to ridicule them. It thus joins the long line of satirical novels that combine the high and the low in a burlesque fashion. Moreover, the narrative structure refuses to follow the disciplined, cause-and-effect plotting that we associate with realistic fiction. Rather than having an orderly and tightly controlled beginning, middle, and end, *Islay* is somewhat rambling and disjointed, even though in outline the plot seems relatively linear. Once again, Bullard plays the mainstream literary tradition off the vernacular storytelling tradition.

In large part the loose structure, or rather lack of conventional structure, derives from the disjointedness of Sulla's travels, which makes the book seem like a travel narrative or a kind of picaresque novel.[5] Bullard has Sulla leave Washington, D.C.; spend a few days in Islay; travel across the country, stopping here and there to find Deaf recruits; and arrive in California for a brief stay. Then, Sulla flies back East, throws himself into campaigning (after clearing himself of the accusation of real estate fraud), and within a few months is elected governor. Throughout the novel he is flying, driving, walking—in constant but not always logical motion.

Such ambulatory writings are common in American literature, whose heroes often head to the wilderness to discover their destinies.[6] Huck Finn speaks for many when he declares at the end of his narrative that he's "got to light out for the territory" before Tom Sawyer's Aunt Polly has a chance to "sivilize" him.[7] The desire to head off—usually west—to pursue a dream, to find riches, or just to thumb one's nose at conventional social mores runs deep throughout the history of the United States. Sometimes the wanderings partake of the mythical quest; in this century, the tradition was perhaps most famously or infamously continued by Jack Kerouac in *On the Road* (1955). But this notion of traveling is especially important in Deaf American literature, for Deaf people themselves have long been wanderers and questers.

Deaf American literature also draws on this tradition of roaming. Indeed, as noted in chapter 3, wandering or traveling is a feature of twentieth-century Deaf popular culture, for Deaf Americans have long been accustomed to travel. Before present-day technology such as TTYs, relay services, and e-mail became available, Deaf Americans relied heavily on face-to-face contact to transact everyday business; they therefore had to do a good deal of moving about. Those errands and travels, in turn, are a staple of storytelling in Deaf culture. When Deaf Americans gather, often one or more in the group goes on at length about his or her travels or errands, touching on places visited and people encountered and frequently highlighting (with exaggerated aggrievement and description) the mishaps that result when minority and majority cultures intersect. Such narratives easily become digressive, as the storyteller is interrupted by one listener, reminded of something by a co-traveler that leads him or her to a self-correction, and so on. In other words, these tales do not evidence a clear-cut structure with a logical, linear progression from beginning to middle to end.[8]

The formlessness and episodic quality of *Islay*'s plot recall this kind of storytelling: a rambling, rather disconnected tale of adventures and misadventures. The plot is ostensibly "realistic," but quite a few times we have the impression of moving from one unconnected episode to another—a movement much truer to what we experience in everyday life than the neat cause-and-effect plotting that realistic fiction demands.[9] For instance, we are not made privy to Sulla's meeting with his in-laws at the beginning of the story: the story leaps from his wife's urging that he approach them for financial backing to his driving to Islay in a new Lincoln. Moreover, in this age of TTYs, no explanation is given for Sulla's decision to travel across the country to California rather than calling to make his case or even to give advance warning of his arrival. The cross-country itinerary as a whole seems rather aimless and spotty; there appears to be no logic behind Sulla's choices of stopovers and encounters. Only gradually does it become clear that Sulla and his fellow Deaf Americans plan not only to take up residence and establish businesses in Islay but also to take over the state, as unlikely a prospect as that might seem. After a series of wonderful events and coincidences, however, we see that—as is typical in the picaresque novel, according to Stuart Miller—"it all works out in the end,"[10] with the election of Lyson Sulla as governor. Despite all the uncertainties of real life, *Islay*'s plot moves toward an improbable end that its readers welcome (and indeed the improbable often does happen).

Though *Islay* may appear formless by conventional criteria, unifying devices more typical of oral and Deaf American storytelling knit the novel together. Recurrent images, sets of thematic contrasts, circular patterns, and the interweaving of secondary characters superimpose an order on Sulla's seemingly episodic adventures. For instance, the NFSD underwriter appears in the beginning and the end of the story, and a family of peddlers that is met on the road shows up again in Islay. Such patterns exemplify a kind of dance pattern: people come together, move apart, and come back together. Sulla's travels across the country to spread the word also have a unifying function, as they knit together the whole narrative.

This kind of structure or semistructure mirrors Deaf culture, which is united and yet not united. Although the community is scattered and internally heterogeneous, the state schools, state and national associations, and athletic organizations give it some cohesiveness and structure. Until very recently, Deaf society was made up primarily of state school alumni who continued to meet one another at state and national conferences, school reunions, and athletic competitions. Here too we find a dance pattern of people coming together once and then again, six or twelve months or even several years later, often as they converge for the ubiquitous "fair" (see chapter 3). In its narrative form, Bullard's novel thus accurately reflects the Deaf experience.

Upending Decorum

Islay is very much like many early (and modern) novels in largely ignoring conventions of discourse and decorum. In contrast to the more ideal and spiritual realms associated with epic romance (e.g., the *Song of Roland*) and prose romance (i.e., fictions more concerned with the stylized and archetypal than the individuated and social), *Islay* highlights the material level of existence in all its exuberance and vitality.[11] Many details or asides relate to the functions and anatomy of the lower body (which is opposed to the upper body or head and its associations with reason, logic, and spirit); intake of food and drink is much discussed, particularly the imbibing of alcoholic beverages (and the consequences of overindulging). In addition, the very married protagonist attracts

women like bees to honey. The frequent "Will he or won't he" sce-
narios are endlessly engrossing. Not only the hero but also all the
seemingly more proper characters are as subject to human failings
as any person alive. Bullard's approach—and he seems to take a cue
from the early novels—illustrates a recognition that life is all-
embracing. High-minded ideals and strivings intertwine with the
more mundane needs of human beings, who, along with plants and
animals, constitute the vital, teeming life on earth.

Not surprisingly, the Bakhtinian linkage of festivity, food, and
drink to life fully lived in popular culture (especially in contrast to
the dead, drab state of affairs in Islay) is much in evidence here.[12]
In this novel numerous parties, parades, and celebrations occur. As
noted above, when Sulla and his wife move into Islay, they buy a
big "castle," dress up, and throw a ball to which everyone is cor-
dially invited—and everyone comes. At the postelection celebration, people "danced round and round the bandstand. Beatrice and
Sandy whirled round and round. Susan and Randy fell into each
other's arms. Everyone danced and leapt for joy. Fires were started
on the beach and chickens set roasting and crabs boiling. Bottles
popped and frothed and spilled" (324). Very rarely is Sulla alone
with just one other person. We have community here and communal intake of food and drink. Thus, Bullard focuses on the communal body, not the introspective, brooding individual. By highlighting physical needs and functions, the novel portrays Bakhtin's
"grotesque" or collective body.

Bullard does not exclude the body's needs and functions even
when they are rather undignified. For instance, at Sulla's first meal
in Islay he "tore into his dinner. . . . he cleaned his plate with a
piece of bread and gave out a belch" (26). The lower part of the
body gets its humorous respect. Throughout the novel there are
recurring images of excrement, the sexual organs, and the body at
its least formal. Bullard is in especially fine form in his depiction of
Sulla's stopover in Utah. In Salt Lake City, Sulla is a guest of a couple who give a dinner party to which he is invited. A long table on
the lawn is covered with barbecued spareribs, baked potatoes
wrapped in foil and covered with butter, corn on the cob, tomatoes
broiled with mayonnaise, cheese cubes, celery, carrots, orange

slices, and, to wash it all down, grape juice and a good red wine. Sulla delights in this bountiful feast and in the camaraderie expressed on the faces and hands of the dinner guests as they converse. "With such a bounty assailing his eyes, nose, and taste buds, Lyson was very happy. He attacked his food and gorged himself; soon he became satiated and aware of a warmth and dampness against his hips and in his thighs pressed tightly together" (176).

During Sulla's trip west, his high-minded mission is sprinkled with many an earthy incident. Manure-encrusted cowboy boots prominently adorn the very large feet belonging to the bodyguard of the Deaf club president in Obeke, Iowa. In Salt Lake City, at the genealogist's home, Sulla interrupts his host and hostess in amorous embrace in the kitchen when he is on his way to a toilet. The characterization of Gene Owles, the NFSD officer and Sulla's Deaf opponent in the gubernatorial election—"That old satyr with the rear half of a horse and the devil's smirk out front" (xvii)— could hardly be less refined. Though Owles is in fact charming, he leaves no doubt that he does not plan to be as accommodating as Sulla when it comes to an integrated society in Islay: "Deaf establish things then hearing take over. Alexander Graham Bell wanted to sterilize deaf but I (clutching crotch) will hold on to my *jewels*" (273). *Islay* is vulgarly, festively, and ludicrously down-to-earth.

Images of and allusions to animals contribute to the narrative's grounded and ribald quality. In the early part of the novel, we are introduced to Mortima Gooser, the gossip who beards Sulla in his den and who has a talent for digging information out of people. Her response to Sulla's extreme embarrassment: "She just never thought to be embarrassed by it, not any more than a bull is by the chewed swallowed digested processed and passed remains of hay drying on its rump raising a stink and a whirring cloud of flies" (xiii–xiv). In Islay, the maid denounces Sulla as a pig when he inadvertently floods his hotel room with bubble bath, and he has a run-in with what he takes to be a rabid squirrel who scurries over his briefcase. In Iowa, a tête-à-tête with a young woman ends with Sulla lying on his back, embraced not by her but by a horde of stinging ants. The soothing waters of the nearby river offer only temporary solace before he hastily exits to avoid what he takes to be numerous snakes in its depth. On his return to Islay, the Deaf Americans gather at the bandstand for Sulla's announcement of his gubernatorial candidacy—and, as noted above, hundreds of wasps quickly cut short the celebration and run them off.

Upending the High Moral

Islay tweaks the whole concept that the novel should have a high-minded moral. To be sure, *Islay's* overriding main theme—the search for a homeland—is the stuff of religion, legend, and history. Think of Moses leading the Israelites out of Egypt and into the Promised Land, of European refugees braving the long ocean crossing to seek religious freedom in the New World, of countless wars past and present fought to gain or preserve a homeland. Yet here that lofty goal is taken down a peg or two. Rather than being legendary or historic, *Islay* has a modern theme, modern setting, modern actions, and an ordinary, even bumbling "hero." Though Sulla's ordinariness takes the novel out of Northrop Frye's category of "high mimetic comedy," as exemplified by Aristophanic Old Comedy, *Islay's* basic form and function are strikingly similar to those that Frye attributes to the Greek playwright:

> In Aristophanes there is usually a central figure who constructs his (or her) own society in the teeth of strong opposition, driving off one after another all the people who come to prevent or exploit him, and eventually achieving a heroic triumph. . . . We notice that just as there is a catharsis of pity and fear in tragedy, so there is a catharsis of the corresponding emotions, which are sympathy and ridicule, in Old Comedy. The comic hero will get his triumph whether what he has done is sensible or silly, honest or rascally. Thus Old Comedy . . . is a blend of the heroic and the ironic.[13]

Sulla is a modern-day Moses who travels cross-country spreading the word and his business cards (emblazoned with "Islay Company") as well. He stops at a Deaf club in Iowa and meets a variety of grassroots Deaf Americans, including a young woman who encourages him to let down his hair. On his visit to Salt Lake City,

Sulla parties almost into the ground. In Wyoming he encounters some kindred spirits: a family of peddlers. Finally, in California, the terminus of his journey, he persuades a minister to move to Islay and a Deaf business to set up a branch on the East Coast in—where else?—Islay. His recruiting expedition is all rather silly and aimless, and Sulla, though endearing, is hardly a heroic leader. Nevertheless, this improbably bumbling savior leads Deaf Americans out of the wilderness of mainstream society and into the Promised Land of Islay.

On its face, Islay bears little resemblance to a land of milk and honey. The state is moribund: it has little industry, the roads are in disrepair, and many homes are boarded up. What's more, its ineffectual old governor merely sits in his wicker chair imbibing mint juleps, making inane remarks, and letting the governorship be stolen right out from under him. Mythically, Islay is a wasteland in need of a Fisher King bringing fertility and eventual restoration. It thus provides the setting for what Frye calls the mythos of romance, whose conflict takes place in a world where "the opposite poles of the cycles of nature are assimilated to the opposition of the hero and his enemy. The enemy is associated with winter, darkness, confusion, sterility, moribund life, and old age, and the hero with spring, dawn, order, fertility, vigor, and youth."[14] Sure enough, as soon as the youthful and ambitious Lyson Sulla and his merry band move into the state, they effectively if hilariously turn it around, bringing in commerce, industry, and new residents. These new residents—many of them Deaf families and their lively children, who communicate animatedly with their hands—eagerly buy the boarded-up houses. What was on the brink of death and decay becomes fertile and full of vigor. Carnivalesquely, the old order is turned on its head and replaced by a new order.

Upending the Hero

Lyson Sulla succeeds despite being seen as a fool both by mainstream society and initially by Deaf society. Indeed, Sulla's wife, Mary, whom Bullard portrays as more astute than her husband, is at first embarrassed by her husband's antics. In the prologue, Mary is dismayed when she comes upon her husband attacking a scale model of the Islay bandstand with toy soldiers: "She'd known all along her husband was a fool, but never could she have dreamt he could be so foolish. Yet, there it was, this enormous enormity entrenched in her home! Grotesque!" (xv). Mary keeps the door to her husband's den locked at all times, so nobody will see his plans. When visitors come while Sulla is in the den busy with his bandstand, she hides his obsession by blaming his absence on his keen interest in a hobby. Nevertheless, the gossip Mortima Gooser rises to the challenge and manages to get hold of the key. To her immense amusement, on slipping into the den she beholds the perspiring Sulla busily storming the toy bandstand with his toy soldiers and triumphantly proclaiming himself governor of Islay. It is not long before others know of and are laughing at Sulla's antics. He is considered decidedly off balance by his wife and their many friends, and it is some time before she and others tender their support for the establishment of a Deaf state.

For Deaf Americans, being considered "fools" or nincompoops by mainstream society is nothing new. Those who have little contact with deaf people but see them "gesturing" usually misunderstand their behavior. The hearing onlookers tend to consider them none too bright and unable to take care of themselves and function fully in society. Thus, mainstream society feels it needs to take these Simple Simons under its wing and decide what is best for them, often ignoring what Deaf Americans have to say. For instance, Sulla comments on the utility of hearing aids that, he asserts, help only a few but that mainstream society enthusiastically promotes: "They never ask us. When we do volunteer an opinion they just smile and whisper among each other" (90).

Deaf Americans are invisible to most hearing people; and when they are "seen," they are not heard on matters that concern them—and hearing aids, loop systems, and cochlear implants are just a few of those concerns. Thus, their treatment as "fools" pervades the novel. For example, when Sulla meets with the governor as part of his effort to investigate business opportunities in Islay, his ambitions are met with incredulity: surely such a well-dressed young man (too well-dressed for the town and the season) cannot possibly be a "deaf-mute." Governor Wenchell takes him to be a prying FBI agent masquerading as a deaf person (and thinks that the TTY is a high-tech coding machine). Nor does he believe his security officers when they inform him that the Deaf Americans plan to take over the state, for how could deaf people do such a thing?

During their meeting, when Sulla resorts to writing notes after his initial effort at speech, the governor goes along with the supposed charade and suggests, "Maybe the Asylum for the Deaf and Dumb down at Crewe can help you learn to speak and read lips" (23). For his part, Sulla is mystified when Wenchell has his security officer read the notes: he leaves wondering "if the governor could read and write. Impossible! An illiterate in such an august position!" (24). Thus, on the one hand, Wenchell's assumption that deaf people are helpless fools leads him to take Sulla for something other than what he is; on the other hand, Sulla suspects that the governor is an illiterate fool. A gleeful two-way burlesque of both an authority figure and an anti-hero is at work here.

By casting Sulla's character as somewhat foolish, Bullard is again playing with narrative conventions. Through the centuries, the fool has been viewed in both a positive and a negative light.[15] This figure was originally and literally a simpleton—a resident of the town or village who was mentally deficient and who therefore acted and talked in strange ways. Because fools could not comprehend what was going on, they did not fit into the social fabric; their behavior was often inappropriate and outside the norms. But at the same time, the "simple-minded" fool was seen as lacking cunning and as being more "natural" and more spiritual; thus his or her intuitions were respected. So the fools were given a wide latitude to say and do unorthodox things. We should not be surprised if some individuals, taking advantage of this license accorded the fool, took on the role deliberately so that they could act more freely and say unconventional but perceptive things. Indeed, the fool or jester became a fixture of many feudal courts; they provided both entertainment and a mocking take on the status quo, protected (at least up to a point) from punishment by the powerful because of their unique status. Thus, in the Middle Ages the fool, jester, or clown was often a quite subversive element.

Like those earlier fools, Sulla is a subversive element in Islay; because he is or is perceived as a fool, he can act and speak in ways that mainstream society would not usually countenance. In taking on this persona, he becomes a kind of trickster; those in authority, who do not take his scheme seriously, are caught off balance and are helpless to stop him and his cohorts. In this case, conventional stipulations and attempts to maintain the status quo are no match for the intuition and "craft" of the common people, the deaf people—the "fools." Both the governor and the oral school superintendent are ousted from office and somehow, absurdly, a total inversion of the social, political, and cultural order is effected.

Sulla's apparent stupidity contrasts with the pseudo intelligence of the authority figure or intellectual, which, as typically happens when polemical incomprehension enters the novel, it unmasks.[16] The governor and his officials, who are supposed to be intelligent, are shown to be moronic. It is Sulla who has the intelligence to achieve his goals. He proceeds largely by instinct, step by step: he meets with people and explains what he wants to do, and many of them, responding to his earnestness and sincerity, get onto the bandwagon. As a man of the people—in this case, a marginalized people aspiring to their own homeland and improved economic and cultural status —he is like a Yankee in the American colonies rebelling against English rule. The Yankee trickster, as Constance Rourke pointed out in *American Humor: A Study of the National Character*, is "a symbol of triumph, of adaptability, of irrepressible life—of many qualities needed to induce confidence and self-possession among a new and unamalgamated people."[17] So too Sulla quickly and astutely adapts to circumstances as he brings together Deaf Americans. Before the powerful realize what is happening, things have changed because the trickster/fool has made people begin to think and act differently. In other words, the Deaf "fools" get the upper hand over the supposedly more knowledgeable and shrewd hearing people.

Sulla's fool persona is a parody of the hero of tragedy or romance, who nobly leads and boldly takes appropriate actions on a grand scale.[18] Sulla "leads" by muddling along and allowing things to fall into place; it is all as frantic and farcical as a Marx Brothers movie. Whenever he finds himself in an awkward position, he apologizes desperately and profusely. Sulla is more of an anti-hero in his very humanness, and yet he is quite heroic in what he manages to accomplish.

In an essay on picaresque narrative, Barbara Babcock describes how the conventional hero of romance who has fallen on hard times must work his way back up the ladder;[19] so, too, Sulla moves up the social scale, bumbling about and enduring many a pratfall in the process. But instead of starting high, falling low, and then returning to the heights, as his conventional counterparts do, Sulla begins very low: as a deaf person lucky enough to have a government job in Washington, D.C. And as we have seen, his progress up the social ladder is marked by absurd ups and downs, from his new Lincoln that runs out of fuel, to the accusation of real estate fraud at the moment of his triumphant return to Islay, and finally to his successful campaign for governor.

This trajectory could also be seen as a laughing inversion of what Northrop Frye believes to be the messianic hero's career path.[20] Just as other messiah figures in the past traveled through labyrinths, wandered in the wilderness, endured various trials, and resisted various temptations, so Sulla endures comic temptations and absurd trials as he travels into Islay and then across the country. The funds (and the new Lincoln) that he gains from his in-laws are a temptation, but he does not let his improved position go to his head. Remaining loyal to his wife, he resists the allures of women along the way who find him attractive. Nor does his new status as the leader of the advance into Islay and eventually its new governor turn his head. Sulla resists all temptations and perseveres through many a trial to make possible a heaven on earth for his fellow Deaf Americans. The heroic progression of Sulla and his cohorts is further burlesqued, as every step along the way his compatriots rally to his call to pursue the dream of a homeland—but it's a call they must take on faith, given Sulla's questionable approach.

Playing with Characterization

Sulla's extensive travels allow Bullard to dish up a panoramic cross-section of representatives of both mainstream and Deaf society.

They are types drawn to elicit laughing recognition rather than fully drawn characters, and include, on the mainstream side, the paternalistic administrator, the school superintendent, the interpreter, the child of Deaf adults, the hearing mother, the baffled hearing school principal, and the helpful hearing government workers; on the Deaf side, the gossip, the worrywart wife, the very educated oralist, the deaf peddler, the vulgar ladies' man, the government worker, and the businessman with a highly assertive partner—his wife. These are stock characterizations of Deaf American narrative; the skillful storyteller enthralls and entertains by how she or he describes them minutely and enacts them skillfully.

Again, Bullard is playing the conventions of mainstream literature off those in vernacular ASL storytelling. The psychological depth and nuance of modern realistic fiction is created by giving the reader access to characters' inner thoughts and feelings; ASL storytelling must take a different approach. Unlike the writer, the storyteller cannot use words to take the listener or viewer into the mind and heart of the characters. However, since ASL storytelling is performative, the skillful storyteller works to reveal inner states by way of enacting characters' thoughts and emotions—the more skillful the narrator, the more detailed and apt the enactment. In this performance, enactment in service to characterization can verge on the slightly exaggerated. Such hamming can give a vernacular narrative a burlesque quality.[21] Even fairly straightforward narratives, such as those by Ben Bahan and Sam Supalla (discussed in detail in chapter 9), have a parodic and satirical quality. The ASL storyteller enjoys going a little overboard in attempting to be as vivid and detailed as he or she can in enacting a character—especially if this narrative has to do with the relationship between the minority and majority cultures.

Peddlers, the ultimate wanderers, constitute one of the most representative types in Deaf culture and literature. Not surprisingly, some of the most significant and memorably amusing of the diverse Deaf Americans Sulla meets on his cross-country trip are members of a peddler family. This family, man, woman, and child, survive by their wits. Often relying on begging, theft, and deception, they have no compunctions about duping hearing people out of their money. Indeed, the family takes the attitude that if certain members of mainstream society want to be paternalistic, then let them be paternalistic by handing over their money and possessions. To be sure, achieving that end may require duplicity. For instance, the man may function as a decoy, drawing away the attention of security personnel while his wife and child happily grab up various items. At other times, the three individually approach people with ABC fingerspelling cards, wearing the appropriate demeanor and getup to elicit not only pity but also very welcome cash.

For Deaf Americans, working-class and middle-class alike, finding employment within mainstream society poses quite a few obstacles. More than a few are relegated to wandering about the streets, seeking handouts or selling tokens and alphabet cards. The peddler, not surprisingly, is viewed by members of the Deaf community with some ambivalence. On the one hand, the community bemoans the image of shiftlessness and isolation that the peddler conveys. On the other hand, it has a grudging respect for the peddler's duplicity—earning good money at the expense of mainstream society's gullibility, while flouting majority mores. In Bernard Bragg and Eugene Bergman's *Tales from a Clubroom*, a peddler says, "You accuse *me* of stealing money? Who, me? No, you're wrong. I'm only taking back what hearing people took from me because I'm deaf."[22]

Though in many ways representing the path not to take, the modern peddler has the distinction of being "true Deaf": that is, he or she goes his or her own way rather than seek employment in mainstream society, preferring not to meet mainstream expectations or to do things the hearing way, such as use speech or written English on a daily basis. Although mainstream society on the whole looks down on the use of ASL and fingerspelling, the peddler goes ahead and peddles ABC cards, making good money in the process. Deaf Americans would much rather have their own community and their own businesses, and exclusively use their own language. Because they cannot, they feel a sense of loss; they feel taken. But the peddler takes from mainstream society, in the way of cash for ABC cards.

Peddlers subvert mainstream maxims and practices. They forswear the bourgeois qualities of diligence, practicality, rationality, patience, stability, prudence, and honesty as they travel about, always on the road. Except for the daily solicitations, they steer clear of mainstream society because they do not feel at home in it. In the new Islay, however, with its increasing Deaf population, it will be a different story.

The peddler family in Bullard's novel, neither isolated nor doing badly, will no doubt settle down or at least stay a while in this new Deaf homeland. When the woman and child first encounter Sulla, approaching him for a handout, they do not know that he too is a Deaf American. He is taken aback, but he passes over a goodly sum along with his "Islay Company" business card. Sure enough, this family heeds the call and eventually arrives in Islay in their well-tooled van. The members dive into the social and political arena and feel right at home in getting the best of mainstream society. After all, they have in their blood a hilarious disregard for majority customs and practices.

Another representative mainstream character is the deaf school superintendent, mocked for his all-too-scrupulous regard for majority practices. School superintendents (more so in the past) notoriously spend half their time attending conferences and keeping up with new trends, while remaining ignorant of Deaf Americans and their needs, aspirations, and daily lives. The superintendent in Islay heads a special school attended by the Deaf children, inappropriately called the "Institute for Communicative Disorders." Staunch advocate of oralism that he is, he goes around slapping the hands of people who are signing, even those who can hear—and even himself when he gestures. He says, "I am the leader of the speaking deaf . . . the speaking deaf are normal like you and I" (253).

But the Deaf mothers in Bullard's novel, still another representative type, have no use for this superintendent and take their children to the public schools. Their approach is sensible and matter-of-fact, and they refuse to give in to categorization and "normalization." One mother insists on her children attending a public school near home; and when the principal suggests otherwise, she throws down an information booklet on PL-142, the Education for All Handicapped Children Act. Very soon other mothers refuse to have their children sent to the Institute for Communicative Disorders and converge on the local school, demanding equal access and throwing the educational system into an uproar. All this leaves the superintendent at a loss: "He had a sinking sensation that they were taking command and that he was becoming the outsider, even in his own school" (223). Indeed, these children's mothers are a force to be reckoned with and soon overturn the conventional structure of the educational system.

Bullard also satirizes two preeminent professions, medicine and ministry. Sulla makes it to California, and he quickly makes a beeline for the home of a clergyman who was formerly his wife's minister in the East. When Sulla and his current traveling companion, a doctor, arrive at Reverend Dowie's residence, he is down on his knees in his study praying. "Quickly [Dowie] went to the desk and hid the bottle of whiskey in its drawer. His shot glass was already filled for his morning toast. He didn't like to rush the toast; he liked it to be leisurely and thoroughly enjoyable" (187). The desk is not the only piece of furniture serving as a hiding place, and while Sulla and the minister go off to discuss Islay, the doctor serendipitously discovers that the ottoman is doubling as a well-stocked liquor cabinet. The reverend's unintended hospitality is much appreciated by the good doctor, and the liquor doesn't remain unimbibed for long. When the reverend and Sulla later return to the living room, they find the doctor greatly intoxicated, much to their mutual concern and chagrin.

By satirizing and skillfully describing typical members of both the Deaf community and the mainstream society, Bullard engages his Deaf readers, who no doubt have encountered similar characters during their own travels. The author's vivid descriptions of events are a lively and festive critique of the two-world situation in which Deaf people find themselves.

A Festive Criticism

The novel, especially the picaresque novel, is a form well suited for commenting on mainstream and minority societies. Alexander A. Parker notes that in picaresque novels "the world is made grotesque in order to reveal the distortions and unreality of human social life in the self-conceit and hypocrisy of men."[23]

In *Islay*, Bullard makes the world grotesque to provide a window onto the contemporary manners, morals, and idiosyncrasies of both hearing and Deaf people. The lauded brotherhood of a minority group is laughed at as witnesses in the rivalry and competition within the community. The famous independence of peddlers is undercut when a family of peddlers comes to settle in the new homeland of Islay. The supposition that Deaf Americans are better off in a place of their own and do not need the help of mainstream society is turned upside down when many of Islay's hearing residents go out of their way to assist Sulla and his band. Despite the goal—a Deaf homeland—eventually Islay will be an integrated state. This playful, burlesque depiction of the two-world condition is essentially carnivalesque: finding all things comic as it mixes high and low, official and popular—but reversing the usual hierarchies so that the powerful are brought low and the oppressed are lifted high.

Islay is a rarity, a full-length novel by a Deaf American in written English and ASL glosses. Almost two decades after its publication, *Islay* still stands alone as an example of the genre. During this time, Deaf American narrative has been in either short story or documentary form—either in written English or in ASL. Because translations of ASL dialogue take much away from the story (as the language is intrinsic to the characters and the culture), it takes a writer with a foot in both worlds to come up with a Deaf American novel in written English. As ASL is a visual, performative language, it is likely that most Deaf American narratives will continue to be in ASL, will remain comparatively short, and will be performed in front of either a group or a video camera.

Notes

1. Douglas Bullard, *Islay: A Novel* (Silver Spring, Md.: TJ Publishers, 1986). Specific page references to this work are hereafter cited parenthetically in the text. One book by a hearing author, Joanne Greenberg's *In This Sign* (New York: Holt, Rinehart, and Winston, 1970),

is wholly concerned with Deaf culture, and a number of others feature deaf characters.

2. M. M. Bakhtin, *The Dialogic Imagination: Four Essays*, ed. Michael Holquist, trans. Caryl Emerson and Michael Holquist (Austin: University of Texas Press, 1981), 3.

3. Ibid., 4–8.

4. Ibid., 6. See also Jay Clayton, *Pleasures of Babel: Contemporary American Literature and Theory* (New York: Oxford University Press, 1993), 95.

5. Originally the picaresque novel was the realistic story of a peripatetic rogue (*picaro*), but in later use the wanderings are emphasized and the crafty hero or heroine often becomes an attractive character—though generally of lowly birth—whose adventures and misadventures we follow with interest but without deriving a clear-cut moral. For example, see Daniel Defoe's *Moll Flanders* (1722).

6. See J. Lee Greene, "Black Literature and the American Literary Mainstream," in *Minority Language and Literature: Retrospective and Perspective*, ed. Dexter Fisher (New York: Modern Language Association of America, 1977), 20–28.

7. Mark Twain, *The Adventures of Huckleberry Finn* (1884; reprint, New York: Bantam Classic, 1981), 281.

8. Carol Simpson Stern and Bruce Henderson, *Performance: Texts and Contexts* (New York: Longman, 1993), 48.

9. Northrop Frye, *The Secular Scripture: A Study of the Structure of Romance* (Cambridge, Mass.: Harvard University Press, 1976), 47.

10. Stuart Miller, *The Picaresque Novel* (Cleveland: Press of Case Western Reserve University, 1967), 12.

11. See Northrop Frye, *Anatomy of Criticism: Four Essays* (Princeton: Princeton University Press, 1957), 305–6, 308.

12. See Mikhail Bakhtin, *Rabelais and His World*, trans. Hélène Iswolsky (Cambridge, Mass.: MIT Press, 1968), 18–19.

13. Frye, *Anatomy of Criticism*, 43–44; on the high and low mimetic modes, see 33–34.

14. Ibid., 187–88.

15. See Olive Mary Busby, *Studies in the Development of the Fool in the Elizabethan Drama* (Philadelphia: R. West, 1977). The following discussion relies largely on her account. See also Vicki K. Janik, preface and introduction to *Fools and Jesters in Literature, Art, and History: A Bio-Bibliographical Sourcebook*, ed. Janik (Westport, Conn.: Greenwood, 1998), xiii–xv, 1–22.

16. Bakhtin, *The Dialogic Imagination*, 403.
17. Constance Rourke, *American Humor: A Study of the National Character* (New York: Harcourt, Brace, 1931), 31.
18. Barbara Babcock, " 'Liberty's a Whore': Inversions, Marginalia, and Picaresque Narrative," in *The Reversible World: Symbolic Inversion in Art and Society*, ed. Babcock (Ithaca, N.Y.: Cornell University Press, 1978), 101.
19. Ibid., 98.
20. Frye, *Anatomy of Criticism*, 190–91.
21. Stern and Henderson, *Performance*, 4. Bruce A. Rosenberg notes this same tendency toward heavy characterization in vernacular storytelling in *Folklore and Literature: Rival Siblings* (Knoxville: University of Tennessee Press, 1991), 37.
22. Bernard Bragg and Eugene Bergman, *Tales from a Clubroom* (Washington, D.C.: Gallaudet University Press, 1981), 113.
23. Alexander A. Parker, *Literature and the Delinquent: The Picaresque Novel in Spain and Europe 1599–1753* (Edinburgh: Edinburgh University Press, 1967), 58.

Chapter

8

Poetry

A good poem reaches us on several different levels. It feeds our senses, stirs our emotions, and fires our imagination. It makes us see, hear, feel, and think at the same time. The total effect of a poem, therefore, is a special union of technique and substance, of artful form and meaning.
APPRECIATING LITERATURE (1989)

LONG BEFORE the fourth century B.C.E., when Aristotle attempted his systematic analysis of literary genres in the *Poetics*, listeners and readers recognized the power of poetry to tantalize and intrigue. Over the millennia, poets have been viewed as prophets, imaginative geniuses, seers, and subversives—so powerful that Plato banned them and their lies from the ideal state described in his *Republic*. Poetry has traditionally been considered a higher art form than the novel, which is an upstart genre, relatively speaking; even during the nineteenth and early twentieth centuries, when the novel was thriving, the general respect and attention lavished on poetry and poets far exceeded that accorded to writers of prose fiction. Through most of the twentieth century, however, popular interest in the genre diminished, and it became almost a coterie activity.

147

While poetry's star has seemed to wane in mainstream culture, the art form has fascinated and often baffled Deaf Americans introduced to it at an early age. In elementary and high school many of them have gravitated toward haiku, imagist poetry, and the works of those poets, such as Robert Frost, whose seemingly plain and straightforward writing captures a quality of the oral vernacular. Many, intrigued by this much-vaunted as well as much-beleaguered form, have tried their own hand at it; a number have produced some respectable specimens, as the works of Laura Searing and Rex Lowman demonstrate.[1] It did not take long for their interest to cross over into ASL, where modern poetics and vernacular principles have combined in contemporary "ASL poetry." It is this ASL poetry that introduced the world to "ASL literature," captured the attention of a fair number of mainstream poetry critics in the 1980s, and found its way onto videotape in the early 1990s.

Especially noteworthy is a 1990 videotape series, *Poetry in Motion: Original Works in ASL.* Each of its three videotapes features a single poet: Clayton Valli, Patrick Graybill, and Debbie Rennie, respectively.[2] In this sampling, we can see how ASL poetry intermingles aesthetic principles and rhetorical practices from two very different traditions: Western literature (the written), on the one hand, and ASL rhetoric (the "oral"), on the other. Composing a work to orally narrate to a live audience is quite different from composing a written or videotaped narrative. These two rhetorical traditions have different principles and functions. The older oral rhetorical tradition echoes in even the new ASL poetry; indeed, it shares equal billing with the written tradition in *Poetry in Motion.*

The Development of Western Poetry

As we saw in chapter 2, authorities on oral literature have stressed that before the spread of literacy beyond a small minority of the population and before the printing press was invented, spoken or oral forms were dominant in the West.[3] These oral forms varied from region to region, and only the most general claims can be made about their characteristics. It is difficult to distinguish oral poetry from other narrative forms—if those other (prose) forms even existed. Indeed, the narrative of the past may actually have been a kind of oral poetry, although it was not either prose narrative or poetry in the modern sense. Because there was likely little distinction then between oral narrative and oral poetry, the combination of the two might be termed *dramatic poetry*. Lois Bragg has pointed out that the Scandinavian eddic poems, which are narratives about mythological figures, appear to have been dramatic poetry that functioned as a kind of sacred liturgy.[4]

Dramatic poetry is structured performance unlike either the poetry or prose (which are dependent on the written page) with which we are familiar. The oral performer had to compose and render his or her material without the aid of pen and paper or recording equipment. Bruce Rosenberg and other researchers studying the effects of these constraints on the resulting work have found that much oral literature was heavily structured, or patterned, for ease of composition and recall.[5] Though the specific patterns varied from region to region, this basic compositional mode was "poetic," often relying to some degree on parallelism. Many oral forms today continue to make use of formulaic phrases, themes, incidents, and plots that can be combined and recombined on different occasions. For example, Dennis Tedlock has found patterned repetition of words, phrases, and episodes in early Native American oral narrative.[6]

Little of this performed, structured narrative has come down to us in an unadulterated form. Those early oral poetic forms that have been preserved in writing necessarily were transformed somewhat in the process. Many early written compositions are similar in style to narratives/poetry intended for oral performance, making it difficult to distinguish the oral and written features. For instance, the Greek epics, originally oral productions, are known to us in their written form; and though *Beowulf*, the earliest preserved English poem of such length, followed the oral tradition of Norse legends, we know it as a literate composition.[7] The *Canterbury Tales*, composed by the extremely well-read Geoffrey Chaucer, nevertheless preserves the oral frame story. In the Middle Ages, as we have seen, few groups were literate and in many ways the culture was still oral. There was thus much interpenetration between the two modes: the written word was read aloud, and literary works were commonly composed for oral performance and circulated by word of mouth.[8] Even the Yugoslavian oral narratives still being recited in the early twentieth century, which appeared to be purely oral works (and have some "poetic" elements), did not escape literary influences.[9]

Western poetry as we know it today, like prose, is "literature": something written and read. It has developed as literacy has become widespread. Thus poetry deemed worthy of modern critics' respect has lost much of its earlier oral or vernacular characteristics and often shows little trace of its origins in song and chant.[10]

Yet popular verse seems to have retained some of those earlier features. For instance, a prayer that appeared in the eighteenth-century *New England Primer* is still familiar to most Americans:

Now I lay me down to sleep,
I pray the Lord my soul to keep.
If I should die before I wake,
I pray the Lord my soul to take.

This poem evokes the image of a person, most likely a child, making an earnest and heartfelt appeal before retiring for the night. It is understandable and memorable from its very first line, primarily because of its narrative flow and the singsong quality that results from the strict meter and rhyme. These qualities make it easy to recite and recall, as does the repetition of "I pray the Lord" and the internal assonance—features that also make the four lines seem like a song.

Set this stanza against the first eighteen lines of one of the iconic poems of the twentieth century, "The Waste Land" (1922) by T. S. Eliot:

April is the cruellest month, breeding
Lilacs out of the dead land, mixing
Memory and desire, stirring
Dull roots with spring rain.
Winter kept us warm, covering
Earth in forgetful snow, feeding
A little life with dried tubers.

Summer surprised us, coming over the Starnbergersee
With a shower of rain; we stopped in the colonnade,
And went on in sunlight, into the Hofgarten,
And drank coffee, and talked for an hour.
Bin gar keine Russin, stamm' aus Litauen, echt deutsch.
And when we were children, staying at the arch-duke's,
My cousin's, he took me out on a sled,
And I was frightened. He said, Marie,
Marie, hold on tight. And down we went.
In the mountains, there you feel free.
I read, much of the night, and go south in the winter.[11]

Rhyme and a good deal of the traditional rhythm and meter have been dispensed with. Though the imaged vignettes are vivid, there are practically no narrative links between them. Instead, the poem's multilayered meaning depends on connotations, allusions, and symbolism. It requires much exegesis—indeed, in what may have been a slightly self-mocking gesture, the poet himself supplied annotations when the poem was first published in book form—and even then it is not quite decipherable. Here Eliot expresses his own critical vision of fragmented modern civilization; he is not concerned with speaking for (or to) the community as a whole and capturing the shared disillusionment of readers who have suffered through World War I.

"The Waste Land" is high modern written poetry—a different animal from "Now I lay me down to sleep" and nothing at all like traditional oral poetry. Writing has made a number of changes possible. By putting marks on paper, the writer makes possible an exhaustive craftsmanship, for he or she (or even someone else, as was famously the case in "The Waste Land") can later review and amend the poem. As Walter Ong points out in *Orality and Literacy*, such a constant reworking leads to added complexity and sophistication.[12] There is more layering and compression, and a more intricate interplay of figures of speech, allusions and intertextual references of all sorts, and symbols.

Writing changes not just the method of composition but also the method of reception. The permanency of words on paper allows poems to be reread and analyzed in depth, encouraging the poet to add layers of meaning and a good deal of figurative language.[13] The poet *expects* that the reader will have the interest, patience, and the time to reread the text, perhaps multiple times, and diligently dig through all the implied meanings. The guideposts generally characteristic of oral poetry, such as logical sequence, narrative, or expressions of clear-cut cause and effect, can be dispensed with. Mnemonic devices such as meter and rhyme may also be dropped, since they are no longer needed to help with recall. Moreover, some poets may see these formal requirements as unnecessary restrictions that interfere with the free play of the individual poetic sensibility.

Writing also distances the writer or poet from those he or she seeks ultimately to reach. The poet simply writes a poem, has it published, and hopes that someone will read it in the not-too-distant future. Thus, instead of communicating—after all, it is rather difficult to carry on a conversation with an imaginary reader—the writer ends up talking primarily to him- or herself.[14] Such writing becomes more personal expression than public communication, for the poet more often than not focuses on matters of individual interest rather than on issues of communal importance.

This distancing also makes the poet less answerable to his or her ultimate audience: he or she feels less need to be crystal clear and universally understandable. "The Waste Land" was and is an intellectual and imaginative tour de force, and Eliot shows little concern that the general reader will almost surely find it difficult going. Such modern poetry with its complexity is actually a rather elitist product created for a very few well-educated, literate, and informed readers who are willing to find the time to sit down and tackle a poem.

In contrast, traditional oral poetry was almost always recited to a group on a particular occasion. The poet would be expected to communicate to an audience, to appeal, to make a lasting impression, to be understandable from the very first line. Without these qualities, people would not have come to listen and surely would not have stayed to the very end of the performance. Because listeners cannot review or "reread" what they hear, the oral poet must draw on a number of strategies to make the poem immediately understandable. Rather than being complexly embedded and compressed, information in an oral poem needs to be continually added, so that it accumulates slowly.[15] As already noted, repetition in its many forms—the recurrence of sounds, words, phrases, lines, or whole stanzas—makes the content of a work much easier to grasp. (Witness the ballads, epics, and poetry with heavy rhymes and refrains that have come down to us from the past.) Perhaps most important for making a poem attention-getting and memorable is to make a story out of it or arrange information in a logical and sequential fashion.

Oral poetry, instead of being composed and then read alone, is a communal experience.[16] People are not drawn to a presentation because the poet is physically attractive, or because what he or she has to say is so scintillating or profound; they gather at some event of importance to their society, or they go for the experience, for the feeling of being with others who have similar needs, expectations, and dreams. Accordingly, the oral poet is more likely to produce poems that appeal to a particular group of people rather than write what is of interest only to him- or herself. By treating more universal themes or experiences and events that affect the entire group, the poet hopes to draw the community closer together. Moreover, the experience is immediate: rather than being a mysterious and disembodied presence behind or within the printed poem, the oral poet stands in person before an audience. We can imagine—although the degree of rapport may depend on the circumstances and the particular form of the presentation—that the oral poet shakes out the welcome mat, opens up his or her arms, and gathers everyone in. During the performance, he or she uses everything available—eye contact, gestures, body language, facial expressions, and impromptu props—to communicate with and fully relate to the audience. At intervals the oral poet may interact with listeners or viewers and let fly with queries and asides of quite a personal nature. After all, this oral poet is typically either a member of the community or a figure familiar to it.

Judging oral poetry from our literate viewpoint, we may view it as fairly simple and straightforward, but that impression may well be mistaken. The original performance relies on the poet's presence—a later transliteration on paper may not make note of extratextual or contextual aspects. The person making the permanent record may overlook the poet's use of gestures, a particular tone of voice, repetition or rephrasing, timely facial expressions, and expressive body movements. All of these intangible elements provide an extra dimension, but they cannot be transmitted via pen and paper. In addition, an outside observer not privy to a group's shared cultural knowledge may miss a good deal of the actual subtlety of oral discourse.[17] Little things that add complexity and enhance oral discourse do not show up in the written version. Thus what may appear simple in fact manifests a different kind of compression and a different kind of complexity.

Walter Ong is among those scholars who stress that because oral poetry is performative, it is evanescent—impermanent. There can be no fixed or authoritative version of a particular oral poem.[18] An oral poem will vary from one rendition to the next, as not even the same poet can re-create the same performance each time. His or her energy level changes, the audience changes, the context changes. As a result, no single presentation can be held up as the one invariable, most masterful version.[19]

Deaf American Vernacular Poetry

Although some oral poetry still exists today, especially as a part of folklore, it is a disappearing form of discourse. Moreover, as noted above, what does remain has been somewhat "contaminated" by written literature and literacy. But because of the unique nature of the Deaf American visual vernacular, ASL poetry or poetic forms have been relatively unaffected by writing and literacy. This "oral" art is thus flourishing and bears many similarities to the oral poetry of the past. One of the most fundamental similarities is that ASL poem-like forms are signed—that is, rendered or performed— before a group of spectators.

A number of organizations at Gallaudet University carry on the vernacular tradition, and at their gatherings through the years many productions have featured the clock tower on Chapel Hall, one of the oldest and most venerable buildings on campus. Because the Tower Clock is a landmark at Gallaudet, it is seen as emblematic of the Deaf postsecondary academic experience. Here is a translation of the beginning of one particular rendition, performed with the Tower Clock as backdrop:

Out of the Tower Clock
Wings furling, unfurling
Soaring and sailing
Diving and gliding
Lifted upon breeze after breeze

Storm clouds roiling
Lightning flashing, crackling
Thunder rumbling and booming
Wings beating, straining
Buffeted and blown.[20]

A never-specified winged creature (most likely a dove or seagull) is caught up in a thunderstorm, struggling to survive. It is buffeted and blown about by strong winds and endangered by lightning strikes. However, it persists mightily and courageously until at last the storm gradually abates.

This presentation, which we can title "The Tower Clock," often varies: perhaps the seagull alights on the casement at some point, or fluffy white clouds and blue skies are added either before or after the storm, or the moon rises later on. The audience may be shown the size of the winged creature, which can range from that of a smallish chickadee to that of an imposing hawk; this bird may be featured alone or may interact with several other beings. Even the ending can change. Yet in every variant the Tower Clock supplies the architectural framing for the aerial acrobatics.

"The Tower Clock" has not only an external architectural framework but also an internal architectural design. Particular signs are selected and used according to their handshape, movement, and orientation in an arrangement that somewhat recalls the composition of an impromptu painting or improvised modern dance. Here the choreography takes the form of spatially localizing and balancing the signing. For instance, the Tower Clock is first situated and "shaped" by being visually detailed. Then the winged creature soars out from the middle of the clock, glides from one side to the other, and descends to a lower altitude. Its balanced soaring and gliding are expressed in harmoniously similar handshapes and movements that flow into one another.

As in oral poetry, with its procedural aesthetics that emphasize the process of telling, in "The Tower Clock" the performer puts all effort into the artistic use of ASL to convey this storm and the bird's predicament. In this vernacular tradition, form takes precedence over content: *how* the presentation proceeds and catches up the viewers is more important than whatever it may have to say. In fact, more often than not, a presentation like this may not be saying anything much at all. An ASL poem is simply, and movingly, a shared experience.

Thus "The Tower Clock" is a performative and communicative act arising out of a specific occasion. It may be part of the entertainment at a formal gathering or at an informal celebration marking the end of probation for fraternity pledges. This act consists of context (the celebration), text (the presentation), teller (the performer or poet), and community (viewers). The experience is collective (probably full of camaraderie) and immediate: the pride and joy that the performer exhibits in the masterful use of the language arouse a corresponding joy and pride in the spectators themselves.

Another vernacular ASL poem is "Butterfly," whose English translation again cannot convey the felicitous selection and spatial arrangement of signs. One must imagine the poet's facial expressions conveying the lightheartedness of someone playing a delightful little prank.

> *Butterfly, butterfly,*
> *flutter, flutter anon*
> *Butterfly, butterfly*
> *alights upon a bell.*
> *Clang goes the clapper,*
> *peal! peal!*
> *Butterfly, butterfly*
> *flutter, flutter away.*[21]

In this scene, observed through the eyes of a young, mischievous girl, a graceful butterfly alights upon a bell with a clapper the size of a human fist. When the girl rings the bell, the butterfly is disturbed and hastily flutters off.

Like "The Tower Clock," "Butterfly" is performance; here the visual imagery is evocative of the fragility and exquisiteness of a butterfly. These qualities are conveyed not by words but by a concrete approximation of a butterfly's motion, as the performer uses apt hand configurations and movements. The viewers can see the butterfly, its dimensions, and its actions. Its nonlinear path—fluttering here and there, flitting up and down—seems to indicate playful curiosity and lighthearted adventurousness. When the butterfly lands on a bell that unexpectedly moves and sounds out, it takes off, most likely in pursuit of other adventures.

This poem, too, has an architectural design determined by the composition and arrangement of carefully selected signs. Only four signs are used altogether. Once the bell image is conveyed with the two hands (shaping it from the bottom up and then meeting, palms down, at chest level), the butterfly flutters in (F handshape) from one side. Then, the clapper swings (full arm ending in the S handshape moves across the body) and the butterfly flutters off (F handshape again) to the other side. The signs are carefully placed and balanced: we see the bell from bottom to top and the butterfly moving toward the bell from the far right. This movement to the right is continued both by the clapper swinging right to left across the body (where the bell had been positioned) and by the butterfly fluttering off to the right.

"Butterfly" has no point beyond the signer's or poet's pleasure—as well as the viewers' pleasure—in the masterful, artistic, and even rhythmic use of ASL. All the artist's effort goes into the imagery, architecture, and enactment: that is, into the procedural aesthetics. The repetition of the hands showing the shape of the bell and the butterfly's movement gives the work exquisite rhyme and rhythm. The horizontal and vertical balancing of sign placement is perfectly appropriate: harmonious at some times and jarring at others. The overall effect is enhanced by the mischievous and lighthearted persona assumed by the signer.

Another vernacular poem by the same performer displays a marvelous lyricism.

Walking
Moon, stars above
Walking
Trees all around
Walking
Path curving, angling
Walking
Moon in sky
Moon in pond

Thunder rolls
Raindrops fall
Raindrops in pond
Drip, drip, drop
Circle into circle
Into circle
Rain plashes, pours
Going, going, gone.[22]

Someone—we'll assume it is a man—is simply walking and taking in the trees and the pond in which a shining reflection of the moon can be seen. The spell is broken when it begins to rain and the man hurries off. This brief scene is the only layer of meaning. We can read other interpretations into the poem, such as one's pleasure in the beauty of nature at night; the relaxation inherent in a leisurely stroll—albeit rudely interrupted—along a wooded, moonlit path; or, a little more deeply, the recognition that life is not just a walk in the park. However, these more complex interpretations have not been sought or contrived at.

The poem sets a scene that incorporates a number of smaller actions and observations; in this vignette, events occur in a sequential and accumulative manner. The work is not as highly structured as are some ASL poems, such as "Butterfly." Nevertheless we still see the careful selection of signs and the careful repetition of handshapes and hand movements. The two-handed 5 handshape

WALKING leads into the balanced arrangement of two hands doing the 5 handshape TREES on the left and on the right. The signer then depicts the path curving and angling, as her (and the viewers') eyes move along it and up into the night sky where the bulbous moon hangs. The moon becomes a ball-shaped reflection in the quiet waters of the pond, as first MOON IN THE SKY is signed with one hand and then the other hand is raised to indicate the ball-shaped object up above the head. Both hands—still indicating a ball shape—are lowered to the level of the waist, where the pond was previously imaged. This careful patterning of the signs also has a rhythm: a quiet two-beat is visible in WALK-WALK, trees on both sides, and the moon in the night sky and the reflection in the water.

Examples of Contemporary ASL Poetry

Many ASL vernacular productions appear to be what we may call "lyrics"; their effect resides mostly in the emotion and the description. They have little or no plot or narrative, and accordingly make little reference to a relevant real-life situation. The three poets in the *Poetry in Motion* videotape series draw on this vernacular tradition in Deaf culture and combine many of its qualities with those of modern written poetry. In so doing, they create deliberately poetic productions that go beyond ASL vernacular forms in the competing and merging of two languages, two rhetorical traditions, two modes of communication, and two cultures. In forming a felicitous (or not) union of such different elements, the medium of videotape itself plays an important role: it is responsible for transforming the "oral" or vernacular into the "written" (as discussed at greater length in chapter 9).

Patrick Graybill's "Liberation"

In modern English poetry, the interplay between the written form of a poem and what is heard in the mind's ear creates multiple levels of meaning. Similarly, in modern ASL poetry the interplay between the form of a poem on videotape and what is seen in the mind's eye makes possible added levels of meaning.[23] Consider Patrick Graybill's very artful, highly figurative "Liberation":

English English
Prodding, prodding
Hand pushing down head
Signing, signing
Later chained, chained
Anger, anger
Comes to a head
Free at last!
Signing, signing
Confrontation, you and me
Resolved, let us bow
Clasp hands
Peace at last
Wonderful
Mine and yours
Let us bow
Equal in all.

The poem represents Graybill's feeling of liberation in being able to freely use ASL as his mode of communication. It describes the struggle on the part of Deaf Americans, who, having lost the freedom enjoyed in the nineteenth century to use sign language, happily recovered it in the late twentieth century.

As we have seen, the point of vernacular ASL poetry is that it has no point but "merely" is an experience shared through the masterful use of the language. But modern ASL poetry such as "Liberation" has a point, though its meaning is often veiled. Indeed, "Liberation" both *is* and *means*, thereby merging the vernacular ASL and the written poetry traditions. In performing this poem Graybill achieves a rapport with his viewers, thus drawing them into the poem; his skillful use of ASL also holds his viewers' attention and heightens their experience of the poem.

Because "Liberation" has multiple levels of meaning, viewers may not immediately grasp the poem's complete message. We are used to treating a modern poem like the proverbial Chinese box, looking for meaning within meaning. If their search for the innermost meaning leads readers or viewers to completely different interpretations, so much the better. To dig through the layers, the possibly befuddled viewer of "Liberation" can replay the tape to "reread" the poem and catch what was missed the first time through, analyzing at length the complex symbolism and abstraction as well as the allusions and figures of speech.

At the same time, Graybill wants to be understood: he wants to communicate clearly. Though this aim is not always shared by modern English poets, it is a goal of the vernacular ASL tradition. Although the narrative is abstract, it plays out like a story. The progression of thought is logical: English and along with it speech are emphasized, frustration and anger result, but when the people's vernacular is recognized the final reconciliation becomes possible. Behind the story lies the historical chronology: Laurent Clerc brings sign language to America, where its use becomes widespread; sign language is denounced in the 1880s and suppressed for almost a century; William Stokoe gives ASL legitimacy in the 1960s, which fuels the increasing empowerment of the Deaf community in the later decades of the twentieth century.

"Liberation," like vernacular ASL poetry, shows a preoccupation with the poetics of expression, but it takes that preoccupation to a higher, more artful level—one made possible by the medium of videotape, which plays a role similar to paper in encouraging more artful language play and composition. The poem exhibits remarkable craftsmanship in the careful selection and use of signs to achieve highly intricate visual rhymes. Graybill's poem uses only three different handshapes in a total of seventeen signs. The first three lines use the slightly cupped handshape that the upper hand takes in the ENGLISH sign. The next several lines use the SIGNING handshape, in which the fingers are more bent, in a number of different movements and orientations. The last half of the poem is in the B handshape—flat and fingers all together—but again with different movements and orientations. The similarity in the handshapes provides a visual rhyme that, along with the mostly two-beat measure interspersed with full one-beat stops, gives "Liberation" a musical quality. This musical quality of the rhythm and rhyme as well as the poem's repetitions makes it easy to follow, comprehend, and remember. That it is even fairly easy to imitate—that is, for someone other than Graybill to perform—is another characteristic of vernacular poetry.

Although "Liberation" has the complexity and artfulness of modern poetry, it does not have a private, confessional, or cryptic quality. It expresses not only Graybill's desire as an individual to use ASL freely but also the desire, frustration, and anguish of others within the Deaf community. On one level it is about Graybill's personal experience; on another level it is about the experience of many children who were subjected when very young to the "oral method." Finally and more broadly, "Liberation" relates the historical experience of Deaf Americans as a whole. The poem thus has a relevance and a communal value to Deaf Americans as a people and a community.

Clayton Valli: The Deaf Robert Frost

Clayton Valli, the second of the three ASL poets in the *Poetry in Motion* series, might be called the Robert Frost of Deaf American poetry because of the way he combines vernacular features and modern symbolism. Like Frost's poetry, a majority of Valli's poems have some connection to nature or natural forces. Consider the titles of those included on the videotape:

"Cave"
"Lone Sturdy Tree"
"My Favorite Old Summer House"
"Windy Bright Morning"
"Snowflake"
"Dandelion"

Even "Hands," the only poem whose title lacks an obvious connection to nature, uses the cycle of the four seasons as a main theme and structuring device. Valli lives in New England, where Frost spent most of his life, and early in his career he attempted to model his poetry, written in English, on Frost's. The influence is clear in Valli's later ASL poetry as well.

Frost, probably the best-known poet in America in the first half of the twentieth century, crafted an apparently simple poetry that was in some ways a deliberate rebuke to the modernist obscurity of poems such as "The Waste Land." He also crafted his own persona as a traditional, rural New Englander (though born in California), using everyday language and formal metrical patterns that gave much of his poetry an oral, vernacular quality.[24]

Frost was able to use oral vernacular to create poems that are more compressed, with richly suggestive imagery. Take, for example, the classic "Stopping by Woods on a Snowy Evening":

> *Whose woods these are I think I know.*
> *His house is in the village though;*
> *He will not see me stopping here*
> *To watch his woods fill up with snow.*
>
> *My little horse must think it queer*
> *To stop without a farmhouse near*
> *Between the woods and frozen lake*
> *The darkest evening of the year.*
>
> *He gives his harness bells a shake*
> *To ask if there is some mistake.*
> *The only other sound's the sweep*
> *Of easy wind and downy flake.*
>
> *The woods are lovely, dark and deep,*
> *But I have promises to keep,*
> *And miles to go before I sleep,*
> *And miles to go before I sleep.*[25]

Although "Stopping by Woods" does have a narrative quality, it is noteworthy for the use of rhyme and rhythm characteristic of oral poetry. Yet its figurative language firmly links it to the complexity of modern written poetry.

Valli is very like Frost in combining the old with the new, the vernacular with the written. One of his more widely known poems, "Cave," which is included on the *Poetry in Motion* videotape, illustrates this point well. Two people are walking (each hand in the 1 handshape, moving forward side by side) and then split up. One goes off alone, while the other continues on his or her way and comes upon a cave. The poet enacts this person, possibly a young man, who steps into the cave, descends rough nature-hewed steps, and sets foot upon the uneven floor. Inside the cave are stalactites dripping from the ceiling and stalagmites rising from the floor; one has an especially large treelike and bulbous column. The young man makes his way through the tunnels and eventually reaches the back of the cave. The poet then enacts one or more workers who cut the steps into geometric rectangles, smooth out the rock formations from the ceiling, and add lights to illuminate the room. Other formations from the floor are completely removed so that the surface can be made even and level. Fans are installed to halt the condensation dripping from the ceiling. Guardrails are added at the entrance and a big chandelier emitting yellow, orange, and green flashes of light is hung within. A blue carpet is laid, and red and white seats are placed in rows. When all is ready, people line up and enter for a lecture; and the lecturer goes on and on about the great work that has been done (the "improvements" inside the cave). The poem culminates when Valli signs CAVE BLACK on his forehead and then turns in profile and positions his hands (in the shape for CAVE) over his right ear.

Rather than being aggregative in the traditional vernacular manner, "Cave" contains much analogical (symbolic) play. The story line helps the viewer immediately grasp that on the surface, the poem is about going into a cave and dressing it up. But in contrast to a vernacular production, where little of importance goes on below the surface, the viewer has to figure out the whole point of this exercise.[26] Valli poses a challenge to the viewer, expecting him or her to actively analyze the work—and replay the tape as many times as is necessary—to unearth the hidden messages or meanings. Instead of "simply" experiencing the presentation in a communal spirit, the viewer must interpret and analyze with a finger heavy on the rewind button.

The meaning of "Cave" is multilayered because the images in the poem function on several levels. Most broadly, they point to the opposition of "art versus nature" or "the artificial versus the natural." The poet images a natural cave being jollied up with all the trappings of a conference room or auditorium: guardrails, chairs, banners, and the like. It is thereby transformed into something "else," made to approximate something more elaborate and more artificial. On another level the journey into a cave represents a deaf person opting to have a cochlear implant; the lecturer at the end stands in for proponents of cochlear implants who proclaim success and impress hopeful parents of deaf children. On still another level, images and actions sprinkled throughout the poem have specific symbolic resonance, such as the red and white of the chairs and the blue of the carpet.

In "Hands," a shorter poem, Valli describes the cycle of the four seasons.

Snow falling
Flowers blooming
Sun shining
Leaves falling
All presented
To you.

At the same time, "Hands" also portrays the capacity of ASL to convey each of the seasons in all its distinctiveness and beauty. The last two lines, "All presented / to you," signify that an artistic and linguistic feat has been accomplished—a feat made possible by using the hands to communicate.

The architecture of "Hands" recalls the composition of vernacular ASL poetry cited earlier. In imaging each season, Valli moves from north to east to south to west in a cyclical motion that imitates the progress of the seasons. By giving each season a different spatial location—one for each direction of the compass—he nicely balances and structures the presentation. The work culminates in the center, thus implying life, nature, God—or perhaps for Deaf Americans the center of all things is the vernacular itself. These last two lines depict something very like the classic depiction of God's cupped hands as strong, generous, and encompassing. These hands are powerful in another way, for they make possible this means of communication and language.

Also recalling the vernacular tradition in this ASL poetry is the strong sense of a musical rhythm, very noticeable in "Hands" as in most of Valli's poems. It is conveyed primarily by the poem's visual rhyme scheme and architecture as Valli repeats a number of hand-shapes, hand movements, and hand orientations. For instance, in "Hands" Valli almost exclusively uses signs formed from the 5 handshape. Rhyme also is visible in the hand movements, such as that of the snow falling and that of the leaves falling, as well as in nonmanual signals. Facial expressions can rhyme: for example, when a performer uses similar expressions (delight, appreciation) at differ-ent points in a poem. The poem's rhythm is emphasized by the cyclical movement in "Hands," as the signing moves up, left, down, right, and back to the middle from one spatial location to another.

Like Frost, who turned the living speech of men and women into poetry, Valli has made the visual vernacular sing to and of Deaf Americans in "Hands" and "Cave." On videotape, he speaks to viewers and wins them over with his affability, intrinsic humor, and apparent simplicity. In "Hands," in particular, Valli begins with a simple idea—the seasonal cycle—and then he leads his viewers to extend its implication more broadly and deeply. He also follows Frost in that his poems exhibit superb craftsmanship: the careful selection of signs, the intricate architectural layout, and the apt symbolism. Valli too gives significance to the apparently insignifi-cant, illuminating things as common as seats in a row ("Cave") or as natural as rain or snow falling ("Hands").

As Frost's poetry is known for its way of uniting opposites, revealing the contradictory nature of the world and the human beings in it, Valli's works similarly touch on the contradictions in the two-world condition of Deaf people (e.g., examining cochlear implants in "Cave"). Despite their seeming casualness, intimacy, and exquisite lyricism, Valli seeks to get at and reveal the truth, the moral of things, in Deaf culture. "Hands" is not merely about snow falling and flowers growing but also about the wonderful expressiveness of ASL and, by implication, of the Deaf people who use sign language.

Debbie Rennie

Debbie Rennie's "Black Hole: Color ASL" on her *Poetry in Motion* videotape also displays much analogical (symbolic) play:

Ladder, rungs, ladder upright
I walk, come to ladder, climb up
See pots of red paint, yellow, blue, green
Blue skies, dip into paint, splatter paint
Ladder shakes, people shake, I totter
Paint spills, the ladder shaken to dislodge, paint spills
Black hole looms, and I am endangered, paint spills
I flail and stagger, black paint spreads, I flail
Ladder is pulled down, I stagger and flail, struggle
Black looms, black looms, black looms
I fly and soar, colors all over, I fly
Colors all over, I fly, I soar

In this poem, we see a basic narrative framework: a person makes the climb out of the hearing world and discovers ASL. Ecstatic, she (or he; the poem is translated using first person for convenience) is in her element; but the ladder is soon shaken, for people in the hearing world desire her return. Struggling to remain on the ladder, she feels at risk not just of falling but of being pulled into an immense, looming black hole. The deaf person perseveres, and even as the ladder is pulled down she takes off into the ASL world of "color," experiencing the freedom to express herself.

Rennie has also compressed and layered the meanings in this poem. Overall, the climb up the ladder and the attempt to dislodge the climber represent the rise of ASL in the nineteenth century and the efforts to eradicate it in the first half of the twentieth century. At the same time, as noted above, the poem is the story of an individual who discovers ASL and struggles to use it freely. The black hole is both the unknown and the plight of the deaf person without a vernacular and without a cultural identity. Within this framework, the paint colors represent the vitality and vividness of ASL as a language, while on another level underscoring that ASL is a visual vernacular. Finally, the poem is also a personal statement: Rennie was an art major and is using paint colors to make a connection between the visuality of ASL and that of the plastic arts.

"Black Hole" has a very intricate architecture based on repetition. The poem as a whole is given a tripartite structure by the three spatial locations represented: in the first part of the "story," a person climbs the ladder and paints; in the second part, the ladder is shaken and pulled downward; and in the third part, the beleaguered person triumphs. Within each part, things seem to happen in threes, as the poem's translation makes clear: each line has three segments or actions. A final reinforcement of this tripartite architecture is provided by the repetition of three basic handshapes: the O and C handshapes (which are similar enough to count as one shape), the B handshape, and the 5 handshape. We see the slightly open O handshape for LADDER—almost a C handshape—and the fully open C handshapes for CLIMBING UP and THE POTS OF COLOR. B handshapes are used for the sky and for the action of painting, and 5 handshapes appear in BRIGHT, SPLATTER, SWAYING, COLORS, FLAILING, SPILLING, SPREADING, LOOMING, and so on.

The Communal Function of ASL Poetry

Despite their deliberate artfulness and complexity, features associated with individualistic modernist poetry, many of the poems in *Poetry in Motion* have a cultural function that is more characteristic of vernacular poetry. Valli's "Cave" and "Hands," for instance, respectively argue against cochlear implants for deaf people and point up the beauty of ASL and the cultural value of the hands. These poems are works of relevance to the members of the culture as a whole. Similarly, Rennie's "Black Hole: ASL Color" and Graybill's "Liberation" are not private outpourings of individual imaginations but general expressions of Deaf people's desire to use their vernacular freely.

A number of presentations in the videotape series, such as Valli's "My Favorite Old Summer House" and "Windy Bright Morning," spring from more personal roots. The medium of videotape, which (like paper) allows the separation of poet from audience, makes the demands of community relevance less pressing; it eliminates the interaction between an oral poet and his or her audience. In the future, as more ASL poets compose for videotape, we may see an increasing tendency toward more and more subtle and individual modes of expression.

However, the ASL poets on these tapes have not abandoned their roots in vernacular ASL discourse. For example, a brief autobiography and a lecture by each poet—an overview of the general poetic principles to which he or she adheres—are inserted at the beginning of each tape. Additional explanations interspersed throughout the tape include the imperative common in Deaf American culture: "Watch (me)." These cues give the impression that the poets are talking to the viewer(s) rather than indulging in private raptures or anguish. Moreover, even though videotape distances teller and viewer, it is inherently more directly engaging than are black marks on a page. The three ASL poets are seen "in person" performing these poems, supplying background information, explaining poetic principles, and simulating interaction with viewers. Each poet maintains eye contact while touching on themes, values, and experiences that are common in Deaf culture.

The videotape series as a whole has a communal function in that the producers as well as the poets want the public at large to understand and value this new development in ASL literature, which they believe deserves as much recognition as literature produced by and for mainstream society. To aid in the appreciation of what is to many an unfamiliar art form, the producers and poets have created these "video textbooks" to explain what this ASL poetry involves. Most collections of poetry or short stories aimed at the general public simply gather together and print the selections, perhaps including a brief introduction or biographical sketches. In contrast, *Poetry in Motion* is intended to teach Deaf Americans as well as interested hearing people about its contents. As a result, the series presents a striking mixture of artistic and didactic, transcendent and mundane, abstract and concrete, high and low.[27]

The producers of this poetry anthology may be specifying an "ASL poetry"—making the kind of generic distinctions familiar from the history of Western literature—but the tapes are in fact quite heterogeneous. Indeed, as we have seen so often in this study, Western generic distinctions—poetry, novel, short story, drama, and so on—cannot be readily applied to a visual discourse. The Western literature we know today is the textualized form of a discourse that was originally oral and aural. In contrast, vernacular

ASL art forms reflect a visual discourse that has remained primarily "oral." In any case, what good are generic distinctions when such two different rhetorical traditions are merged (or yanked together, if you will)?[28]

This ASL poetry is carnivalesque: a dynamic intermixing and interplay of diverse modes, rhetorical practices, art forms, and what have you. It is a hybrid, but it is still poetry: signs (read "words") are variously grouped according to particular patterns of sight, "sound," and logic, all combining to musical effect. ASL poems evoke sensory images that stimulate our senses and minds, eliciting in the process the emotions and thoughts that we associate with those images and experiences.

Notes

1. See Jack Gannon, "Laura Searing," in *Gallaudet Encyclopedia of Deaf People and Deafness*, vol. 3, ed. John Van Cleve (New York: McGraw-Hill, 1987), 11–13; Howard Glyndon [Laura Searing], *Echoes of Other Days* (San Francisco: Harr Wagner, 1921), particularly "One Perfect Day" (264) and "Christmas Greetings" (280); and Rex Lowman, *Bitterweed* ([Bentonville, Ark.]: Bella Vista Press, 1964).

2. *Poetry in Motion: Original Works in ASL*, Burtonsville, Md., Sign Media, three videocassettes, 60 min. each, 1990. All the poems by Valli, Graybill, and Rennie cited in this chapter are drawn from this collection.

3. See Walter Ong, *Orality and Literacy: The Technologizing of the Word* (London: Methuen, 1982); Ruth Finnegan, *Literacy and Orality: Studies in the Technology of Communication* (Oxford: Blackwell, 1988) and *Oral Poetry: Its Nature, Significance and Social Context* (New York: Cambridge University Press, 1977); and John Miles Foley, *Immanent Art: From Structure to Meaning in Traditional Oral Epic* (Bloomington: Indiana University Press, 1991).

4. Lois Bragg, letter to author, spring 1999.

5. Bruce A. Rosenberg, *Folklore and Literature: Rival Siblings* (Knoxville: University of Tennessee Press, 1991), 135–36.

6. Dennis Tedlock, "Toward an Oral Poetics," *New Literary History* 8 (1977): 507–19.

7. Lois Bragg, letter to author, spring 1999. See also Dennis Tedlock, *The Spoken World and the Art of Interpretation* (Philadelphia: University of Pennsylvania Press, 1983), 250–51; Rosenberg, *Folklore and Literature*, 135–43.

8. Finnegan, *Literacy and Orality*, 26.

9. See Albert B. Lord, *The Singer of Tales*, Harvard Studies in Comparative Literature, 24 (Cambridge, Mass.: Harvard University Press, 1960).

10. P. J. Laska, "Poetry at the Periphery," in *A Gift of Tongues: Critical Challenges in Contemporary American Poetry*, ed. Marie Harris and Kathleen Aguero (Athens, Ga.: University of Georgia Press, 1987), 327.

11. T. S. Eliot, "The Waste Land," in *The Norton Anthology of Modern Poetry*, ed. Richard Ellmann and Robert O'Clair, 2nd ed. (New York: Norton, 1988), 491–92.

12. Ong, *Orality and Literacy*, 104–5.

13. See Christopher Collins, *The Poetics of the Mind's Eye: Literature and the Psychology of Imagination* (Philadelphia: University of Pennsylvania Press, 1991).

14. Ong, *Orality and Literacy*, 105.

15. Ibid., 38.

16. Ibid., 45, 74.

17. Tedlock, *The Spoken Word and the Art of Interpretation*, 35–36. See also Finnegan, *Literacy and Orality*, 79.

18. Ong, *Orality and Literacy*, 35.

19. Finnegan, *Literacy and Orality*, 88–89.

20. A variant of a Kappa Gamma fraternity rendition, performed by Samuel Hawk in June 1998. This, and all other translations in this chapter are mine.

21. This poem was rendered at the Mill Neck School for the Deaf and then reenacted by a recent Mill Neck graduate, Jin-Kyoung Kim, at Gallaudet University in spring 1998; her performance is translated here.

22. Performed by Jin-Kyoung Kim at Gallaudet University in spring 1998.

23. Trenton Batson, "Poetry in American Sign Language," in Van Cleve, *Gallaudet Encyclopedia of Deaf People and Deafness*, vol. 3, 222–24.

24. See, for example, Robert Frost, "Two Witches: The Witch of Coös," in *Collected Poems, Prose, and Plays*, ed. Richard Poirier and Mark

Richardson, Library of America (New York: Literary Classics of the United States, 1995), 187–88.

25. Robert Frost, "Stopping by Woods on a Snowy Evening," in *Collected Poems*, 207.

26. Samuel Hawk, conversation with author, summer 1998.

27. Perhaps this mixture is most notable in Rennie's tape, which contains both fifty-some minutes of aesthetic poetry and a rather vulgar narrative about European nose-picking.

28. Lois Bragg has pointed out that both traditional oral poetry and ASL vernacular poetry differ from representative modern poetry in that they do not require "school learning"; they therefore cannot be adequately judged by the traditional criteria of Western literary criticism. Bragg, correspondence with author related to Clayton Valli's views on poetry, fall 1998.

Chapter
9

From Orature to Literature: The New Permanence of ASL Literature

FOR CENTURIES Western cultures have had the means not only to record their vernacular forms but also to distribute them with relative ease. They have been able to record on paper and later to publish—and thus distribute—their poems, stories, and plays. In contrast, Deaf Americans have only very recently acquired this same capacity to record and easily distribute their vernacular forms to the Deaf public at large. A few ASL stories, speeches, and art forms were captured on film in the early twentieth century, but these films were not widely distributed. Only when home videocassette recorders became ubiquitous in the 1980s did a large number of ASL videos begin to be created and widely disseminated. Even more were produced and distributed in the 1990s; and with the new availability of affordable videocameras and video computer technology, the upward trend is very likely to continue.

As increasing numbers of ASL art forms are recorded, video-tape is becoming more than simply a means of preservation. Works are being adapted to the medium and even composed explicitly with this format in mind. As the discussion of *Poetry in Motion* in the preceding chapter suggests, the use of videotape is already leading to changes in ASL vernacular forms, in the very indigenous rhetorical tradition itself. Such changes in fact parallel those that occurred in early European vernacular forms centuries ago during their transition from orality to literacy, described in chapter 2. As the use of writing spread, mainstream oral forms vanished or took on a literary ("written") cast. A similar transition is occurring in Deaf American literature, and as this transpires we can see the inter-mixing of two very different rhetorical traditions.

Bahan and Supalla: New ASL Literature

Aspects of the transition from "oral" vernacular forms to "literary" forms can be observed in DawnSignPress's remarkable videotape ASL Literature Series. The first and to date only installment appeared in 1992; it consists of two entertaining narratives, Ben Bahan's "Bird of a Different Feather" and Sam Supalla's "For a Decent Living," each about twenty minutes long.[1] Both are ASL stories that have been adapted for video distribution with students of ASL as a second language in mind. Bahan's narrative was created in 1982 for a live performance at a confest. Supalla's fictitious narrative was developed over fifteen years through his one-man show before a live audience.[2]

In the early 1990s when the videotape first came out, the two ASL artists held a number of workshops around the country that focused on the characteristics of ASL literature in general and on the literary features of these two narratives in particular. Through these workshops, Bahan and Supalla helped make a case for the value of ASL itself in showing that literature is no less possible in a visual than in an aural language.

"Bird of a Different Feather," the first narrative on the 1992 videotape, was briefly described in chapter 3. The fable concerns an eagle couple that find among their hatchlings two eaglets with "normal" beaks and one eaglet with an "abnormal" beak. Anguished over their "odd" eaglet, the couple searches far and wide for a cure, consulting both the medical and the religious establishments—but to no avail. At their wits' end, the parents are reduced to placing their offspring in a special school at which he is to learn "eagle behavior." There he will be taught how to swoop and hunt, though he lacks the physical capacity to do so successfully. Nevertheless, the eaglet practices and practices, and practices some more, in an effort to compensate for his physical limitations. Eventually the eaglet graduates and attempts to take his place in eagle society, but attempt is the best he can do. As his family relocates to the West, the eaglet by chance encounters some songbirds (a lower and denigrated species). From them, he learns to sing and eat berries, and he feels in his element. Yet despite his luck at finding such compatible companions and a more suitable lifestyle, the eaglet accedes to the urging of his family and undergoes an operation to reshape his beak, an operation that everyone hopes will make him fully "eagle." This operation does give him a hooked beak, but he still cannot hunt or swoop like other eagles—and he forever loses his ability to sing and eat berries. At the end of the narrative, no longer able to find any compatible companions, the eaglet flies off into the distant mountains very much alone.

Bahan's "Bird of a Different Feather" is an animal fable, a form common in vernacular storytelling.[3] Everyone is familiar with Aesop's fables. They invariably entertain as they endeavor, often by using animals that speak and act like human beings, to drive home a useful truth. This practice of anthropomorphizing animals doubtless harks back to prehistoric times; the extant tales often involve a trickster-figure who deceives or is deceived.[4] These fables are also common in minority literatures, which have vernacular roots even if the living vernacular tradition has been lost: witness the Brer Rabbit tales of African American literature and the Coyote narratives of Native American literature.[5] Such fables or passing references featuring various anthropomorphized creatures are likewise common in Deaf American literature where the creatures' lives and treatment represent those of Deaf Americans.

In Deaf American literature, animal fables combine the didacticism of Aesop with the tricksterism of Coyote, providing an indirect way for this minority culture to show up the majority culture. Although Ben Bahan, our Jester, never indicates that his tale has human implications, no Deaf American will miss his point—that while parents often try to "fix" their child's deafness, many Deaf Americans do not believe that deafness is something that needs to be fixed (and indeed view the "fix" as often worse than the "problem"). The deaf child/eaglet simply needs a different approach to communication and life.

On the same videotape is Sam Supalla's "For a Decent Living," the story of a young man from the country who leaves home to seek his fortune in the big city. He meets up with an older Deaf American who fills him in about the local deaf club and then accompanies him there. At this club the young man is at first viewed with suspicion, as members take him to be a peddler. Once everything is cleared up, they welcome him warmly. When he asks about job opportunities, they tell him of various openings, including those at a big factory near town—yet they warn him that the factory is unlikely to hire a Deaf employee. Rising to the challenge, the young man heads for the factory and persists through numerous rebuffs to finally meet the manager. Fortuitously this manager knows some fingerspelling, and he takes a chance on the young man. The young man settles down happily in his new job and is a model worker. Although the work quickly becomes repetitive and monotonous, he works diligently until he has a rather absurd accident—he falls into a large hole, injuring himself and losing consciousness. After coming to in the hospital, the young man—still confused and not knowing where he is—staggers out of the building, back to the factory, and back to work. All this makes a very favorable impression on the manager, and the narrative ends with many of the young man's Deaf friends being given the same opportunity to show what they can do.

These two remarkable narratives were performed explicitly for videotape, not taped at performances before audiences. Both are clearly derived from but different than traditional oral literature. Bahan's animal fable is an original narrative, but it is based on a traditional form.[6] The Supalla narrative, a composite of stories the narrator/performer "listened to" during childhood, is put together in an original way.[7] Moreover, as is common of oral forms, variants of "Bird of a Different Feather" and "For a Decent Living" have spread all across the country—largely because the artists encouraged their workshop participants to attempt imitations, particularly of the animal fable.

Nevertheless, when writers intend vernacular narratives to be preserved, whether on paper or videotape, their narratives inevitably undergo changes, for the medium of storytelling has changed. In Western aural cultures the process began centuries ago and was very gradual, taking hundreds if not thousands of years.[8] This very same process, however, seems to be happening much more quickly now in Deaf culture and literature as a result of larger trends in contemporary American culture and rapid advances in technology.

The Transition from Orality to Literacy

Before the widespread use of writing and reading, many oral storytellers traveled about and told stories to comparatively small groups of people, usually as part of some ceremonial occasion, fair, or festival.[9] For generations these oral forms coexisted with writing, for few in the audience (and indeed among the storytellers) were literate. Vernacular forms were rarely recorded, both because potential readers were scarce and because even access to "paper" (first wax tablets and later papyrus) was problematic, as the medium was either cumbersome or rare. When Homer's *Iliad* and *Odyssey* were first written down, Western culture was primarily oral. Writing was reserved mainly for official use in government and business. But over time, more orally communicated matters were recorded, and more discourse was simply written from the start. This process of textualization—the writing down of what once was transmitted orally—part of the larger shift from orality to literacy, has been documented by a number of scholars, perhaps most notably Walter Ong and Ruth Finnegan.[10] We primarily understand "text" to mean something written or printed, such as writing or printing gathered to make a book. The word derives from the Latin *texere*, "to weave," so it implies in its basic sense words "woven together" on a page. Such interwoven, printed words create a quite different medium from words communicated orally.

Scholars generally believe that the process of textualization has been gradual; people cannot change their way of communicating (and of thinking) overnight. As Ong notes, early writing had many of the characteristics of oral communication.[11] Over time, as people became more familiar with the new medium, its oral quality faded and it increasingly took on textual or literary features. These two modes, with their two rhetorical traditions, have continued to compete and overlap.[12] As noted in chapter 2, contemporary scholars call more formal oral communication *orature*; it includes storytelling, oratory, sermons, oral poetry, and much contemporary folklore. *Literature*, a word derived from the Latin term for "letter," refers to all formal communication in letters: originally everything written or printed, ranging from histories, legal documents, philosophical treatises, and speeches and sermons composed first on paper to poetry, novels, and the like. The term now is usually applied more narrowly to aesthetic forms such as short stories, novels, playscripts, and poetry.[13]

Different cultures and periods have approached writing differently and have assigned different values to the kinds of literature produced, but we can make some generalizations about the "higher" forms of writing in Western cultures (and, as the authors of *The Empire Writes Back* point out, in those cultures that once were colonized by Western powers).[14] Their concepts of literature are largely derived from classical and neoclassical theories, particularly those that rely on the writings of Aristotle. To be sure, contemporary "postmodern" criticism has complicated the picture considerably; but traditionally the most attention has been paid to the works that are the "best" (variously defined, when defined at all). These make up the literary canon: works of high aesthetic worth that exhibit masterful use of the language, unity of structure, universality, and humanistic values and that, at least in modern times, are attributable to the individual, imaginative genius of one author. Though such "masterpieces" have not been the only texts printed and circulated among the public, literary works of *art*—high-caliber narratives, plays, and poetry—have been considered the only literature worthy of serious attention.[15]

As we have seen throughout this study, orature or storytelling has quite different properties from those of written literature. They are not so easy to list, both because the study of orature is still relatively new and because orature is by its nature evanescent and local. While written literature tends to be a product of an educated elite infused with high, national culture, orature is a discourse of the people and thus shows much variation between regions. However, as has been frequently noted, a few generalizations can still be made about orature. It is performative, and because it requires an audience, it usually arises out of particular social circumstances that draw a group of people together. Thus orature is by nature more communal or collective than literature, which is generally consumed by individual readers; moreover, because other people are physically present, the performer or storyteller must be concerned with keeping their attention. Finally, an oral performance has no authorized version, for every time it is presented (even by the same person) it varies from earlier renditions.[16]

The Emerging Textualization of Deaf Vernacular Discourse

Because Deaf Americans are primarily an oral people, their attitude toward communication resembles that of oral cultures before the invention of writing. As Ben Bahan (who is a scholar as well as an ASL performer) notes, their oral rhetorical tradition will probably continue, because their language continues to be more interactive than those that rely on writing.[17] However, because Deaf Americans are able to record and distribute their ASL productions with ever-increasing ease, ASL vernacular stories are being transferred in greater numbers to the new medium, videotape. As more and more ASL works are composed for videotape, the differences between traditional vernacular stories and videotape stories may grow increasingly marked. Videotape is making possible the "textualization" of ASL works performed by a flesh-and-blood signer. Just as an oral spoken story becomes text when it is put on paper, taking on some of the characteristics of the medium of the written page, so an ASL story becomes "text" on videotape, acquiring characteristics of (written) "textual" works and losing some of its oral or vernacular characteristics.

Loss of Interaction

In their study of performance, Carol Simpson Stern and Bruce Henderson observe that all oral storytelling is performative, not textual (i.e., not on paper).[18] As performance, ASL storytelling goes even further than mainstream storytelling because of the nature of ASL itself. Although the mainstream modern storyteller may use some gestures, body language, and mimicry, he or she usually relies primarily on the voice;[19] in contrast, the ASL storyteller not only tells what something looks like but also shows or enacts what it looks like, creating a small play in front of the viewers' eyes.

Storytelling also involves an interaction between storyteller and audience, or viewers, gathered together at a specific place and time. The storyteller does more than recite: he or she engages with those who have gathered to hear or watch. Many ASL storytellers go out of their way to interact with their viewers. For example, the late Stephen Ryan would make a "Hello everybody!" entrance and conclude a live storytelling session by waggishly fingerspelling "T-H-E E-N-D" in midair. In between, he would make comments and throw out asides to individual spectators. For example, during one storytelling session Ryan mentioned that a character was very much like his beloved wife, and by the way she's there in the room. "So, let's all give a big hand for the little lady!" he suggested, and then went on with his narrative. On the same occasion, Ryan narrated a highly interactive story of King Kong, who claps his hands joyfully after grabbing the young woman he loves—and inadvertently flattens her into a mess in his gigantic hands. He immediately called out for a handkerchief to wipe off the imaginary blood and gore. Very much caught up in the action, one of the spectators tossed him a handkerchief while everyone looked on in shared merriment. Seemingly heedless of the audience's reaction, Ryan fastidiously wiped his hands clean both on the handkerchief and on his well-worn denim jeans. This kind of interaction continued throughout the session. After the session, to the delight of everyone in the room, Ryan socialized with his audience.[20]

The viewers are usually not passive observers (as readers are often characterized) but active participants who keep their eyes on the storyteller and indicate with their body language that they are (or are not) following along. The storyteller in turn watches the spectators (as maintaining eye contact is particularly important in ASL storytelling), judges their reactions—yawning, restlessness, delight, engrossment, comments, questions—and responds by adjusting the story accordingly, perhaps adding a little humor or a personal touch to draw them back in. At moments of high drama, the storyteller makes sure of the spectators' rapt attention and plays the moment for all it is worth. In this way, the storytelling is the product not of one person but of both the storyteller and the audience or viewers.[21] Feedback—whether conscious or unconscious, whether deliberate or accidental—causes the storyteller to make major and minor adjustments. Thus, in contrast to the creative process in textual literature, whose author sits down alone to write a book or stands in isolation to narrate a story on videotape, the creative process in storytelling is collaborative, active, and ongoing.

A story that is told—especially in informal ASL storytelling—is quite different from a story that is written. The storyteller is physically present and there is no separation between what the storyteller is saying and the storyteller him- or herself. In contrast, written stories do away with the storyteller: we have only the words on the page, and behind them a disembodied persona that is often very vague. At the same time, written stories do away with the physically present audience. The result is that the individual readers (audience members) are more removed from the storyteller.

This removal of storyteller and audience has been part of the process of textualization in mainstream literature, but in ASL literature on videotape the process differs in one respect: the storyteller remains.[22] A mode of communication that uses the hands, arms, body, and face must have a person visible and communicating. Therefore, on videotape the ASL storyteller—though not always his or her whole body—can still be seen. Sometimes to provide a clearer view of the signing, the camera must zoom in closer to the storyteller, rendering only the torso visible. Still, the viewer never loses sight of the person telling the story, and thus ASL discourse on videotape largely avoids the divorce between author and text suffered by literature in print.

However, ASL literature on tape does lose the immediacy of the relationship between storyteller and audience, whose members have in effect disappeared. Usually the story preserved on film is taken out of context (or given no context) and adapted for the taping. No "audience" is involved, or at least none is visible; the storyteller has no viewers unless we take the camera to be representing people "out there," or count the cameraperson and prompter as an audience.

In the videotaped performances by Bahan and Supalla, the narrators stand pokerfaced and silent before a neutral backdrop before they commence signing. A Deaf American watching the tape may sense less of the accustomed engagement in this vernacular, interactive discourse. Many may not notice the reduction immediately because the two narratives are in themselves vastly entertaining. However, the absence of the real-life interaction characteristic of vernacular storytelling creates some artificiality and detachment that continue until the conclusion of each narrative, when both narrators break eye contact with the camera and stand motionless and expressionless until the video ends.

Viewers may be more fully engaged with Supalla's narrative and with its narrator because it is more straightforward than Bahan's allegorical animal fable. Supalla makes interjections from time to time that seem to be directed at imaginary viewers. Additionally, the camera zooms in a little closer to him during "Decent Living" than to Bahan during "Bird," making his facial expressions more readily visible. Because these techniques convey a stronger feeling that the narrator is relating to the viewer(s) personally, Supalla's narrative seems a bit more comfortable, immediate, and interactive than Bahan's. But as storytelling becomes professionalized and textualized, the distance between the storyteller and the audience always becomes greater.[23]

A New Permanence

A storyteller both responds to audience feedback and adjusts to the *kind* of audience that he or she is facing. For example, one story-teller in the Washington, D.C., area, Mike Kemp, has rendered "Cinderella" in many ways, in different contexts and for different viewers.[24] He doesn't adjust the story to take the audience's deaf or hearing status into account, but does modify his narrative to suit the audience's age range. For an audience of teenagers or adults, "I can get far-fetched in terms of how Cinderella dresses," Kemp says. "She can have a long gown or a pair of tight leather pants and a tight sweater that has 'I love you' signs all over." He might enter-tain children with a gentle Cinderella and a courtly Prince, or indulge adults with a more ribald version of the story.[25]

In an oral culture, storytellers and performers typically have available a stock of stories and other forms (such as folklore) that they can draw on at their convenience. A storyteller can adapt a story such as the Cinderella narrative to fit the viewers and the cir-cumstances, or he or she can imitate an earlier rendition by anoth-er storyteller. Original stories, too, become stock narratives and then can be imitated or modified by other storytellers. Every story-teller has his or her idiosyncratic delivery, so no two stories are ever alike. Moreover, because no one person is likely to reach every seg-ment of the population, other storytellers feel even more free to take another's story and render it to suit themselves, their circum-stances, and their viewers.

In such oral storytelling, stories are fluid, repeatable, variable forms.[26] Even the same story told the very next day by the same storyteller to the same audience will be rendered differently. Text or written literature, in contrast, has a permanence (although less so in this electronic age); it stays the same under all circumstances. Rather than adjusting the story to a particular audience, a writer labors to create one version that is the most imaginative and mas-terful to be published and distributed; all other versions (inferior "drafts") are discarded. Copyright protects this work once it is published; it is an original work of art, the property of one person or a publishing company.[27]

ASL narratives on tape have similar permanence and copyright protection, another change resulting from the process of textualization. Because they are preserved on videotape, Bahan's and Supalla's narratives become fixed, authoritative, artistic objects. Once a particular story is taped, every viewer will see precisely the same performance, which is held to be *the* story and valued as *the* definitive work. Presumably it was rehearsed and perhaps there were earlier takes, but the best work is preserved and no other variants are distributed. The resulting narratives thus become suitable models for others, though of such high quality that other storytellers might be discouraged from attempting the same stories.

Ben Bahan and Sam Supalla themselves have resisted this "inscribed in cement" quality that textualization threatens to bring to ASL stories. At their San Diego ASL Literature workshop in 1993, the two did everything possible to instill the idea that what they narrated on tape was not fixed but instead, like any vernacular ASL story, is available for imitation and adaptation. Workshop participants were encouraged to participate in the storytelling experience and to imitate and modify sections of "Bird of a Different Feather" however they wished. Furthermore, Bahan and Supalla renounced their copyright on the videotaped narratives (keeping it only for the accompanying workbook). The two men stressed that part of Deaf culture is the handing down of stories and their numerous variants and that they wished to see such "oral" transmission continue.

An Emphasis on the Individual

As noted above, when textualization separates the audience from the art form, leaving only the writer or the signer and his or her text, then storytelling becomes less a communal activity and more an individual enterprise. Rather than using traditional stories that are carriers of cultural mores and values, the writer or the signer on videotape tends to treat matters of personal importance, writing or signing out of his or her experiences, imagination, and needs as an individual. Such a focus on a single person is foreign to oral storytelling, whose stories are selected or composed to appeal to the community, to bring it closer together, to move it to action, and to inform it of outside affairs. As Stern and Henderson note, such storytelling conveys myths, religious tales, and history that tell the community what it is, how it should feel and think, and what it should do.[28]

Even though the narratives by Bahan and Supalla are not performed in a communal setting, they largely retain the communal function of oral storytelling. Both address the central issue of Deaf culture: living as a minority within the majority world. Bahan's animal fable concerns the often-bungling integrationist approach of mainstream American culture and Supalla's tale touches on general job discrimination. Indeed, Supalla's protagonist could represent the Deaf Everyman as he blithely kicks in the door and perseveres in the face of hardship. He is a cultural hero who faces up to the hardship and discrimination that many Deaf Americans experience and by doing so helps others gain employment. Yet he is not the lone hero of middle-class mainstream literature but a representative figure: *the* Deaf American hero. Thus Supalla's story is one that a majority of Deaf Americans would relate to and would want to have told to them again and again.

The Bahan narrative is also very popular with Deaf Americans as a whole. As a fable, it is a work that says more than it seems to say. Bahan is our Jester here, and his fable is a metaphor for the two-world condition of Deaf Americans. H. J. Blackhorn in *The Fable as Literature* comments that "a fable does not state; it shows."[29] Fable is occasioned; cultural conditions, either political or philosophical, make it possible or timely. Opinions may be clothed in the form of a fable to deceive or confuse the official mind, although the message is clear to its intended audience.[30] Bahan teases and entertains his viewers, but he effectively shows the familiar in a new light.

We should note that these two narratives are part of a series and that the tape contains *two* narratives, not one. Indeed, most of the ASL literature available on videotape is presented in the form of series and collections. Whether the presentations are narratives, autobiographies, poetry, or other art forms, we tend to have a set of this and a set of that. Rather than being the single, autonomous creation so typical of mainstream written literature, an ASL work is distributed as one of a collection of works or performances and thus presented in a manner more typical of vernacular discourse. The experience of watching a videotape set of ASL literature is much like observing a group of fairgoers interacting and having a high time—taking in now a ride, now a sideshow, all the while encountering a variety of people and behaviors. For instance, *ASL Storytime*, a collection of eight videotapes, features a multitude of American storytellers—female, male, black, white, Hispanic, Native American, Asian American, gay, straight, oral, mainstreamed, and Deaf children of Deaf parents—as well as a number of immigrants.[31] The collection emphasizes the community as both unique and diverse, not the solitary individual that is the focus of so much written literature.

By weakening the personal relationship between the storyteller and the audience, textualization reduces the immediacy of the storytelling experience. Instead of being a member of or a frequent visitor to the community, the writer or signer on videotape may well be a stranger, whose background, circumstances, and motivations are unknown. The Deaf community is comparatively small, and many of its members have met or at least heard of Bahan and Supalla; thus in viewing this particular videotape, not much intimacy is lost. But as more and more videotaped narratives and the like are produced, featuring artists who are not so well known, the feeling of being "one big family" may disappear. As the writer's or signer's relationship with a particular community weakens, his or her productions will lose immediacy and communal purpose.[32]

Increase in Aesthetic Play

As noted in the discussion of ASL poetry in chapter 8, literacy and its product (the printed text) enable us to go back and review what has been written as many times as we wish, an impossibility in purely oral cultures. Similarly, the writer can review his or her work and make changes while composing. In this way, textualization and professionalization bring more aesthetic play to storytelling. Before a live audience, the storyteller has an immediate purpose: to communicate and, usually, to communicate clearly. Left with only the text, the storyteller is inclined to polish the language and perhaps to go outside the usual rules of language and communication. As famed ASL storyteller Ella Mae Lentz puts it, artistic forms derive from standard forms "but they 'twist' or 'break' linguistic rules of standard forms. . . . Artistic forms are used chiefly for the expression of values, feelings, and ideas whether or not the addressee understands immediately. Standard forms are used for clear communication."[33]

Lentz differentiates between two kinds of ASL discourse: informal storytelling and more artistic ASL literature, which is often formal and professionalized. Storytelling that puts a premium on communicating clearly must use standard forms; but signers composing with videotape, no longer feeling the need to get everything across in one telling, will tend to play more with the language. They will become more interested in art for art's sake.[34]

That is not to say that ASL vernacular stories are simple and unartistic; in fact, they display much creativity and playfulness.[35] But what is intuitive in storytelling becomes conscious and contrived in text-based literature.[36] Indeed, as Deaf American artists have become more self-conscious and analytical about ASL (and the videotape medium as well), they have incorporated more deliberate aesthetic play in ASL discourse in recent years, giving many recent ASL works an "artful" or "literary" quality.

Increasingly, the *language* (and videotape) is not simply a transparent medium of storytelling but the focus of presentations. For instance, "A Little Dictionary of Slang" in *My Third Eye* is a demonstration of the properties of ASL; these include, according to one National Theatre of the Deaf performer, its capacity for a "condensation" in poetic forms not possible with English words. Another NTD performer demonstrates this quality by signing BLACK TREE SHADOW ON HOUSE. First he depicts a tree using his left hand and arm propped at the elbow on his right arm, which is held straight out at chest level and parallel to the ground. As the sun rises, the shadow of the tree lengthens and expands up the side of a house: the right hand becomes the shadow, moving to the left and upward.[37] This is more aesthetic play than meaningful communication.

Similarly, the narratives by Bahan and Supalla showcase ASL in all its beauty and versatility. The medium of videotape allows more deliberate aesthetic play along with more complexity and layering of meaning. Because the narrators can go back and revise the work, it becomes more of an artistic production. Indeed, the two Bahan/Supalla narratives are highly crafted, lengthy, and heavily symbolical. The Bahan narrative in particular is a finely crafted beast fable, basically allegory and effectively satire, summing up the political and social conditions affecting Deaf Americans as a minority group. It is a highly polished tale utilizing ASL aesthetics. The selection of the mighty eagle to represent members of the majority culture and the songbird to represent Deaf Americans requires more artful subtlety and planning than is usually the case in vernacular storytelling. And the symbolism extends beyond the outer layer of allegory. For instance, it is not just that the eagles represent hearing people and the songbirds Deaf Americans, but that the eagles are the lords of the skies and the earth, and the songbirds are its sensitive and artistic denizens. And suffusing this symbolism is the irony of using songbirds, noted for their singing, to represent deaf people who are not at all noted for singing or even for using basic speech.

The writer or signer taking advantage of the permanence of paper or videotape can indulge in the greater artistry and complexity that he or she finds pleasurable and challenging, confident that readers or viewers will be able to ponder and analyze the completed work by rereading and re-viewing it at length and in depth. For instance, Bahan adds layering and irony as well as additional symbolism to his story because he knows that his viewers will be able to replay the taped story. He knows they will be able to slow the tape down and stop it at will, as they endeavor to understand every nuance and every symbol. "Literature," whether of the mainstream or ASL variety, could not exist without this permanence of text. Contemporary literature in particular demands of its audience a back-and-forth review of text that has multilayered and hidden meanings. Thus, not only have Bahan and Supalla introduced ASL literature (specifically, ASL narrative) to the world, but they have also helped provide the impetus for ASL literary studies. Videotape permits conventional literary analysis of signed discourse, something that was not practical in the past.

Uniformity of Structure and Homogeneity of Content

Another feature of textualization, notes Walter Ong, is a move toward the more uniform and rigid narrative structure characteristic of conventional (written) literature.[38] Replaying the Bahan and Supalla tape, we can see that their productions are lengthy narratives containing few of the personal comments and digressions that often occur in the informal byplay between storyteller and live audience. Like commonplace written narratives, they are more conventional in structure; they exhibit a logical sequence of actions and have a more linear movement than does the more rambling and interactive vernacular ASL storytelling.

Often sequence is not of paramount importance in oral or vernacular ASL storytelling, because many of the audience or viewers already know the plot of the story, which is likely to be a variant of a traditional tale.[39] If they have not heard or seen a particular story, they most likely have at some time encountered a variant with a similar plot or narrative element. Therefore, both storyteller and audience take pleasure not so much in what happens in the story as in how it happens, enjoying the performance and the interaction. Indeed, as we have seen, storytelling presupposes a relationship between the storyteller and the spectators that often amounts to a process of co-creation. This relationship and the performance itself are more important than the story being told.

In addition, linear logic is not as important in traditional storytelling as in written texts because the shared knowledge among members of a community provide order and unity external to the story.[40] Relying on this shared knowledge, the storyteller often avoids explicit exposition in favor of implying, insinuating, and alluding. He or she may use vivid and concrete narrative detail (examples of people acting in such and such a way) stitched together without supplying an overarching framework. To outside observers, such seemingly haphazard narration comes across as episodic and disconnected; but the implicit links are clear to those within the culture. Therefore, vernacular storytelling often presents episodes from the "whole story"—many small plot segments whose resolution is not important—rather than a complete biography or account of events with transitional phrases to help the reader along.[41] Consider this "disjointed" narrative from *Bill Ennis: Live at SMI!*:

> My favorite . . . cat. I had a cat, this big. Bigger? This big. It was a tomcat and its name was "Nitty." It was born in the country: Staunton, Virginia. Gallaudet people brought it and gave it to us. Why call it "Nitty." Why not "K"? Right. Can't pronounce "K." How did I find out? I wish you told me. The person who told me was the little one, John Mark. John Mark has seven children. True! Six girls and one boy, the last one. Six darlings! The boy is six months old now and called Mark, Jr. From the baby we go all the way up to the oldest girl who is seventeen and in high school. The second oldest girl, LA or Leigh Ann, loves her aunt. She goes to her aunt and stays one week. Remember the cat Nitty? Her aunt decides to call it, "Here, kitty, kitty, kitty." I'm not using my voice. The cat may run here from Staunton, thirty miles away. The girl is fifteen, eleven? twelve? No, fourteen. She tells her aunt that if she calls the cat this way, it won't come. Uncle Bill always pronounces it "Nitty." She caught it somehow. Call "Nitty, nitty, nitty" and the cat will show up. You know what I mean. The cat can be awfully confused. With a "K," the cat will wonder, "Me?" A cat is very sensitive. On the other hand, when I use ASL with you, I zoom along, frequently go off the point, and mess it up. But it still works.[42]

This is not a straight narrative with a beginning, middle, and end. It appears choppy and incoherent because much information that one would expect in a written narrative is omitted. For instance, we are not told exactly how the Ennis family obtained the cat—not that the details are relevant.[43] Nor is it clear that John Mark is Ennis's brother. On paper the narrative seems full of gaps, digressions, and irrelevant information, and sadly lacking in transitions; but in performance it seems coherent and artistic to Deaf viewers. As soon as Ennis mentions "Nitty," the viewers immediately know that the narrative has something to do with "deaf speech," a favorite topic of Deaf Americans.[44]

In this way, informal ASL storytelling is more a visual and subjective experience than a presentation of objective facts or straight narrative. In a similar vein is the following English translation of Mary Beth Miller's "New York, New York" (which cannot do justice to her exuberantly visual story):

> I planned to stay one year, two years, stayed twenty years.
> I have black lungs. A lot of pollution, things flying
> around—*free* newspaper!—dirty stuff. A lot of people,
> bikes, and dogs. Dogs look like their owners. Must pick up
> poop. Good thing it's not elephant; dog not bad. A lot of
> noise. People become hard of hearing. All kinds of people,
> animals, all sizes and heights, some with boom boxes. Big
> man goes to steak lunch. Different people walking, differ-
> ent faces, get on subway. Hot, no A.C. there, worse than
> sardines in can, underarm smell at seven in the morning,
> then too tired, sick and hot to work. That's New York.
> You know what a ballet dancer looks like? Conductor
> below is always practicing and never sees the sun. Contrast
> woman dancer and male dancer with his big thighs. [Goes
> through a short performance.] People applaud lightly like
> rain on the palm, not like you shaking the house. The
> Metropolitan Opera House has a stage three football fields
> big and a curtain one mile long. There are five tiers of
> seats with the people in the cheap fifth tier using binocu-
> lars to see the big mouth on stage. Hearing are strange.
> [Miller mimics an opera singer getting ready to sing and
> then singing. She uses her hands to show the pitch like a
> dog baying.] When it's over, Bravo, bravo, bouquet, thank
> you, thank you. Very refined.[45]

This heteroglot vernacular performance is a lively, multifaceted discourse that avoids univocalism and purity of content. Rather than adhering to the principles of written narrative, the storyteller is the merry rogue playing with language and discourse structures, mixing them up, and even parodying and burlesquing them. This vital, interactive, unrestrained play leads to a performance that is more vigorous and less restricted than conventional narrative.

The comparison with the stories by Bahan and Supalla is telling. Both men render straightforward narratives and remain throughout in the role of the conventional narrator. They tell a story from beginning to middle to end and nothing else; they are on tape simply to render that story, which is a self-contained work. That well-crafted story is what matters, not the storyteller or the audience (or viewers). In producing this tape, Bahan and Supalla knew their two stories would be analyzed: that was their express purpose in adapting the stories for videotape dissemination. So they concentrate primarily on telling a story and not on entertaining their viewers (though of course in the process the viewers are entertained). Their approach is quite unlike that of the vernacular storyteller, who has no compelling reason to narrate a story straightforwardly from beginning to end, or indeed to tell a story and nothing else.

A vernacular storyteller revels in metamorphosis—switching from one role or format to another, from the functional to the artistic, from rudimentary stories to ASL art, from seriousness to hilarity.[46] Many of the other *Live at SMI!* videotapes illustrate this multifacetedness. The six entertainers/storytellers in the series tell stories, perform ASL art, and joke, sometimes singing and using rhythm. Some are more serious and earnest than others, or more concerned about serious and meaningful content and about being "artistic." Overall, however, they display a heterogeneity that is customary in the vernacular storytelling tradition and culture.

Bill Ennis: Live at SMI!, for example, opens very casually with "Dumbo." This ASL narrative, about a baby elephant who wants to fly but lacks the necessary self-confidence, begins with many digressive comments about Ennis and his family; yet it has profound implications for Deaf Americans as a whole. Ennis then tells of beginning school at a very early age and relates his experiences there, followed by the story of "Nitty" translated above. Intermixing with and succeeding each of these narratives is personal information frequently flavored with "low" details. The next narratives return to Ennis's childhood: first back at the school again, as a little boy at odds with the dorm supervisor over proper attire; next visiting his grandparents in the singsong "Mississippi Squirrel Revival" (discussed in chapter 4); and then back home, when his mother learns sign language and Ennis and his brother play Little League baseball. After performing slow-motion renditions of various players—catcher, pitcher, batter, and fielder—he changes sports but not speed, switching to basketball and track. The subsequent narrative from his boyhood has to do with the art of urinating into a toilet bowl and Ennis's lack of awareness of the noise he makes (see below). The performance closes with the singsong "St. Valentine's Day Massacre," two ABC story-poems, and a golfing piece in which Ennis enacts all the characters, including the golf ball, rounded off by a narrative about sign language interpreting. Ennis is playing the veritable Jester in a lengthy session of narratives, jokes, mimicry, and ASL art that includes songlike pieces and visual-kinetic language play.

Whereas the first installment of the ASL Literature Series features two homogeneous, straightforward narratives, the tape by Ennis presents a kind of small-scale vaudeville. The performance fuses and juxtaposes diverse forms (high and low), genres, and performance styles. Ennis is a versatile performer able to switch from personal reminiscence (storytelling), to ASL art, to jokes and riddles, to cultural enlightenment. The result is heteroglot and inclusive, with a commingling of two different modalities: the aural and the visual. His performance also intermixes two cultures and their rhetorical traditions in a carnivalesque hodgepodge of fiction and fact. The aesthetic and the didactic are either side by side or intermeshed in any given moment, scene, or performance. This tape highlights ASL discourse's inclusivity, its mix of the serious and comic. In Deaf American storytelling, the serious and comic often intermingle in a popular festive discourse that meets the requirements of collective performance and contemporary everyday needs and has little in common with conventional, classical Western literary practices.

Such inclusiveness and heterogeneity, with the concomitant intermixing of the serious and comic, were common in many cultural forms, including writing, until the eighteenth and nineteenth centuries. Then, neoclassicism took hold; and, as Olive Busby observes, the "intrusion" of the comic fool was no longer encouraged by "many writers whose taste and sense of propriety were outraged by the intrusion of the buffoon into the sphere of serious drama in flagrant defiance of classic precedent." She goes on to argue, however, that "to intermingle merry jests in a serious matter is no 'indecorum' but rather a more faithful representation of nature than drama that is wholly comic or wholly tragic."[47] Much Deaf American storytelling, with its carnivalesque discourse, provides just such a faithful representation.

This intermingling of the comical and the serious also reflects the requirement of oral presentations to "tell a good story." Writers of printed literature may and do keep the comical and serious apart, but performers have to find ways to maintain viewers' attention. As Sybil Rosenfeld says of the theater in the London fairs, popular taste "was conservative, 'clinging to the old tales.' . . . It demanded the ancient relief of comic interlude, revelling in swiftly alternating contrasts of marvelous feats and knockabout farce, fustian and slapstick. . . . It required an admixture of singing and dancing, so that all the elements of the Elizabethan jig (which was Fool entertainment) survived in the booths."[48] A long story can be a lot of work for the performer as well as hard on the eyes; but the mixing of the high and low provides physical, comic, and visual relief.

Sanitization of Textual Discourse

Farce, vulgarity, and foolishness are generally not encouraged in written literature. In fact, textualization often involves a sanitizing of narrative. In *The Preservation of Sign Language*, a 1913 film produced by the National Association of the Deaf, George Veditz signs with great dignity in English word order.[49] His deliberate signing reflects a common result of making a concerted effort to record, preserve, and disseminate sign language videotapes. Those venturing into the larger public arena naturally tend to refine and put a good face on ASL discourse. The somewhat sanitized discourse and body image seen here parallel what happened to literary texts in the eighteenth century: that is, the creation of a sublimated public body without smells, coarse laughter, and sexual organs.

A similar dynamic is at work in the videotape featuring Bahan and Supalla. They are well-groomed, well-behaved young men narrating two stories from Deaf culture that can benefit all, in "clean" versions that are appropriate for all ages. Although both stories are comic, this quality is kept within bounds and not allowed to veer off into farce and burlesque, as it could easily do if these narratives were part of a storytelling session in front of a small group. With an intimate crowd—the usual setting for vernacular storytelling—just about anything goes, especially when the viewers are adults in good spirits. However, with ASL literature on videotape, the performance is sanitized: the vulgar, low, jokey storytelling common in day-to-day ASL discourse is cleaned up and made decorous.

When a particular group of people come together to tell and retell stories, they generally touch on their everyday, personal concerns. There is talk both of high, dignified activities and of low, "vulgar" activities. The storyteller performing before a marginalized group is especially apt to turn to farce and burlesque—perhaps caricaturing members of the majority culture, especially authority figures, and making fun of their misunderstandings, misperceptions, and misconceptions. Moreover, since marginal groups themselves are often systematically identified with "low" aspects of existence (obscenities, excrement, dirt, etc.), the storyteller may well turn these elements to his or her comic advantage. In *Live at SMI!*, for example, Bill Ennis intermingles the vulgar and aesthetic graphically and happily:

> I dunno you have the same experience but I'm happy to tell you a story. I bare myself. Every block had a playground in New York. I went to play basketball on the street one time but had to take a break. It's time. Have to go. [He mimes the need to urinate.] The boys knew instantly what for and said for me to go on. I headed home. I wanted to make bubbles. I love bubbles. Bubbles! When I got home and into the bathroom, my mom was on the phone. I would try to urinate and make a perfect circle of bubbles. When I passed Mom on the way out, she reprimanded me. "Bill! You make too much noise! It's like a horse urinating on a flat rock." No one told me. She showed me, my *mother* showed me, where to do it in a

particular spot. It's hard to break a habit. But it takes
more skill to do it that way, more training. But when no
hearies are around, clap, yah!

This is not the kind of narrative that most parents would want told
to their young children, but in the context of adult viewers it is
both typical and highly appreciated.

Moreover, such narratives are typical for Deaf Americans
because ASL is inherently graphic. Its expressive body use and
imagery may appear vulgar from the viewpoint of conventional literature and society. In vernacular storytelling, the bathroom,
vomit, blood, acne, cigarette-flavored coffee, nostrils, ear hairs,
excrement, pregnancy, bed-wetting, and strange animals all crop
up, and often do so quite artistically. Consider the following narrative, in which Elinor Kraft, one of the *SMI Live!* storytellers,
describes an ocean cruise:

> At twelve midnight we are treated to a buffet on tables
> stretching from here all the way down to there. At the top
> are vegetables, salad, tomatoes, cucumbers, onions,
> pineapples—tables piled with food. There is a huge turkey
> with a full, rounded breast and detailed feathering that is
> made out of solid butter. I take a knife and slice off a dol-
> lop only to have a waiter inform me that it's not for use.
> It's just a sculpture, a pretty design. I try to return the
> dollop but that part of it is marred. Sorry. I didn't know. I
> fill up my plate with more food—meat, potatoes and cake.
> My plate becomes full. But a waiter takes my plate to my
> table and I start filling up another plate. Among the cakes
> are some designed to look like mice. The mouse cake is
> such a pretty cake I can't eat it. Then, in the middle of the
> table is an alligator. It's bread; French bread.[50]

This narrative is not in itself offensive or risqué. It is informative and at the same time amusing and physical in its imaging of
tables brimming and swimming with food. The turkey sculpture is
a particularly apt example of how Kraft bodies forth material
objects as she uses her own chest to depict the curved, full breast
and the detailed feathering. Moreover, Kraft shows what eating a
mouse-shaped cake entails, biting off the head and then gulping

down the body, with its tail disappearing into her mouth and down her throat. Going on a cruise may seem glamorous, as one imagines beautifully coiffed men and women dressing for dinner and remaining elegant at all times; yet Kraft focuses on the food, the gambling, and the physical injuries she endures, bringing it all down to a material, popular level. Starring in her description of the buffet are mice, a turkey, and an alligator. These animal images could hardly convey more tellingly the Bakhtinian linkage of feasting, animal life, and festivity.

In the narratives by Bahan and Supalla, we can see a conscious merging of the mainstream literary tradition and the indigenous storytelling tradition in Deaf culture. This deliberate interanimation, facilitated by the use of videotechnology, results in the vernacular storytelling being textualized—not surprisingly, as mainstream literature is after all a textual literature and videotape in ASL literature functions much like paper and pen do in written literature. With such textualization, ASL literature takes on many of the features of conventional, written literature. In this interanimation much is lost, but what is gained is increased artistry and complexity.

Notes

1. Ben Bahan and Sam Supalla, *Bird of a Different Feather and For a Decent Living*, ASL Literature Series, San Diego, Calif., Dawn Pictures/DawnSignPress, videocassette, 60 min., 1992.
2. Ben Bahan, conversation with author, December 1999.
3. E.g., see Umberto Eco, "The Frames of Comic 'Freedom,'" in *Carnival!*, ed. Thomas A. Sebeok, assisted by Marcia E. Erickson (Berlin: Mouton, 1984), 2.
4. Richmond Y. Hathorn, "Fable," in *The Encyclopedia Americana* (1998), s.v.
5. On African American Trickster tales, see John W. Roberts, *From Trickster to Bad Man* (Philadelphia: University of Pennsylvania Press, 1989), 42; on Coyote narratives, see Wolfgang Karrer and Hartmut Lutz, "Minority Literatures in North America: From Cultural Nationalism to Liminality," in *Minority Literatures in North*

America: Contemporary Perspectives, ed. Karrer and Lutz (New York: Lang, 1990), 11–64.

6. Ben Bahan, e-mail to author, February 1999.

7. Numerous storytellers have related stories about the 1940s, often driving home the point that in the war years many doors to steady employment were first opened to Deaf Americans. On that history, see John Van Cleve and Barry Crouch, *A Place of Their Own: Creating the Deaf Community in America* (Washington, D.C.: Gallaudet University Press, 1990); Robert M. Buchanan, *Illusions of Equality: Deaf Americans in School and Factory, 1850–1950* (Washington, D.C.: Gallaudet University Press, 1999).

8. Walter Ong, *Orality and Literacy: The Technologizing of the Word* (London: Methuen, 1982), 10.

9. Ruth Finnegan, *Literacy and Orality: Studies in the Technology of Communication* (Oxford: Blackwell, 1988), 88.

10. See especially Ong, *Orality and Literacy*, and Finnegan, *Literacy and Orality*.

11. Ong, *Orality and Literacy*, 2.

12. Ibid.

13. Arnold Krupat, *The Voice in the Margin: Native American Literature and the Canon* (Berkeley: University of California Press, 1989), 42.

14. Bill Ashcroft, Gareth Griffiths, and Helen Tiffin, *The Empire Writes Back: Theory and Practice in Post-Colonial Literatures* (New York: Routledge, 1989), 6.

15. In the late twentieth century the notion of "the canon" has come under attack from a number of fronts, as recent titles suggest: for example, see, *Multicultural Literature and Literacies: Making Space for Difference*, ed. Suzanne M. Miller and Barbara McCaskill (Albany: State University of New York Press, 1993); *Out There: Marginalization and Contemporary Cultures*, ed. Russell Ferguson, Martha Gever, Trinh T. Minh-ha, and Cornel West (Cambridge, Mass.: MIT Press, 1992); and Paul Lauter, *Reconstructing American Literature* (Old Westbury, N.Y.: Feminist Press, 1983).

16. These views are widely held; for example, see Ong, *Orality and Literacy*, 36–68. On the communal nature of storytelling in oral cultures, see p. 69.

17. Ben Bahan, "American Sign Language Literature: Inside the Story," in *Deaf Studies: What's Up*, conference proceedings, October 24–25, 1991, ed. Jackie Mann (Washington, D.C.: Gallaudet University, Continuing and Summer Studies, 1992), 153–66.

18. Carol Simpson Stern and Bruce Henderson, *Performance: Texts and Contexts* (New York: Longman, 1993).

19. Ruth Finnegan, *Oral Traditions and the Verbal Arts: A Guide to Research Practices* (New York: Routledge, 1992), 93. See also Bruce Rosenberg, *Folklore and Literature: Rival Siblings* (Knoxville: University of Tennessee Press, 1991), 27, 143, and Stern and Henderson, *Performance*, 14–15.

20. Stephen Ryan at "Deaf Comedy Night" at the International Express in College Park, Maryland, 1995.

21. Finnegan, *Literacy and Orality*, 88–124.

22. Ong, *Orality and Literacy*, 1–3.

23. Rosenberg, *Folklore and Literature*, 22–24.

24. Mike Kemp, e-mails to author, winter 1995 and fall 1999.

25. Mike Kemp, e-mail to author, October 1993.

26. See John Miles Foley, *Immanent Art: From Structure to Meaning in Traditional Oral Epic* (Bloomington, Ind.: Indiana University Press, 1991), 43.

27. See Finnegan, *Literacy and Orality*, 72; Rosenberg, *Folklore and Literature*, 160.

28. Stern and Henderson, *Performance*, 75.

29. Harold John Blackham, *The Fable as Literature* (Dover, N.H.: Athlone Press, 1985), 252.

30. Ibid., xviii.

31. *ASL Storytime*, prod. Department of Sign Communication, Gallaudet University, eight videocassettes, 60 min. each, 1991.

32. In interpreting the work of an unknown signer, we would have to make the same decisions as when faced with a text by an unknown writer: do research into the author's motivations and background (at the risk of becoming more interested in the individual than in the body of work), concentrate only on the tape or text itself, or choose some other approach.

33. Ella Mae Lentz, "Signs: Artistic/Storytelling," in *Gallaudet Encyclopedia of Deaf People and Deafness*, vol. 3, ed. John Van Cleve (New York: McGraw-Hill, 1987), 126.

34. Cf. Trinh T. Minh-ha, *Woman, Native, Other: Writing Postcoloniality and Feminism* (Bloomington, Ind.: Indiana University Press, 1989), 13–15.

35. Carol Padden and Tom Humphries mention that at the beginning of the twentieth century George Veditz, a leading early advocate of sign language, compared signing to a beautiful painting or sculpture. He

saw an order in how the parts came together, but he did not attribute this order to linguistic rules and the ability to use ASL grammar correctly. See *Deaf in America: Voices from a Culture,* ed. Padden and Humphries (Cambridge, Mass.: Harvard University Press, 1988), 62.

36. Ibid., 208.
37. *My Third Eye*, dir. J Ranelli, the National Theatre of the Deaf, 1971–72. Shown on WTTW-TV, Chicago, videorecording, 58 min., 1973.
38. Ong, *Orality and Literacy*, 40.
39. Foley, *Immanent Art*, 8–14.
40. Ibid., 38–40.
41. Viv Edwards and Thomas J. Sienkewicz, *Oral Cultures Past and Present: Rappin' and Homer* (Oxford: Blackwell, 1991), 196–98.
42. Bill Ennis, *Bill Ennis: Live at SMI!*, Burtonsville, Md., Sign Media, videocassette, 60 min., 1993.
43. We might note that Gallaudet students commonly hide pets in the dormitories. Then, when they are caught or when they graduate, they must find the animal a new home or take it to a shelter.
44. Because a nasal quality common in Deaf speech tends to turn the *k* sound to *n*, Deaf Americans would likely say "nitty" rather than "kitty."
45. Mary Beth Miller, *Mary Beth Miller: Live at SMI!*, Burtonsville, Md., Sign Media, videocassette, 60 min., 1991.
46. Franchot Ballinger, "Ambigere: The Euro-American Picaro and the Native American Trickster," *MELUS* 17 (1): 32–34.
47. Olive Mary Busby, *Studies in the Development of the Fool in the Elizabethan Drama* (Philadelphia: R. West, 1977), 5, 6.
48. Sybil Rosenfeld, *The Theatre of the London Fairs in the Eighteenth Century* (Cambridge: Cambridge University Press, 1960), 149.
49. George Veditz, *The Preservation of Sign Language*, n.p., National Association of the Deaf, videocassette, 15 min., [1913].
50. Elinor Kraft, *Elinor Kraft: Live at SMI!*, Burtonsville, Md., Sign Media, videocassette, 60 min., 1993.

Chapter

10

Conclusion

THE MOMENT when a society must contend with a powerful language other than its own is a decisive point in its evolution. This moment is occurring now in American society, which has only recently discovered American Sign Language and ASL literature. It has discovered that the rather complex gestures used by Deaf citizens are integral to a legitimate national language. Many things change under the pressure of this newfound polyglossia. As Mikhail Bakhtin notes, "Two myths perish simultaneously: the myth of a language that presumes to be the only language, and the myth of a language that presumes to be completely unified."[1] In American society, English is not the only language—nor for Deaf Americans is ASL the only language. Moreover, neither English nor ASL is completely unified; each is an aggregate of elements of other languages. So too is Deaf American literature a polyglossic aggregate of various discourse structures.

These multiple discourses that make up and stratify every language—differences of genre, register, sociolect, dialect, and their interpenetrations—constitute what Bakhtin calls *heteroglossia*.[2] In the dialogic interaction of these elements, Allon White explains, the high languages (as opposed to those associated with children, immigrants, deviant subcultures, etc.) "try to extend their control and subordinated languages try to avoid, negotiate, or subvert that control."[3] Thus, polyglossia is a heteroglossic phenomenon on the national level: a dominant language (English) seeks to exert control and another language (ASL) twists, squirms, tries to escape, and gets back at that control.

Such twisting, squirming, and jesting help make Deaf American literature an incredibly rich and multifaceted body of works. It is uniquely bicultural, bilingual, and bimodal—even trimodal. Many national literatures draw on both oral and literary traditions; so too ASL literature has an oral performative component rooted in traditional vernacular forms and a print component based on the aural language of the majority culture. But no other literature has a visual-kinetic component: a visual vernacular that enables ASL to create a visual literature, or *visuature*. This visuature has properties so far outside what is usually considered "linguistic" that only analogies with dance, graphic art, cinema, and drama can do it justice.

Every literature is evolving, but Deaf American literature is experiencing changes that are particularly numerous and significant. In a way, it is less than half a century old, for ASL, after generations of suppression, first achieved recognition as a legitimate language in the 1960s. The vernacular of its visual component, too, is comparatively new, dating to the early nineteenth century (and Old French Sign Language, from which it borrowed heavily, is just a century older). However, its visuature—its ASL literature—is working to catch up with literature in English. More and more Deaf Americans are creating increasingly sophisticated and artistic productions, and eagerly making use of videotechnology both to record and distribute and also to compose these works. With the help of new technology, Deaf Americans are experimenting with innovative graphic enhancements, both live and recorded, as Ella Mae Lentz's *Treasure* video demonstrates.[4]

Another way in which ASL literature is evolving is in its gradual transition from the "oral" to the "literary," a transition undergone by many literatures before it. Until quite recently, there was a sharp division between print literature and ASL "deaflore," the culture's traditional vernacular productions. Yet the burgeoning ASL video-tape literature now has assumed many of the properties of a print literature. How far will this trend go? As more ASL videotape literature is produced, will deaflore diminish or even vanish? Watching this evolution in action helps scholars better understand the world-wide transition from orality to literacy in the distant past—and also, ironically, today's growing orality, fostered by advances in telecommunications. The evolution in ASL literature is momentous, but there should be a concerted effort to locate and record the traditional ASL forms before and if they disappear.

We can see promise in where Deaf American literature is going: more masterful and artistic use of ASL, more use of videotapes, and more use of traditional vernacular forms in composing artistic works. Perhaps if vernacular forms are more widely distributed, more Deaf Americans will utilize them as a basis for composing increasingly complex works. As its sophistication and complexity grow, Deaf American literature may become more like a written literature and lose its vernacular qualities. Deaf American literature is likely to become a complex, sophisticated, and "artistic" literature.

The Deaf community itself is coping with two contradictory trends. On the one hand, advanced technology is making it increasingly possible for deaf people to communicate without the need for fluent English. A video relay service is now in the experimental stages, and software programs can automatically correct many errors in English. There are vocalizers being developed that may be able to convert a deaf person's writing or speech to fluent written or spoken English. Greater numbers of interpreters are being hired by businesses and schools. At least one university in the northeast no longer requires written compositions in its English courses, allowing instead an interpreter to translate a Deaf student's signing into English. As such accommodations become more widespread, Deaf Americans appear to be achieving successful integration into American culture. The spread of literature on tape may diminish the immediacy of renditions and the interaction between teller and viewer. ASL literature today is an art form driven by its culture, but this may not always be the case.

On the other hand, powerful influences are endangering the Deaf community and along with it ASL and ASL literature. Advancing technology applied to and not for Deaf Americans, such as cochlear implantation and bioengineering, is having a staggering effect. Mainstreaming is tearing at the fabric of the Deaf community as fewer children are going to schools for the deaf and being exposed there to ASL; instead, they are being scattered in public schools, never with very many in any one place. Some of these children, if their hearing loss is not severe, do not come within a mile of a school for the deaf or see any kind of sign language. Others may have sign language interpreters but no exposure to the Deaf community and to the collective, fluent use of ASL. Many of these youngsters, in a linguistic regression to the 1960s and 1970s, are therefore using a kind of manually coded English. To make matters worse, many Deaf adults have been drawing together into smaller groups and watching cable at home. As those more skilled in ASL gather in on themselves, other deaf children and adults will find scrambling for contacts in the Deaf community even more difficult to locate than in the past. Many of them will not even make the effort, increasing the danger that fewer deaf people will use ASL very fluently.

As they splinter into little groups, Deaf Americans may gather less often for "carnival" with its intertwining and competing social structures and discourses. The Deaf community has long been unique in retaining carnival as a vital part of cultural life. Carnival by its nature is not just a party or a festival; it is the counterculture of the dominated.[5] It offers a different view of the world—one from below—and makes possible the symbolic overthrow of oppressive social structures. It helps demystify all forms of dogmatism and oppression: aurality, patriarchy, and so on. To be sure, civic festivals also display conservative practices that maintain the status quo; but those exist beside the subversive and festive participation of the populace that is carnival. Such gatherings have nearly vanished from mainstream American culture, reduced to a few scattered rallies and weekend festivities that no longer function as a collective cleansing.

Rather than drawing together the society as a whole, carnival today gathers together only smaller groups (such as the Hispanic and gay communities and their discourses), who draw indirectly and symbolically on the soul of carnival to register their opposition to and criticism of the mainstream. As we saw in chapter 3, carnival has played an even more vital role for Deaf Americans than for other marginalized minorities: as a visually oriented people, they need to gather together to keep their visual vernacular and culture in force. But as the trends enumerated above continue, the Deaf American carnival may disappear. Fewer Deaf Americans may go to state conventions; fewer Deaf American storytellers will feel the need to mediate for and guide this less cohesive community.

Carnival may already be starting to disappear, replaced by the more personal and artistic works of Clayton Valli, Ella Mae Lentz, Peter Cook, and many others. The carnivalesque may just become—may already be—a literary echo. This is thus the right time to look at Deaf literature: where it was, where it is now, and where it is going.

Will ASL and ASL literature thrive? Or will the language become endangered, so that a small group must make a concerted effort (perhaps supported by the government, as has happened with the successful revival of Welsh) to prevent its disappearance by ensuring that it is taught in schools? We might imagine a few schools and colleges beginning to teach ASL at every level, instead of or along with English. Along with this instruction would be exposure to traditional ASL art forms and rhetoric.

Perhaps this small community, aided by new technologies, will enjoy a new sense of freedom: no longer forced to learn English, Deaf people will be able to remain in easy contact with one another via telecommunications. As television channels multiply, some will become available for the use of Deaf Americans; a future national channel could nurture cultural identity and cultural forms including ASL and its literature. Both vernacular forms and more sophisticated ASL literature would gain exposure, but we should expect the literature to become less of a minority literature.

The end of carnival would certainly not mean the end of Deaf American literature, but it could end the use of vernacular and oral techniques so important in the literature's current form. As the impact of the two-world situation of Deaf Americans becomes less powerful and "oppression" by the hearing majority less frequent,

Deaf American literature will no longer need to negotiate between English and ASL, between hearing and Deaf cultural norms. "Deaf literature" may come to refer more fittingly to literature *by* Deaf Americans rather than to a literature *of* Deaf America.

Notes

1. M. M. Bakhtin, *The Dialogic Imagination: Four Essays*, ed. Michael Holquist, trans. Caryl Emerson and Michael Holquist (Austin, Tex.: University of Texas Press, 1981), 68.
2. Ibid., 262–63.
3. Allon White, *Carnival, Hysteria, and Writing: Collected Essays and Autobiography* (New York: Oxford University Press, 1993), 137.
4. Ella Mae Lentz, *The Treasure*, dir. Lynnette Taylor, prod. Cheri Smith, Ken Mikos, and Ella Mae Lentz, n.p., In Motion Press, video-cassette, 60 min., 1995.
5. Robert Slam, *Subversive Pleasures: Bakhtin, Cultural Criticism, and Film* (Baltimore: Johns Hopkins University Press, 1989).

Index

Abbé de l'Epée, 38, 48

ABC story-poems, 6, 12, 27–28, 55–58, 92, 110

Academic conferences, 35

Acting, 62, 113

Adapting mainstream art forms, 116

Adventures of Huckleberry Finn, 128, 129

Aesthetic play, 186–89. *See also* Language play

Aesthetics: classical, 90, 178; procedural, 54, 156

African American literature, 2, 11; animal fables in, 175; and authorization of texts, 127; oral nature of, 20; and playing the dozens, 54; polyglossic nature of, 8; Trickster in, 9

Alice in Deafinity, 106

Alphabet, English, 27–28, 55–58

Ambulatory writings, 129–30

American School for the Deaf (Hartford, Conn.), 5

American Sign Language (ASL), 3; advantages of, 59–65; artistic use of, 7, 157; body in, 19, 26, 45; diglossic nature of, 6; recognition of, 6–7, 52, 80, 202; status in nineteenth and early twentieth centuries, 5; unwritten nature of, 4; as visual-kinetic vernacular, 18, 19, 58, 91, 122, 202. *See also* Deaf American literature; *headings beginning with "ASL"*

Animal fables, 175–76, 185, 188

Architectural concepts in ASL art, 61–62, 155–57, 165, 167–68

Aristophanic Old Comedy, 134

Asian American Literature, 2, 20

ASL. *See* American Sign Language

ASL Literature Series, 8, 174, 193

ASL novel, 121–46. *See also Islay* (Bullard)

ASL poetry, 7, 154–72; communal function of, 168–70; examples of contemporary poetry, 159–68; rhythm, rhyme, and tempo, 161, 165–66

ASL Storytime, 186

Audience participation. *See* Spectator participation

Auerbach, L., 84

Authorization of texts, satires on, 127

Babcock, B., 139
Bahan, B., 12, 52; "Bird of a Different Feather," videotaped storytelling by, 49, 174–77, 182, 184–85, 188, 192, 194–95, 197; on communal nature of storytelling, 185; as a humorist, 26; on importance of storyteller to story, 84; as narrative storyteller, 8, 13, 140; on orality, 179; on permanence of stories, 184
Bakhtin, M.: on carnivals, 10, 17, 21–22, 32–33, 93, 132; on challenging authority, 23–24, 47; on degradation in comic activities, 84–85, 89, 90; festive critique of, 101; on folk humor, 24–25, 87–88; on the grotesque body, 89, 105, 132; on heteroglossia, 201–2; on light associated with carnival, 48; on literary and nonliterary modes of expression, 41, 54–55; on novels, 127–28; on polyglossia, 8, 92, 201; on spectator participation, 40, 111
Baldwin, K., 6
Baldwin, S., 112, 116
Ballard Literary Society, 79, 107
Bangs, D.: and collaboration in ASL art, 111; and Deaf American drama, 7–8, 105–6; and staging of ASL theater, 115. *See also A Deaf Family Diary; Institution Blues*
Barliowek, A., 70
Beowulf, 149

Bergman, E., 3; *Tales from a Clubroom,* 42, 97, 100, 141
Biculturality, 3–4, 10–11. *See also* Two-world condition of Deaf Americans
Bienvenu, MJ, 26, 61
Bill Ennis: Live at SMI!, 190–92, 195–96
"Bird of a Different Feather." *See* Bahan, B.
"The Bison Song," 67, 80
"The Black Cat" (Graybill), 81–82, 84–86, 92
Black English, 54
"Black Hole: Color ASL" (Rennie), 166–68
Blackhorn, H. J., 185
Body: Deaf concept of, 91–93; and the grotesque, 24, 86–87, 131–34; and meaning, 83–84; middle class's concept of, 89–91, 194; in song and music, 65–66; use in ASL, 19, 26, 45, 83–87, 196
Body politic, 46–47
Bowling tournaments, 10, 35
Bragg, B., 3, 7, 52; *Tales from a Clubroom,* 42, 97, 100, 141
Bragg, L., 18, 149
Bragg, W., 106–7
Bristol, M., 97, 99
Bullard, D., 3. *See also Islay* (Bullard)
Burlesque, 70–75, 86, 195
Busby, O. M., 26, 193–94
"Butterfly," 156–57

California State University at Northridge, 97
Carmel, S., 6
Carnal relations stories, 57
Carnivals, 10, 106; Deaf American literature in context of,

17–31, 116–17; Deaf culture and, 32–51, 204–5. *See also* Culture, centers of
Carroll, L., 58–59
Cat Spanking Machine (Mow), 97
"Cave" (Valli), 162, 163–65, 168
Characterization, 63, 139–43
Charles Krauel: A Profile of a Deaf Filmmaker (film), 66
Chaucer, G., 149
Chicago Silent Dramatic Club, 107
Children of a Lesser God (film), 113
Chinese American Literature. *See* Asian American Literature
"Cinderella" (Kemp), 183
Cinematic concepts in ASL art, 61–62
Circus of Signs, 27
Classical aesthetics, 90, 178
Clerc, L., 6
Cochlear implants, 165, 168, 204
Cokely, D., 122, 126–27
Collaboration in ASL art, 64–65, 110–15
Comic discourse, 87–88. *See also* Humor
"Coming into the light" theme of the Deaf community, 48–49
Commedia dell'arte style productions, 116
Communal function of ASL art, 168–70, 184–86
Community, centers of, 32–51, 99
Conferences, academic, 35
Conley, W., 3, 97
Content and delivery in ASL art, 53–59, 70
Cook, P., 12, 205

Copyright, 183–84
Counterfeits (Mow), 97
"The Cowboy Story" (Miller), 67–69
Cultural encyclopedias, 104–5, 112
Culture, centers of, 32–51, 104–5, 131, 204–5. *See also* Carnivals
"Curious Circus," 43

Daniels, B., 97
DawnSignPress, 48–49, 174
Deaf American literature: characterization in, 63, 139–43; definition of, 2–3, 10–13; evolutionary changes in, 202–3; forms of, 39–48, 185–86; future of, 201–6; historical development of, 5–8; literary criticism of, 9, 11, 188–89; and orature, 17–31, 40–41; permanence of, 173–200; shared characteristics with other literatures, 3–5; transmission of, 41–42, 43–44; visual-kinetic nature of, 7, 202. *See also headings starting with* "ASL"
Deaf Americans: body concept of, 91–93; centers of culture for, 32–51, 104–5, 131, 204–5; English language and literature instruction for, 3, 5–6, 20–21, 79–80; identity issues of, 36–39, 104; impact of technology on, 177, 203–4; perceptions of, by mainstream society, 101, 136, 141; preferences in art forms, 116; relation to printed English, 84. *See also* Biculturality; Two-world condition of Deaf Americans

Deaf children: and fingerspelling
games, 60; schools for, 5, 37,
48, 78–80, 204
Deaf culture: and carnivals,
32–51, 204–5; festivals in,
25–26, 34–36; identity issues,
36–39; mobility in, 34–36, 38,
129–31
Deaf education and English
instruction, 3, 5–6, 20–21,
79–80
Deaf Expo (conference), 35
A Deaf Family Diary (Bangs), 8,
49; collaboration in, 112–13;
Deaf culture in, 97, 100, 102;
ensemble acting in, 113; high-
low discourse in, 110; staging
of, 115
Deaflit. *See* Deaf American litera-
ture
Deaflore, 6, 202–3
Deafology 101 (Glickman), 44–46
Deaf President Now movement,
7, 47
Deaf speech, 191
"DeafTheatre Showcase," 115
Deafula (film), 100
Deaf Way (conference), 10,
33–34, 36, 42–43, 47–48
Deafywood (Maucere), 97
Decorum, 22–24, 127, 131–34,
194–97
Degradation and regeneration,
84–87, 89–91, 134–35
DeLap, J. *See Institution Blues*
Delivery and content in ASL art,
53–59, 70
Dematerializing the word, 87–88
Diglossia, 6
Discourse: carnivalesque, 24–26,
39–48, 78, 86, 193–94;
comic, 87–88; Deaf American,
10–11, 25–26, 179–97; high

versus low, 63–64, 91–92,
109, 128; official or public,
90; textual, 194–97
Discourse structures, 21, 191,
201
Dissemination. *See* Transmission
of ASL productions
Double-voicedness, 29, 54–55,
72, 101
Douglas, M., 47
Dr. Jekyll and Mr. Hyde, 96
"Drag Racing" (Ennis), 55–57
Drama, 7–8, 42, 96–120; Greek,
98–99, 104, 149; scope of
Deaf drama, 13
Dramatic poetry, 149
Dramatists, Deaf, 110–13
"Dumbo" (Ennis), 192

Eastman, G., 3, 12; *Sign Me
Alice,* 12, 13, 38, 97, 100,
113
Eddic poems, 149
Eliade, M., 47
Elinor Kraft: Live at SMI!,
196–97
Eliot, T. S., 150–52
Emerson, R. W., 87
English language and literature: in
ABC story-poems, 28; in ASL
literature, 7, 53–59, 122–26;
Deaf Americans' relation to
printed, 15n13, 84; dematerial-
izing of, 87–88; instruction in,
3, 5–6, 20–21, 79–80; struggle
with ASL, 80, 202
Ennis, B., 52, 63; *Bill Ennis: Live
at SMI!,* 190–91, 195–96;
"Drag Racing," 55–57;
"Dumbo," 192; "Mississippi
Squirrel Revival," 73–75, 192;
"Nitty," 190, 192; "St. Valen-
tine's Day Massacre," 193

Ensemble acting, 113
Ethnic writers, 2
Eye contact, 73, 82, 115–16, 169, 181

Face-to-face communication, 4, 19, 36, 129
Fairmount Theater of the Deaf, 7, 27, 106
Falling on Hearing Ears (Conley), 97
Farce, 63, 195
Feminization of Deaf culture, 101
Festivals, 10, 131, 204–5; Deaf culture and, 34–36. *See also* Carnivals
Film concepts in ASL art, 61–62
Fingerspelling, 55–58, 60, 70
Fingers That Tickle and Delight (Zola), 27
Finnegan, R., 177
Flynn, J. W., 5
Folk humor, 24–26, 87–88. *See also* Humor
Folklore, 6, 20
Fool in mainstream society, 135–39. *See also* Jester; Trickster's role in literature
Footlight Fever, 106
"For a Decent Living" (Supalla), 174, 176–77, 182
Frost, R., 148, 162–63, 166
Frye, N., 59, 134, 135, 139

Gallaudet, T., 6
Gallaudet University: Deaf President Now movement, 7; and Deaf Way, 33; English and ASL instruction, 20–21, 79–80; performances at, 12, 38, 70, 96–97; student performances, 27, 107; *Telling Stories,* 42, 106; "The Bison Song," 67, 80; "The Tower Clock," 154; and transmission of ASL productions, 44; and vaudeville-like productions, 107
Gallaudet University Press, 44
Gates, H. L., 9, 10, 11
Glickman, K., 44–46
Graybill, P., 52; as ASL poet, 13; on collaboration, 113; and Deaf American drama, 7–8; "Liberation," 159–62, 168; *Poetry in Motion,* 148; and spectator participation, 114, 115; "The Black Cat," 81–82, 84–86, 92; "*The World According to Pat,*" 80–82, 84, 112; "Yankee Doodle Dandy," 81
Greek drama, 98–99, 104, 134, 149
Greek views of poetry, 147

Haiku, 80, 148
Hall, Stephanie, 19
Hall, Stuart, 86
Hamlet, 42
Hand in Hand, Foot in Mouth (Daniels), 97
"Hands" (Valli), 162, 165–66, 168
Hands, use of, 59–60, 158–59
Handshapes, 158–59; and ABC story-poems, 27–28, 55–58; in "Black Hole," 168; in "Butterfly," 157; in "The Cowboy Story," 69; in "Liberation," 161; in *Poetry in Motion,* 60
Harlequin figures, 59
Haunted house stories, 57

Havelock, E. A., 19
Hazards of Deafness (Holcomb), 26
The Hearing Test (Conley), 97
Hearing theater, 107
Henderson, B., 20, 87, 102, 180, 185
Heroes and heroines, 113, 135–39, 185
Heteroglossia, 201–2
High art, 97–99, 116, 178–79
High diver story, 61
High versus low discourse, 88, 91–92; in "The Black Cat," 86; in drama, 109; in novels, 128; and sanitization of textual discourse, 194–97; in "Sign Language Class," 63–64
Hispanic Literature, 2–4, 8
Holcomb, R., 26
Home, desire for, 36–39, 124, 134
Homogeneity, 189–94
Humor, 24–26, 70–75. *See also* Comic discourse
Humphries, T., 38

Identity issues of Deaf Americans, 36–39, 104
I Didn't Hear That Color (Daniels), 97
Imagist poetry, 148
Inside out, logic of, 24
Institution Blues (Bangs and DeLap), 8, 13, 49, 97; collaboration in, 64; as cultural encyclopedia, 104; Deaf culture in, 99–100, 102; ensemble acting in, 113; identity issues in, 37; Literary Night in, 80, 85, 92; staging of, 96, 115; tableaux in, 80, 110

Interanimation between cultures and languages, 55, 75, 80–81, 92, 122–26, 197
I See the Moon (Verhoosky), 97
Islay (Bullard), 12, 13, 39, 121–46; characterization, 139–43; comparisons with other picaresque novels, 126–31, 139, 143–44; decorum ignored by, 131–34; festive criticism of, 143–44; hero in, 135–39; intermixing of ASL and English in, 122–26; mainstream narrative tradition undermined by, 126–31; moral tone and, 134–35; two-world milieu of, 126–39
Italian language, 21
"It's Cabaret," 43

"Jabberwocky" (Malzkuhn), 58–59
Jefferson Memorial, 89
Jester, 43; in ABC story-poems, 27–28; Bahan as, 176, 185; Ennis as, 193; as literary critic, 9, 11–12; and metadiscourse, 29, 117; Miller as, 73; role in Deaf American literature, 13, 26–29; subversiveness of, 137. *See also* Fool in mainstream society; Trickster's role in literature
Jollity Club, 107

Kannapell, G., 66
Kansas School for the Deaf, 80–81
Kemp, M., 183
King of Hearts, 42
Kraft, E., 196–97
Krauel, C., 66

Language play, 53–59, 187. *See also* Aesthetic play
Latin language, 21
Laughter, 26, 44–48
Lefebvre, H., 98, 114
Lentz, E. M., 7, 52, 187, 205; *Treasure,* 202
l'Epée, Charles-Michel, abbé de, 38, 48
Letters from Heaven (Mow), 97
"Liberation" (Graybill), 159–62, 168
Light: in ASL art, 70, 109; as symbol in Deaf community, 48–49
Literacy, 18–21; history of, 20; versus orality, 4, 87, 177–79
Literary canon, 2, 18, 178–79
Literary criticism, 9, 11–12, 188–89
"Literary Night," 12, 13, 27, 78–95
Literature of minority cultures. *See specific type (e.g.,* African American Literature, Hispanic Literature, *etc.)*
"A Little Dictionary of Slang," 187
Longfellow, H.W., 80, 85, 92
Lord, A. B., 19
Lowman, R., 3, 12, 148
Low versus high discourse, 88, 91–92; in "The Black Cat," 86; in drama, 109; in novels, 128; and sanitization of textual discourse, 194–97; in "Sign Language Class," 63–64

Machalski, M., 42
"Magic Night and Roving Magician," 43
Makeup skit, 64
Malzkuhn, E., 58–59

"Manifest," 109
Manually coded English, 39, 53, 80
Martha's Vineyard deaf community, 5
Marx Brothers, 65, 138
Mary Beth Miller: Live at SMI!, 59–60, 62–63, 67–69, 70, 191
Maryland School for the Deaf, 12
Maucere, J., 97
McKinney, C., 70
Meaning in ASL art, 53, 55, 83, 160–61, 164, 167
Metadiscourse, 29, 117
Middle Ages, 21–26, 32–35, 71, 149; carnivals in, 10, 32–33; educative nature of fairs, 34; folk forms and activities, 23–26, 88; languages used, 21
Middle class's concept of the body, 89–91
Middle of Nowhere (Verhoosky), 97
"The Midnight Ride of Paul Revere," 80, 85, 92
Miles, D., 7, 112; "Seasons," 80
Miller, M.B., 52, 70–73; "The Cowboy Story," 67–69; *Mary Beth Miller: Live at SMI!,* 59–60; "The Mouth Story," 62–63; "New York, New York," 191; "Sign Language Class," 63; "The Star-Spangled Banner," 70–72
Miller, S., 130
Mime, 42, 43, 62
Mimicry, 62–63, 87
Minority literatures, 2, 11, 13, 20, 37, 175
Mirror skit, 64–65
Miss Deaf America pageant, 34

"Mississippi Squirrel Revival" (Ennis), 73–75, 192
Mobility of Deaf community, 34–36, 38, 129–31
Model Secondary School for the Deaf, 43
Moscow Theatre of Mime and Geste, 42
Mothers, deaf, 142–43
Motion in ASL art, 70, 83–84
"The Mouth Story" (Miller), 62–63
Mow, S., 97
Multidimensionality in ASL art, 60–64
Multifaceted discourse, 40–44, 191–92
Multifunctionality in ASL art, 60–64
Mundus inversus of carnival, 22–24, 102–3
Music in ASL art, 65–72
"My Country 'Tis of Thee," 70
My Eyes Are My Ears, 106
"My Favorite Old Summer House" (Valli), 168
My Third Eye, 12; collaboration in, 111–12; as cultural encyclopedia, 104; ensemble acting in, 113; "A Little Dictionary of Slang," 187; "Manifest," 109; popularity of, 116; "Promenade," 108; "Side Show," 27, 101–3, 109, 112; spectator participation in, 115; tableaux in, 49, 110; two-world condition of Deaf Americans in, 100–101; vaudeville-like nature of, 13, 97, 105, 108–9

National Association of the Deaf (NAD), 10, 34, 44; *The*

Preservation of Sign Language, 194
National Technical Institute for the Deaf (NTID), 97, 105–6
National Theater of the Deaf, 27, 91, 107–10; *King of Hearts,* 42; *My Third Eye,* 49, 97, 100–101, 108, 111–12, 116; *Parade,* 97, 108, 116; *Parzival,* 108
Native American Literature, 2–5, 8, 149, 175
"New York, New York" (Miller), 191
"The Night of 100 Stars," 42
"Nitty" (Ennis), 190, 192
Novel, 127–28; ASL novel, 121–46. *See also Islay* (Bullard)
"Now I lay me down to sleep" prayer, 150
NTID. *See* National Technical Institute for the Deaf

Oedipus, 42
Old French Sign Language, 5, 202
Ong, W., 19–20, 151, 154, 177–78, 189
Orality, 4, 18–21, 87, 177–79
Orature (oral literature), 4, 178–79; of Deaf American literature, 17–31, 53–54; history and effect of, 18–21; poetry, 148–54. *See also* Storytelling

Padden, C., 38
Panara, R., 106
Parade, 97, 108, 112, 116
Parker, A. A., 143–44
Parodies, 44–48; Ennis's use of, 73–75; Middle Ages, 25, 88
Parry, M., 19
Parzival, 108

Pauses in communication, 72–73
Peddlers, 140–42
Perez Firmat, G., 22, 92, 106
Performative art forms, 41–42, 82, 149–50, 156–57, 180
Phantom of the Opera, 42
Philippine Theatrical Group, 42
Picaresque novels, 126–31, 139, 143–44
Planet Way Over Yonder (Ryan), 38–39
Playfulness, 23–24, 26, 72, 186–89
Playing the dozens, 54
Plays. *See* Drama
Playwrights in ASL theater, 97, 110–13
Poe, E. A., 81–82, 92
Poetry, 147–72; Greek views of, 147; oral, 148–54; rhythm and rhyme in, 66, 150–51; Western poetry's development, 148–54. *See also* ASL poetry
Poetry in Motion (videotape series), 60, 148, 168–69, 174
Polyglossia, 8, 10, 80, 92, 201
Postlingual deafness, 79
The Preservation of Sign Language (film), 194
Procedural aesthetics, 54, 156
"Promenade," 108

Rabelais, F., 90
Ranelli, J., 112
Regeneration, degradation and, 84–87, 89–91, 134–35
Rennie, D.: as ASL poet, 13; "Black Hole: Color ASL," 166–68; *Poetry in Motion,* 60, 148

Residential schools, 37, 78–80, 204
Reunions, 10, 35
Rhythm and rhyme, 150–51; in ASL, 65–70, 75, 157, 161, 165–66
Romero, E., 106
Rosenberg, B., 149
Rosenfeld, S., 194
Rourke, C., 138
Rutherford, S., 6, 7, 27
Ryan, S., 27, 83, 180–81; *Planet Way Over Yonder,* 38–39

Sacks, O., 61–62
"St. Valentine's Day Massacre" (Ennis), 193
Sanitization of textual discourse, 194–97
Satires, 26, 44–48, 128–29
Saturday Night Dramatics Club, 107
Schools for the deaf, 5, 204; history of, 48, 78–80; identity issues of students, 37
School superintendents, deaf, 142
Searing, L., 3, 148
"Seasons" (Miles), 80
senza Parole (theater company), 42
Shakespeare, W., 109
"Side Show," 27, 101–3, 109, 112
Signed English, 6
Signing Exact English, 70
"Sign Language Class" (Miller), 63
Sign languages: Old French, 5, 202; oral language compared with, 19; Signing Exact English, 70. *See also* American Sign Language (ASL)

Sign Me Alice (Eastman), 12, 13; and the collective as hero, 113; Deaf culture in, 97, 100; identity issues in, 38

SignRise Cultural Arts (community theater), 49, 64, 111, 115

SignWave (performing ensemble), 43

Smith, L., 3

Social structures, 21, 98

Sollars, W., 37, 104, 105

Song in ASL art, 65–72

Sonnenstrahl, S., 36

Spectator participation, 46, 54, 114–15, 189; during carnival, 40, 111; lack of in mainstream literature, 98, 152; as literary criticism, 11; loss of interaction in, 180–82, 186

Spinks, C. W., 73

Staging of ASL theater, 114–15, 116

Stallybrass, P., 34, 47, 89, 90, 104–5

The Stand (television mini-series), 101

"Stars of Mime," 43

"The Star-Spangled Banner," 70–72

Statutes, classical, 89

Stern, C.S., 20, 87, 102, 180, 185

Storytelling, 3, 11, 179; animal fables in, 175–76, 185, 188; at festivals, 36; characterization in, 140; episodic nature of, 130, 189–94; individualization of, 184–86; loss of interaction in, 180–82; modalities of, 83–87; and permanence of stories, 53–54, 183–84, 188; tradition in Deaf American literature, 3–4, 6, 36, 52–77. *See also* Orature

Story Theatre, 106

Supalla, S., 12, 52; and communal nature of storytelling, 185; "For a Decent Living," videotaped storytelling, 174, 176–77, 182, 184–85, 188, 192, 194–95, 197; as a humorist, 26; as narrative storyteller, 8, 13, 140, 188, 192; and permanence of stories, 184

Tableaux, 49, 80, 110

Taking breaks in communication, 72–73

Tales from a Clubroom (Bragg and Bergman), 42, 97, 100, 141

Technology, 177, 203–4. *See also* Videotaped productions

Tedlock, D., 54, 149

Telling Stories, 42, 106

Textualization, 151–52, 177–78; of Deaf American discourse, 179–97

Theater. *See* Drama

Theater design, 114

Theaters of the Deaf, 42

Thomas, D., 108, 116

Topic changes in communication, 73

Topsy-turvy world of carnival, 22–24, 102–3

Tournaments, 10, 35

"The Tower Clock," 154–56

Transmission of ASL productions, 41–44, 173, 184

Traveling theme in literature. *See* Picaresque novels

Treasure (Lentz), 202

Trickster's role in literature, 8–10, 52–77, 138, 175–76. *See also* Fool in mainstream society; Jester

TTY (teletypewriter) text,
122–24
Turner, V., 47
Twain, M., 128, 129
Two-handed communication,
59–60
Two-world condition of Deaf
Americans, 13, 39, 166, 185;
in Deaf drama, 99–107, 112;
in *Islay* (Bullard), 126–39; lan-
guage in, 43, 55; "Literary
Night" reflections of, 92. *See
also* Biculturality
Two-world condition of medieval
Europe, 92, 100

Under Milkwood, 108, 116
Uniformity, 189–94

Valli, C., 7, 162–66, 205; as ASL
poet, 13; "Cave," 162,
163–65, 168; "Hands," 162,
165–66, 168; "My Favorite
Old Summer House," 168;
Poetry in Motion, 148; "Windy
Bright Morning," 49, 168
Vaudeville-like productions, 13,
105–7, 115–17, 193
Veditz, G., 194
Vendors of ASL productions,
43–44
Verbal compositions, comic,
24–26, 88
Verhoosky, M., 97
Vernaculars: during Middle Ages,
21; visual-kinetic, 10, 18, 19,
58, 91, 122, 124, 202
Vernacular tradition of ASL art,
3, 13

Videotaped narratives, 8, 12, 13,
39–40, 188
Videotaped productions: as collections of works, 185–86; and
literary criticism, 188–89; and
loss of spectator interaction,
168–69, 181–82; and textualization of ASL art, 173–74,
179–80, 197, 202–3; and
transmission of ASL art,
43–44, 91, 203
Viewer participation. *See* Spectator participation
Visuature (visual literature), 202
Voice communication in the
hearing, 59, 60, 72

The Water Falls (Conley), 97
White, A., 104–5; on educative
nature of fairs, 34, 47; on
middle class's distancing of
popular culture, 89–90; on
polyglossia, 92–93, 201–2
Whitman, W., 87
"Windy Bright Morning" (Valli),
49, 168
Words, dematerializing of, 87–88
"The World According to Pat"
(Graybill), 80–82, 84, 112
World Federation of the Deaf, 35
World Games for the Deaf, 35
Wright, D., 3

"Yankee Doodle Dandy" (Graybill), 81
Yugoslavian oral narratives, 150

Zola, E., 27